Documentary Culture and the Making of Medieval English Literature

Emily Steiner describes the rich intersections between legal documents and English literature in the fourteenth and fifteenth centuries. The literature of this period, from Passion lyrics to Lollard sermons, abounds in documentary language and metaphors. Steiner argues that documentary culture (including charters, testaments, patents and seals) enabled writers to think in new ways about the conditions of textual production in late medieval England. She explains that the distinctive rhetoric, material form, and ritual performance of legal documents offered writers of Chaucer's generation and the generation succeeding him a model of literary practice. Covering a wide variety of medieval texts: sermons, lyrics, *Piers Plowman*, *Mum and the Sothsegger*, *The Book of Margery Kempe*, heretical writings, and trial records, this study will be of interest to scholars of medieval literary studies and medieval studies in general.

Emily Steiner is Assistant Professor in the Department of English at the University of Pennsylvania. She is the editor (with Candace Barrington) of *The Letter of the Law: Legal Practice and Literary Production in Late Medieval England* (2002).

CAMBRIDGE STUDIES IN MEDIEVAL LITERATURE

This series of critical books seeks to cover the whole area of literature written in the major medieval languages – the main European vernaculars, and medieval Latin and Greek – during the period c. 1100–1500. Its chief aim is to publish and stimulate fresh scholarship and criticism on medieval literature, special emphasis being placed on understanding major works of poetry, prose, and drama in relation to the contemporary culture and learning which fostered them.

Recent titles in the series
Margaret Clunies Ross *Old Icelandic Literature and Society*
Donald Maddox *Fictions of Identity in Medieval France*
Rita Copeland *Pedagogy, Intellectuals and Dissent in the Later Middle Ages:*
Lollardy and Ideas of Learning
Kantik Ghosh *The Wycliffite Heresy: Authority and the Interpretation of Texts*
Mary C. Erler *Women, Reading, and Piety in Late Medieval England*
D. H. Green *The Beginnings of Medieval Romance: Fact and Fiction, 1150–1220*
J. A. Burrow *Gestures and Looks in Medieval Narrative*
Ardis Butterfield *Poetry and Music in Medieval France: From Jean Renart to*
Guillaume de Machaut

A complete list of titles in the series can be found at the end of the volume.

Documentary Culture and the Making of Medieval English Literature

EMILY STEINER

CAMBRIDGE
UNIVERSITY PRESS

CAMBRIDGE UNIVERSITY PRESS
Cambridge, New York, Melbourne, Madrid, Cape Town, Singapore, São Paulo, Delhi

Cambridge University Press
The Edinburgh Building, Cambridge CB2 8RU, UK

Published in the United States of America by Cambridge University Press, New York

www.cambridge.org
Information on this title: www.cambridge.org/9780521110532

First published 2003
This digitally printed version 2009

A catalogue record for this publication is available from the British Library

ISBN 978-0-521-82484-2 hardback
ISBN 978-0-521-11053-2 paperback

For Peter, my best friend

Poetry is verse: prose is not verse.
Or else poetry is everything with the exception of
business documents and school books.
                              Diary of Tolstoy

nor is it valid
to discriminate against "business documents and school books."
                              Marianne Moore, "Poetry"

Contents

Abbreviations   *page* xi
List of illustrations   xiii
Acknowledgments   xv

Introduction   1

I   Documentary poetics

1 Bracton, Deguileville, and the defense of allegory   17

2 Lyric, genre, and the material text   47

II   Langland's documents

3 *Piers Plowman* and the archive of salvation   93

4 Writing public: Documents in the *Piers Plowman*
   tradition   143

III   Identity, heterodoxy, and documents

5 Lollard community and the *Charters of Christ*   193

6 Lollard rhetoric and the written record: Margery Baxter and
   William Thorpe   229

   Epilogue: "My lordys lettyr & the seel of Cawntyrbery"   240

Bibliography   247
Index   263

Abbreviations

CCSL   *Corpus christianorum series latina*
CCCM   *Corpus christianorum continuatio mediaevalis*
EETS   Early English Text Society (OS, Original Series, ES, Extra
        Series)
PL   *Patrologia Latina*, ed. J-P. Migne. Paris, 1844–64

Illustrations

1 Augustus Caesar and his surveyors. From the Hereford
Mappamundi, lower-left corner. (c. 1280).   *page* 2

2 The pilgrim reads Reason's commission to Rude
Entendement. From Guillaume de Deguileville, *Le pèlerinage
de la vie humaine*. New York. The Pierpont Morgan Library
MS. M.772, fol. 39. (fourteenth century). (With permission
of The Pierpont Morgan Library).   37

3 Reason presents her commission to Rude Entendement.
From Guillaume de Deguileville, *Le pèlerinage de la vie
humaine*. Oxford. Bodleian Library MS. Douce 300, fol. 46v.
(ca. 1390–1400). (With permission of the Bodleian Library).   38

4 *Short Charter* depicted with a hanging seal. London. The
British Library MS Sloane 3292, fol. 2v. (sixteenth century).
(With permission of the British Library).   78

5 *Short Charter* drawn up as a charter. London. The British
Library MS Additional Charter 5960. (early sixteenth
century). (With permission of the British Library).   80

6 *Short Charter* depicted with a hanging seal. London. The
British Library MS Stowe 620, fol. 12v. (sixteenth century).
(With permission of the British Library).   81

7 *Short Charter* depicted with a hanging seal. Cambridge
University Library MS Additional 6686, p. 271. (ca. 1400–50).
(With permission of Cambridge University Library).   82

8 Christ's crucified body depicted as a charter and inscribed
with the text of the *Short Charter*. London. The British
Library MS Additional 37049, fol. 23r. (ca.1400–50). (With
permission of the British Library).   86

xiii

9 *Carta Dei* inscribed on the dorse of a charter. Oxford.
Bodleian Library MS Kent Charter 233. (ca. 1400). (With
permission of the Bodleian Library).   88

10 The priest examines the Pardon. From William Langland,
Piers Plowman. Oxford. Bodleian Library MS Douce 104,
fol. 44v. (1427). (With permission of the Bodleian Library).   156

11 Charity presents the last will and testament of Jesus Christ;
Penance presents her instruments of torture. From
Guillaume de Deguileville, *Le pèlerinage de la vie humaine*.
Oxford. Bodleian Library MS Douce 300, fol. 19v.
(ca. 1390–1400). (With permission of the Bodleian Library).   160

Acknowledgments

I am fortunate to have had so many individuals help me grow as a researcher and thinker. They have nourished my faith in collegiality and made me thankful to belong to a community of medievalists. I am especially grateful for the stimulating conversation and thoughtful responses of the following people: Candace Barrington, Jenny Davidson, Margreta deGrazia, Elizabeth Fowler, Matthew Giancarlo, Frank Grady, Ralph Hanna III, Traugott Lawler, Lee Patterson, Fiona Somerset, Peter Stallybrass, David Wallace, and Nicholas Watson. It is also a pleasure to acknowledge the participants at the University of Pennsylvania Medieval-Renaissance and History of Material Texts seminars, whose incisive questions forced me to rethink the project several times over. I am deeply indebted to the intellectual labors of Rita Copeland and Andrew Galloway, who read several chapters of the manuscript in draft, and I can never repay Bruce Holsinger, who commented astutely on the entire manuscript. James Simpson and the anonymous reader for Cambridge University Press generously showed me how to push the manuscript to completion, and the energy of my editor, Linda Bree, persuaded me to finish it. The librarians at the Beineke Rare Book Library, Bodleian Library, British Library, Cambridge University Library, and Pierpont Morgan Library accommodated my every request. Sharon Fulton, Stephanie Gibbs, Michelle Karnes, and Stella Singer assisted me invaluably during the last stages of the project.

Support for this project was provided by summer fellowships from the University of Pennsylvania and the Huntington Library/British Institute.

Acknowledgments

Part of chapter 3 appeared as "Langland's Documents," in the *Yearbook of Langland Studies* 14 (2000): 95–107. An early version of chapter 6 appeared as "Inventing Legality: Documentary Culture and Lollard Preaching," in *The Letter of the Law: Legal Practice and Literary Production in Medieval England*, ed. Emily Steiner and Candace Barrington (Ithaca, NY: Cornell University Press, 2002), 185–201.

Introduction

In the lower left corner of the Hereford Mappamundi (ca. 1280) a scribe
has drawn four figures: on the one side is a monarch or ecclesiastic en-
throned, holding the edge of a typical thirteenth-century charter, and
on the other side are three men in robes, presumably surveyors, one of
whom gestures with his right hand to the charter and with his left hand
to a protruding roundel labeled with a red S (Figure 1).[1] The charter, the
seal of which indicates that it has been authorized by Augustus Caesar,
orders the surveyors, "Go into the whole world and report each of its
continents to the Senate, and I have affixed my seal to this document in
confirmation therof."[2] This crowded little scene tells us much about the
dynamics of medieval *translatio imperii* – Augustus's papal tiara and the
charter's papal seal transform Roman imperialism into medieval Christian internationalism. This scene reveals something else, however, about
"cognate forms of documentation."[3] More specifically, the surveyor's
emphatic gesture toward the two texts, the charter and the map, implies
a reciprocal relation between validation and imitation, and between materiality and textual form. From one perspective, the gesture indicates
that Augustus's servants have fulfilled his royal decree: they have successfully issued a report on the continents of the world. They have, in
effect, exchanged documents with the emperor, portraying their service

---

[1] The "S" doesn't indicate a southern direction, but rather it is one of the four letters in
"MORS" that surround the map.

[2] "Ite in orbem universum et de omni eius continencia referte ad senatum et ad istam
confirmandam huic scripto sigillum meum apposui." On the sources for this scene see
Scott Westrem's excellent book, *The Hereford Map*, 8.

[3] Hiett's term for this scene in "The Cartographic Imagination of Thomas Elmham," 863.
Hiett's interest in this map has to do with the ways that both maps and charters make
claims on territorial expansion and the ownership of land.

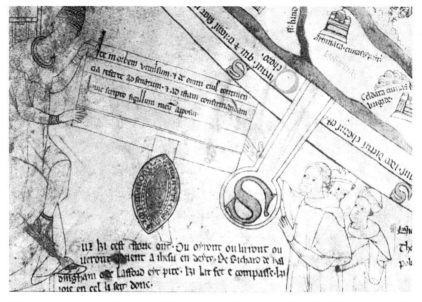

Figure 1 Augustus Caesar and his surveyors. From the Hereford Mappamundi, lower-left corner (c. 1280).

as a diplomatic or administrative event. From a different perspective, the gesture suggests that the emperor's charter is not just an order but a safe-conduct. It is a document that permits surveyors or cartographers to skirt the dangerous territory located between trespass and hubris, and between a geographical and conceptual imagining of a world that takes Jerusalem as its center. Finally, the surveyor's gesture argues for a physical likeness between the charter and the map. The Latin word *carta* would not be used to describe a map for at least two hundred years, yet clearly the scribe of the Hereford map hoped to identify the map with the charter by virtue of their shared material textuality. The surveyor, by pointing with one hand to the S roundel and with the other to the sealed charter (*sigillum*), reminds us that both texts corroborate form and function; it is their material grammar – the disposition of the words on the page, the pictorial devices – by which they claim to be universally applicable and irrefutably authoritative. It comes as no surprise, perhaps, that the map's authorial signature appears at the very conjunction of charter and map. At the bottom of the scene, the Hereford scribe invokes romance and documentary conventions when he implores all those who hear, read, or see this story ("estorie") to pray to Jesus on behalf of Richard of Haldingham who made and measured it.

I propose that just as the charter defines the textuality of this particular map, its origin, appearance, production, and mode, so medieval English writers used legal documents to trace out the contours of their own writing, or an ideal writing, whether political satire or holy scripture. Indeed, the Hereford map might be taken as a starting point for a period in which authors used documents to describe the larger project of writing literature in later medieval England. From about 1350 to 1420, the period in which vernacular poetry re-emerged as a vital and creative force, insular writers were profoundly invested in the idea of a documentary culture, especially those writers committed to social vision or spiritual reform. The literature of this period, from counsel poems to Passion lyrics, from preaching handbooks to Lollard sermons, abounds in documentary terms and metaphors, tales of miraculous charters, and fictive (spurious or literary) pardons, manumissions, feoffments, patents, testaments, and safe-conducts.

The document figures so largely in medieval English literature because it was considered to be an eminently citable text. It was citable, not just because it was precious, authoritative, or true, but also because its *brevity*, by which I mean both its conciseness and portability, made it citable as a writing outside writing, a writing that acts precisely because it is a writing that ends. For one thing, like a social security card or driver's license, the document's brevity made it immediately recognizable to medieval audiences as the smallest unit of institutional writing, even if it turned out to be forged. Whether it was drawn up in a royal or ecclesiastical chancery or it was drawn up between individuals, it was recognizable as an official production because it was written according to certain protocols, and because its distinctive physical shape determined and substantiated its textual form. For another thing, the very quality that made the document citable – its brevity, its ability to be framed as text or within a text – is what made it *instrumental*, and for this reason it might serve as a model of literary practice, as well as a mode of literary reflection. Like a social security card or driver's license, the document's brevity gave it its practical efficacy, the agency to enact legislation, identify persons, grant land, or declare war. This relationship between brevity and instrumentality accounts for the difference between a charter and a chronicle, but also, and more contentiously, between a papal indulgence and the Bible. It is also what crucially distinguishes documents in literature from ekphrasis or stained-glass windows. This is not to suggest that the document, by virtue of its textual agency, transcended or insisted upon the difference between the literary and the non-literary. Rather, as I argue in this book, the document, because it was citable as text, became a means of thinking through intergeneric problems about the status of textuality in late medieval England: how a text might be imagined to itself or classified for others, or how the community of a text might be defined and its effects qualified and measured. By document, then, I don't mean just any text that attests to a culture or a narrative, but rather to its narrowest possible definition: a material object, written on parchment, sealed with wax, carried in sleeves, displayed to witnesses, and stored in the chests, cupboards, and *vasa* that served as archives in medieval England.

The proliferation of documents in medieval English literature was accompanied by a surge in the production of official documents. By the mid-fourteenth century the legal document was clearly one of England's primary texts, and possibly the only written text available to every social stratum. The average layman may have seen liturgical books processed up the nave, glimpsed the tiny Books of Hours in the hands of merchants' wives, or heard sections of the gospel recited in private reading groups. Yet the texts that the majority of administrators, laborers, artisans, and their apprentices (not to mention the upper echelons of society) physically encountered were official documents: certificates of good conduct, land-grants, indentures, proclamations, and indulgences. Michael Clanchy has demonstrated that, by the end of the thirteenth century, members of every social stratum had first-hand experience with legal instruments – by the fourteenth century, even laborers and artisans owned seals – and had come to trust the written record as the primary instrument of proof in a legal transaction. By this period, the charter had replaced traditional symbolic objects such as ancient family knives, which had often accompanied a conveyance of goods or property. A charter might even be laid on an altar during a legal transaction, serving like the Bible or a relic as a guarantor of the transaction as well as its official record.[4] By the late thirteenth century, the jurist Henry de Bracton was complaining that the livery of seisin (the formal occupation of land), a critical step in the transfer of property, had become ancillary to written evidence.[5] In short, the document had become not only important to legal action but the principal agent of that action as well. The production of legal documents increased in the fourteenth century as a corollary to the growth of towns and trade and to a burgeoning interest in efficient estate management.[6] During that period, the royal administration also grew dramatically in size and complexity, and the number of clerks multiplied in the royal household, the court of Chancery, and the nascent Office of the Privy Seal.[7]

Modern scholars have generally supposed that the increasing prominence of the document in all sorts of contracts, in addition to its wider circulation in medieval English culture, compromised the integrity of the judicial system and the flexibility of social relations. They argue that the formalizing of legal rhetoric and the systematizing of legal texts were socially divisive, inequitable, and coercive practices. Thus, according to the legal historian Robert Palmer, the Black Death so frayed social relations that a more coercive form – the written contract – was invented to make people stick to their obligations. Before the Black Death, for example, the contract of debt depended upon a covenantal relationship in which both parties had to produce witnesses should the debt be contested. After this period, it was much more common to contract debt on obligation, based on a sealed bond rather than on witnesses, a practice that gave creditors a better chance of compensation but could often be inflexible and harsh. In order to escape the debt, the defendant had to produce a quittance or prove that the original deed was invalid.[8] In a similar vein, the literary historian Richard

---

[4] Clanchy, *From Memory to Written Record*, 49–52, 260. For more information on the cultural and technological transformations of documentary culture from the eleventh to thirteenth centuries, see Clanchy, "Archives and Memory in the Middle Ages," and "Literacy, Law and the Power of the State."

[5] For a more detailed explanation of Bracton's theories of documentary agency, see chapter 1.

[6] Bennett, "Careerism in Late Medieval England," 21.

[7] Green, *Poets and Princepleasers: Literature and the English Court in the Late Middle Ages*, 15–16. For more information on diplomatics in medieval England, see chapter 2.

[8] Palmer, *English Law in the Age of the Black Death, 1348–1381*, 62–72.

Firth Green argues that documents precipitated a crisis of contractual faith or "trouthe": by the mid-fourteenth century it had become difficult to "maintain an illusion of communal coherence founded on ethical truth in the face of the unwavering insistence of written evidence on a depersonalized intellectual truth."[9] Green offers the example of relations between lord and vassal, which were increasingly organized by indentures of service and maintenance rather than by the ancient trothplight that had confirmed traditional (hereditary) homage.[10] The relationship that Green posits between contractual faith and legal documents is illustrated indirectly by some fourteenth-century reformists, who denounce the partiality and abuse of the law in terms of the law's written culture. The author of *The Book of Vices and Virtues* (c. 1375), for example, berates the scribes, notaries, and lawyers who draw up self-interested ("fals") documents (as opposed to the "true" documents that they ought to be producing): they "maken fals lettres and fals seales and makeþ fals dedes and charteres and many oþere falsenesses."[11] Likewise, in the view of the poet and social critic John Gower, the corruption perpetrated by royal and aristocratic affinities was facilitated by documentary culture. According to his *Cronica tripertita* (c. 1400), for example, Richard II proved his faithlessness by forcing his subjects to seal "blank checks" during the frantic last years of his reign: "Charters were written and read everywhere, and he ordered these to be stamped with seals and honored by all...City, farm, and manor affixed seals to the charters, so that all the poison was scattered to the fullest extent." As Gower explains, these charters made all recipients irredeemably complicit in the king's treason: "Everyone was reckoned as a traitor, for one's established guilt might be made a matter of record by means of a seal."[12]

---

[9] Green, *A Crisis of Truth*, 38–9.

[10] Green, *A Crisis of Truth*, 155–63. According to Green, this "mechanization" of contract debased homage, weakened ties of responsibility, and corrupted the judicial system by creating networks of self-interest. He proceeds to argue that if documents were often venerated in the late medieval period (and especially in literary texts), it was only because they retained some of the aura and symbolic power invested in old common law objects, such as swords or gospel books (264–82).

[11] *The Book of Vices and Virtues*, ed. Francis, 36, ll. 8–10.

[12] "Carte scribuntur et in omni parte leguntur/Hasque sigillari iubet omnibus et venerari... Vrbs, ager, et villa cartis posuere sigilla/Quo magnis ad plenum conspergitur omne

Green and Palmer, among others, have demonstrated the various ways in which documentary culture permeated the legal world of late medieval England, and especially the way it reconfigured relations among lawyers, magnates, merchants, and kings. By contrast, legal and literary historians of the 1381 Peasants' Revolt, such as Christopher Dyer, Rosamund Faith, and Steven Justice, have traced the expansion of legal documents among the illiterate and disenfranchised, demonstrating in the process how documentary culture could frequently be empowering and its uses unpredictable and complex. From the beginning of the fourteenth century, for example, laborers and artisans began to use documentary culture for more sophisticated political agendas, such as proving their rights to free status and to the king's justice. They hoped that documents would help them avoid the arbitrary services and manorial courts of landowners, and as the relationship between lords and tenants grew more strained over the course of the century, the participation of laborers in documentary culture was increasingly disputed. The monastic chronicles of the 1381 revolt attempt to show, for example, that the rebels, in their headlong stampede towards London, destroyed old records out of ignorance of, or hostility towards, the written record.[13] As the same accounts make clear, however, the insurgents were sufficiently well-versed in documents to discriminate between forms and invoke ancient records to support their claims.[14] The king had first tried to appease the rebels with charters of general pardon, which they

venenum/Fallitur ex illo quisquis, cum firma sigillo/Culpa recordetur, qua proditor omnis habetur" (*Cronica tripertita*, III. 49–50, 55–8). The English translation is from *The Major Latin Works of John Gower*, trans. Stockton, 313. The Latin text is from John Gower, *Complete Works*, vol. 4, ed. Macaulay, 331.

[13] See Knighton's description of these activities in *Knighton's Chronicle, 1337–1396*, ed. and trans. Martin, 207–31. The Anonimalle chronicler confirms that when the rebels attacked the Archbishop's palace at Lambeth, they threw in the fire all the chancery documents that they could find: "toutz les livers des registres et rolles de remembrauncez de la chauncellerie illeoqes trovez" (*The Anonimalle Chronicle, 1333–1381*, ed. Galbraith, 140). Walsingham recounts the destruction of documents at St. Alban's in *Gesta abbatum monasterii Sancti Albans*, ed. Riley, 308. For theories of the rebels' anti-literacy see Susan Crane, "The Writing Lesson of 1381."

[14] Dyer, "Social and Economic Background to the Rural Revolt of 1381"; Justice, *Writing and Rebellion: England in 1381*; 55–64. See also Paul Strohm's study of stigmatization and ventriloquism in the chronicles of 1381, "'A Revelle!': Chronicle Evidence and the Rebel Voice," in *Hochon's Arrow: The Social Imagination of Fourteenth-Century Texts*, 33–56.

dismissed as "troefles et mokerie," but he was later forced to hand over charters of freedom ("chartres destre free de toutz maners de servage") when the rebels reconvened at Mile End.[15] Later at Smithfield, rebel leaders attempted to obtain a charter of liberty that would better address the emancipation of serfs: "ut a rege emendaciorum optineret de libertate cartam; displicuerat enim eis carta per regem primitus concessa."[16] And when the king finally dispersed the rebel troops at Smithfield, the townsmen of Somerset had the foresight to send the king a draft of pardon so as to avoid future retribution.[17] Similarly, Thomas Walsingham reports that the townspeople of St. Alban's would not be satisfied until their abbot handed over a spurious charter of King Offa, which they remembered to be decorated with gold and lapis lazuli. Indeed, this absent charter became a major negotiating point for the rebels: when the abbot claimed ignorance, they forced him to write out a new charter that confirmed their free status.[18] Nor was their vigilance without precedent. A few years before the revolt, the tenants of Saint Mary Ottery, Devon, organized a strike based on an exemplification (an official copy) from the Domesday Book, which confirmed the free status of the town.[19]

In each of these examples, the written record played a crucial role in the insurgents' larger political agenda. They assumed that their personal

[15] *The Anonimalle Chronicle*, 143, 145–6.

[16] *The Westminster Chronicle, 1381–1394*, ed. and trans. Hector and Harvey, 7, 11. See also the account of this charter in Martin, ed., *Knighton's Chronicle*, 212–13: "Vnde rex pro bono pacis et temporis ingruencia ad peticionem eorum concessit eis cartam sub magno sigillo quod omnes homines in regno Anglie liberi essent et libere condicionis et ab omni iugo seruitutis et uillenagii exuti pro se et heredibus suis imperpetuum permanerent."

[17] Harvey, "Draft Letters Patent of Manumission and Pardon for the Men of Somerset in 1381," 89–91.

[18] *Gesta abbatam monasterii Sancti Albans*, 308, 317–22.

[19] Faith, "The 'Great Rumor' of 1377 and Peasant Ideology." Villeins began to use the Domesday Book as proof of ancient demesne as early as the last two decades of Henry III's reign. The earliest case concerns a group of villeins from Yorkshire who were trying to establish that they were privileged tenants. Domesday was consulted and their villein tenure confirmed (Hallam, *Domesday Book Through Nine Centuries*, 52). In the fourteenth century, manorial tenants and townsmen increasingly purchased exemplifications from the Domesday Book in order to be excused from paying local taxes under special status upon ancient demesne. The 200-year-old Domesday Book could not answer many of the questions raised, yet it continued to be dutifully searched and extracted from (Galbraith, *Domesday Book: Its Place in Administrative History*, 112–22).

rights were encased in legal documents and must be proven by specific forms. And if their appeals to the Domesday Book were fanciful or uninformed, as the chroniclers would suggest, they nevertheless chose ancient records of privilege over oral declarations or physical acts.[20] Green and Palmer suggest that fourteenth-century legal actors would be right to mourn a bygone world of oral *communitas*, yet those most underserved by the legal system longed for a liberating past of founding documents. In these chronicles, moreover, bureaucratic savvy is nearly indistinguishable from mythic, hagiographic, or even apocalyptic imaginings of the written record. Offa's charter becomes a founding relic glittering in the communal memory, and the Domesday Book, whose reputation was already inflated beyond all utility, becomes a myth of political origins.[21]

The two pictures of medieval documentary culture summarized above – documents derided as instruments of legal and moral corruption and documents employed as instruments of insurrection and repression – together illustrate the juridical and political climate of later medieval England, as well as the controversial role that documents played during that period. Neither, however, makes sense of legal documents as a literary practice, which, I argue in this book, is central to the formation of a documentary culture, as well as to the ways that medieval writers came to terms with the notion of an English literary tradition. This book takes as its premise the idea that a culture's understanding

---

[20] "By the thirteenth century onwards, many documents were given its name [Domesday] to endow them with special and binding importance. Among them were the Domesday rolls of Chester, used for recording charters . . . [and] the thirteenth-century Domesday survey of the lands of St. Paul's Cathedral . . . such wide use of the name to cover many different kinds of documents further enhanced the standing of the original Domesday Book, but also strengthened the common misapprehension that it contained a virtually inexhaustible and encyclopaedic store of useful evidence" (Hallam, *Domesday Book Through Nine Centuries*, 53–4).

[21] Admittedly, the chroniclers were, with the benefit of hindsight, satirizing the rebel's naiveté: the king did end up revoking the charters of freedom (citing extortion), and King Offa's charter probably never existed, as Walsingham takes enormous pains to prove. But the chroniclers took the rebels' charters very seriously and were equally willing to attribute to documents an almost supernatural power and authority. (*Gesta abbatum monasterii Sancti Albani*, 365). Many of the chroniclers copied the rebels' charters of privilege and pardon and gave detailed descriptions of the reasons why these documents were declared legally invalid.

of textuality is revealed both in its literature's reflexive moments, and in its material texts or ritual objects.[22] And it asks, subsequently, not how legal documents undermined the traditional values of the aristocracy, or how they endorsed the goals of the peasantry, but rather how they informed the literary culture of fourteenth and fifteenth-century England by posing challenging questions about the making of texts. This book argues that documentary culture was shaped, in part, by the formal, ethical, spiritual, and political aspirations of late medieval English writers. Conversely, it argues that documentary culture helped shape an identity for English literature: the work it performs, the stories it tells, and the authority that it claims for itself.

Finally, I want to suggest that it is at the intersection between documentary culture and late medieval literature that we encounter distinctly medieval – and even, perhaps, distinctly English – relationships between the institutional and the expressive, the material and the textual, the literate and the literary, and Latin and the vernacular. I call this intersection a documentary poetics, a term that extends not only to poetic theory and composition but also to genre theory, historiography, public writing, textual authority, and vernacular piety. It is this documentary poetics that enabled late medieval English writers to come to terms with their own literary endeavors and to describe the conditions of their own literary moment. This book is divided into three parts. The first part, "Documentary poetics," argues that the document's peculiar relation of textual form to material text made it a rich site of rhetorical and generic experimentation in fourteenth-century religious texts. In the first chapter, "Bracton, Deguileville, and the defense of allegory," I argue that Guillaume de Deguileville, in his popular pilgrimage trilogy (French, 1330s–1350s, English, 1360s–1420s), used documentary writing to defend the spiritual efficacy of personification allegory. In doing so, he was exploring theories of legal person and documentary will developed a century earlier in Henry de Bracton's influential legal treatise, *De legibus et consuetudinibus Angliae* (*On the Laws and Customs of England*) (c. 1230–50). In chapter 2, "Lyric, genre, and the material text," I turn to a uniquely English tradition, the Middle English *Charters of Christ*

---

[22] On this idea, see Derrida, "Of Grammatology as a Positive Science," in *Of Grammatology*, trans. Spivak, 87–8; Goldberg, *Writing Matter: From the Hands of the English Renaissance*; and Lerer, *Literacy and Power*, 27, 158–94.

(1350–1500), a huge corpus of Passion lyrics in which Christ's body is imagined to be a bloody charter granting heaven to true penitents. I argue that the writers of these lyrics discovered in documentary culture a language with which to excavate the poetic subject, unpack the relationship between religious lyric and metaphor, and even speculate upon the limits of genre.

Part 2, "Langland's documents," takes as its subject William Langland's kaleidoscopic dream-vision, *Piers Plowman*, a poem which represents in many ways the culmination of an English documentary poetics. As John Alford observed years ago, *Piers Plowman* "contain[s] several charters, court scenes and hundreds of legal terms and maxims from common, civil and canon law, so that in the whole history of English literature there is nothing even remotely to be compared to it."[23] Indeed, the poem's most urgent concern, the immanence of the divine in the human condition, is imagined as a series of fictive documents of various kinds. As I argue in chapter 3, "*Piers Plowman* and the archive of salvation," Langland used the written record – the clerkly activities that produced it, its ceremonial delivery, and its archival afterlife – to describe the penitential writing of salvation history. Or to put it a different way, Langland's documents, and particularly the scene of Truth's Pardon, show how the transhistorical experience of the divine might be historically apprehended through the social and material practices of documentary culture. Chapter 4, "Writing public: Documents in the *Piers Plowman* tradition," reconsiders Langland's documents from the perspective of post-Langlandian literature: the allegorical letters of insurgent leader, John Ball (1381) and the alliterative counsel poem, *Mum and the Sothsegger* (c. 1400). I argue that *Piers Plowman* presented for these later works a paradigm of public writing wrested from the legal fictions and ritual performances of documentary culture. More specifically, Langland's documents model an ideal of public writing by positing a discursive realm between disclosure (what society reveals about itself, that writing which protrudes from persons and institutions) and address (a writing that meddles, intrudes, or passes judgment upon others). Whereas for Langland, documentary writing remained an ideal never fully realized by the poem, for the rebels of 1381 and the *Mum*-poet, legal

[23] Alford, "Literature and Law in Medieval England," 942.

documents served as a viable mode for demanding political action or offering counsel. Significantly, however, this documentary mode of public writing was first elaborated in *Piers Plowman*, and in many respects sets the terms for a *Piers Plowman* "tradition."

The final part, "Identity, heterodoxy, documents," shows how medieval writers used documents to construct a meaningful relationship between textual authority and spiritual community. This relationship was a primary interest of English catechistic, homiletic, and contemplative literature from the 1350s on, and it was increasingly contested as the Lollard heresy gained the attention of ecclesiastical officials. Chapter 5, "Lollard community and the *Charters of Christ*," argues that documentary culture inspired a language of vernacular piety, which informed orthodox and heterodox texts alike but to startlingly different effects. For orthodox writers, legal documents, and especially indulgences and letters of fraternity, confirmed the intercessory powers of the institutional church at the same time that they emphasized the difficulty of obtaining salvation. For writers sympathetic to Lollardy, documentary culture offered two opposing models of textual authority: the illegitimate documents of the institutional church and the Charter of Christ, a document equivalent to scripture, which authorizes a spiritual community unmediated by ecclesiastical authority and inclusive of all (elect) believers. In this way, documentary culture offered preachers and polemicists of all stripes a language with which to redefine textual authority and spiritual community, ecclesiology, and salvation theology. Chapter 6, "Lollard rhetoric and the written record: Margery Baxter and William Thorpe," further examines the question of textual authority in late medieval polemic but from the perspective of religious identity, rather than spiritual community. It argues that confessed Lollards on trial, Margery Baxter and William Thorpe, purposely disfigured the rhetoric of trial documents and proceedings in order to cultivate their own heterodox polemic.[24]

[24] Nicholas Watson and other scholars have written about the experience of vernacular literacy in medieval England, and they have demonstrated how different languages produce sub-cultures of ideas about reading, theology, and authority. See especially Watson, "Censorship and Cultural Change in Late Medieval England: Vernacular Theology, the Oxford Translation Debate, and Arundel's Constitutions of 1409," and "Visions of Inclusion: Universal Salvation and Vernacular Theology in Pre-Reformation England." I'm less concerned here with vernacularity *per se* than with the ways that late medieval authors, many of whom were writing in English, articulated the problems of writing in that period.

Both Baxter and Thorpe were determined, in other words, to isolate a new documentary rhetoric with which to redeem Lollard polemic from the trial documents of the institutional church. Finally, in the epilogue to the book, "My lordys lettyr & þe seel of Cawntyrbery," I argue that another accused Lollard, Margery Kempe, assiduously collected documents of credence and safe-conduct as evidence both of her orthodoxy and charismatic mission. For Kempe, documents became a way not just of appropriating official authority but also of foregrounding the relationship between textuality and identity.

In short, this book argues that, for medieval English writers, documentary culture was not a fixed entity, something to be represented rather than cited, but rather a shifting set of questions about the ways that texts functioned in fourteenth and fifteenth-century England. As such, it offered these writers a source of validation or authorization but also, and more significantly, a means of inventing new relationships between languages, genres, identities, and communities.[25] Brigitte Bedos-Rezak argues that students of diplomatics, by their very methods of categorization, have artificially detached medieval charters and seals from their original social context: "Through the comprehensive taxonomy of diplomatics, the medieval status and role of charters, which have yet to be assessed, has been changed: from being social phenomena and cultural artifacts, charters have been rendered into data, no innocent term." The task of the critic is now to reinterpret charters according to their operations within society, operations that include being "ambivalent symbols, ritual objects, or sacred monuments."[26] It is my contention that the operations of documents in medieval England were

---

[25] On the relationship between literacy and textuality in medieval England, I am indebted to the work of Brian Stock, who argues that the written text, materially present or absent, was the pole around which certain social relationships were organized. The text, then, whether enacted in oral performance or private reading, became the "common interpretative and ritualistic experience" for communities of literates and non-literates alike (*Listening for the Text: On the Uses of the Past*). See also Joyce Coleman, who, building upon the work of Franz Baüml and Malcolm Parkes, entirely rejects "self-validating" categories of orality and literacy in favor of pragmatic, "culture-specific" systems that address local methods of dissemination and reception. She argues, moreover, that multiple forms of literacy always existed in medieval culture, and that fourteenth-century literates, partial literates, and illiterates participated in a third and highly-regarded mode: aural reading (*Public Reading and the Reading Public in Late Medieval England and France*).

[26] Bedos-Rezak, "Diplomatic Sources and Medieval Documentary Practices," 314–15.

deeply bound up in the re-creation of an English literary tradition. To speak of them as symbols, objects, or monuments is to speak of the ways that medieval authors came to terms with a manifold textuality, drawn from the rhetorical, material, and performative aspects of documentary culture.

PART I

Documentary poetics

I

Bracton, Deguileville, and the defense of allegory

English poetry of the later Middle Ages abounds in references to legal documents, both to the official formulas with which they were composed and to the material forms with which they were circulated. As we shall see in this chapter and the next, documents take center stage in all sorts of religious narratives, where they are instrumental in communicating and corroborating divine truth. Much more interestingly, however, documents in medieval literature do not simply attest to received doctrine or traditional authority, but they also invite vernacular innovation and generic transformation. In the process, they investigate the forms through which doctrine and authority can be disseminated and experienced. As I argue in the next two chapters, medieval writers borrowed, and sometimes even distorted, the textual apparatus of the law to invent a *documentary poetics*, by which I mean the ways in which legal documents – both their external material forms and their internal rhetorical modes – call attention simultaneously to poetic form and cultural practice. More specifically, later medieval poets discovered in documentary culture a theoretical vocabulary for describing the work of vernacular religious poetry, as if, at this moment in literary history, documentary culture generated a theory of poetry at once rigorously formal (how does personification work? who is a lyric speaker? what is genre?) and socially and politically contingent (how are charters distributed, to what effect, and by whose authority?). Chapters 1 and 2 show how medieval authors constructed a poetics from the texts and practices of documentary culture, and further, how documentary culture itself signified within the literature of late medieval piety, from allegorical dream-visions to Passion lyrics.

The relationship I am positing between legal documents and medieval poetics may be better grasped in terms of allegories of the book. Ernst Curtius demonstrated long ago that the book was a popular medieval philosophical and penitential trope, one that was motivated by a number of biblical passages and would live on into print culture as well. Commonly cited examples include Dante's book of memory, creation as a transcendental book, and the heart as a fleshly book to be consulted by the penitent or inscribed by God.[1] As Eric Jager argues in his response to Curtius, this last example, "the book of the heart," speaks to the "incarnational poetics" of later medieval piety, as well as to pre-modern notions of subjectivity.[2] Indeed, earlier monastic and later Franciscan poets often invoke the material book in terms that resonate with manuscript production – the stretching of the parchment, the prick of the pen and ruler, the gushing of the ink – in order to dramatize the relation of Christ's body to the penitential soul. The friar William Herebert (ca. 1270–1333), for example, in a prayer to Christ, puts his faith in a charter drawn up in the Passion: "And helpe he wole, ich wot,/For Love the chartre wrot,/And the enke orn of [ran from] his wounde."[3] In a very different English text, Richard of Bury's *Philobiblon* (1345), the material text trope veers even toward the fetishistic. In this treatise, Bury confesses his acute bibliophilia, a confession that concerns, in Michael Camille's felicitous phrase, "the interpenetration of corporeality and codicology."[4] Bury's books complain of violations that are at once textual and physical, ranging from carelessly executed marginalia, to the "smutty hands of scullions," to the infection of both text and material text by Jews and pawnbrokers whose nefarious practices keep the books' owners living in high style.[5]

Yet the prevalence of *material text* tropes for expressing the relationship between the created and the divine or between the text and its human agents tells us little about how books as *material forms* signify in medieval literature. A book as a written or revealed text (the book of life, the book of the apocalypse) or as a material object (*libri pergamenum*)

---

[1] Curtius, *European Literature and the Latin Middle Ages*, trans. Trask, 302–47.

[2] Jager, "The Book of the Heart." For a study of writing as totality in the Middle Ages, see Gellrich, *The Idea of the Book in the Middle Ages*.

[3] Davies, ed., *Middle English Lyrics*, #28, ll. 19–24.

[4] Camille, "The Book as Flesh and Fetish," 35.

[5] Bury, *Philobiblon*, ed. and trans. Thomas, 47.

might represent totality, memory, vision, or abjection. But exactly what material form does a book (*liber*) designate, and further, what relation does such a form bear to the genre of text contained within (just as in the modern period, the book has come to classify the novel and be classified by the codex)? It is true that Bury, in his confession of a book lover, seems to be chiefly attracted to the book (*liber*) as codex. He is mesmerized by the erotics of the covering, the clasps and the bindings, as well as by the quality of the marginalia, which might be proper in a codex containing a meditative treatise, but which would cause a legal document, no matter how beautifully written, to be thrown out of court.[6] What Bury's treatise demonstrates, then, is that the materialities of codices bear some relation to the texts contained within. They classify genre, or more precisely, they eliminate a number of generic possibilities. That relation, however, is accidental, having to do more with format than with form; it happens that Bury's codices contain texts that probably wouldn't have been issued otherwise. In this sense, a better comparison with Bury's codices would be glossed bibles or canon law texts, often recognized as such by the boldface scriptural verses at the centers of their pages which spin out intricate webs of commentary. It is worth remembering, too, that in medieval parlance words such as book, script, or *liber* – words that indicate a complete text – are not restricted to codices and might refer to any type of material form, such as a codex, scroll, pamphlet, or legal document. I am arguing, finally, that there is no *inherent* relationship in medieval culture between a codex and a book, because the relation of materiality to textuality was generally perceived to be symbolic or practical rather than functional (that is, classifying or performative). Thus medieval artists do not always choose to depict scripture as a codex, unlike their early modern counterparts, in part because the revelatory is often symbolized as a scroll; and in part, perhaps, because the sections of bibles that circulated in the medieval period did not always require a whole codex, nor were they understood to be independent of non-scriptural texts bound between the same covers.

By contrast, the forms of legal documents – by which we may imagine a single sheet stored flat, folded, or rolled, with seals hanging or

---

[6] For more information on interlineation, see Green, *A Crisis of Truth: Literature and Law in Ricardian England*, 50; and *'Piers Plowman': The B-Version*, ed. Kane and Donaldson, Passus II. 303–6.

adherent, and with visually impressive subscriptions and special signs – have an *exclusive* and *functional* relationship to the text contained within. In fact, when it comes to legal documents, the symbolic is absolutely indistinguishable from the functional. Their integrity as texts depends upon the relation that they establish between written text and material form. It is interesting, in that respect, that the same Latin and vernacular terms that designate different documentary forms (charter, writ, *brevia*, *chirographum*, letters patent, schedule) refer neither to other kinds of texts nor to other material forms; a book, as a complete textual act, may sometimes refer to a charter, but a charter can refer neither to a Book of Hours nor to a codex.[7] Thus the legal document's *singular relation of form to text* makes it signify differently than other texts, and consequently, as we shall see in this chapter and the next, it challenged late medieval readers to rethink the meaning of certain literary forms, such as allegory, lyric, and genre.

This documentary challenge is especially visible in two sets of texts widely circulated in late medieval England: Henry de Bracton's formidable legal compendium *De legibus et consuetudinibus Angliae* (*On the Laws and Customs of England*), compiled in the first third of the thirteenth century, and Guillaume de Deguileville's allegorical dream visions, the *Pèlerinages*, composed between the 1330s and 1350s. At first glance, these two sets of texts appear to have very little in common in the making of an *English* poetic tradition. After all, they originate in Latin and French and have no direct influence on each other, although, as we will see, they permeated the pedagogical, professional, and literary environments in which poets like Geoffrey Chaucer and William Langland wrote. Bracton and Deguileville also represent very different ideas of tradition. Whereas Bracton's book of jurisprudence was continually copied in the fourteenth century, it was already anachronistic by the time Bracton died in 1268, and it is by no means a reliable guide to late medieval legal practice. Deguileville, on the other hand, was fashionable among English court poets from the mid-fourteenth through the fifteenth century and was almost immediately translated into English. What is so important about Bracton and Deguileville is that both of them, in mutually illuminating ways, wrested from documentary

---

[7] They are sometimes, however, interchangeable with each other; a writ might refer to a charter and *vice versa*.

culture a language with which to reflect upon the symbolic claims of medieval religious allegory. And in doing so, they helped to lay the groundwork for a peculiarly English documentary poetics.

BRACTON'S DOCUMENTS

De legibus et consuetudinibus Angliae, contemporaneous with Aquinas's *Summa theologiae*, is a huge collection of Roman and common law traditionally attributed to Henry de Bracton, who served as sometime justice of the court of the King's Bench.[8] *De legibus* is perhaps best known for its explanations of dominion and royal prerogative, rather than for its insights into documentary culture. But Bracton was deeply concerned with the agency of legal documents, and especially with how to position the whole document, both text and material text, in relation to juridical agency, the legal act, and its actors. Was the written record considered to be dispositive or probative? Did it establish the act or prove it? How did it compare to other ritual acts within a given transaction, and how else might it signify within the larger narrative of the law? It is true that *De legibus* was passed around Chancery and the Inns of Court in the fourteenth and fifteenth centuries, centuries that failed to produce a successor to, aside from abridgements and vulgarizations of, *De legibus*, as well as other more practical and procedural treatises.[9] Yet *De legibus* is nevertheless a useful starting place to think about the relationship between documentary culture and literary making, not just because it continued to be valuable to late medieval clerks and lawyers, but because

---

[8] Scholars disagree as to exactly how much of *De legibus* has been compiled by Bracton, and whether it really reflects the practice of the royal courts – as opposed to the county courts – either in the 1230s or 1250s. See Barton, "The Mystery of Bracton"; and Brand, " 'The Age of Bracton.' "

[9] Out of 46 known manuscripts Thorne dates 41 of them to 1300 and after. See Bracton, *De legibus et consuetudinibus Angliae*, vol. I, trans. Thorne, 1–20. For more information on the Bracton inheritance, see Clanchy, *From Memory to Written Record*, 107–8; and Harding, *A Social History of the English Law*, 174–7. Harding suggests that, "The Bractonian tradition was remarkably short-lived, probably because these Latin treatises were characteristics of a time when legal education was available only in hybrid Roman-English law schools at Oxford and Northampton. When legal training was provided in the courts and then in the Inns of Court, the treatises in demand were the more practical and procedural ones" (*A Social History of the English Law*, 201). See also Richardson and Sayles's introduction to their edition of the Bractonian adaptation called *Fleta* (ca. 1290).

it theorizes, really for the first and last time, the signifying functions of
the written record. It theorizes the relationships that the written record
establishes between textuality and materiality, and between rhetoric and
subjectivity, and the implications of those relationships for other legal
and social practices.

Bracton repeatedly states in *De legibus* that charters and other documents represent the will of the donor to give a gift, privilege, or liberty.
They do not found the action, he warns; they are not, in legal terms,
dispositive. They are simply one form of evidence among many that the
donor wished a certain action to take place or a gift to be awarded, such
as the transfer of land from lord to vassal. Bracton worries that too much
agency is ascribed to documents – they are wrongly thought to establish
instead of proving the juridical act, and he repeats several times that a gift
is not made valid simply by the drawing up of charters and instruments.
Rather, livery of seisin, the physical transfer or occupation of the land,
must follow. It is preferable to have a charter drawn up so that the gift
may be more readily proved, but a gift may be valid and effective even
without a charter, so long as the donor is present during the transfer,
making his intent very clear, or a sufficient number of witnesses are present to attest to the donor's will, should it be questioned at a later date.

Yet despite his painstaking efforts to defend the prerogative of livery
and delineate the role of charters, Bracton ends up reasserting the
centrality, and even priority, of charters within legal procedure by
theorizing their relation to legal will and, by extension, to legal person.
Indeed, whereas in much of *De legibus* Bracton *seems* to be contrasting
the written record with physical acts, such as the livery of seisin, in fact
he is offering a much more sophisticated theorization of the relationship
between textuality, agency, and will than may first appear.[10] Because the
donor's will is necessary to authorize any transaction – the very principle
of dominion for Bracton – and because the charter serves as a written
transcript of that will, it is seen in some cases to be instrumental to the
transaction and not just another form of proof. The charter may serve
not just as evidence of the intentions of the donor but as the proxy

---

[10] Clanchy argues that for Bracton, "written words were thus entirely inadequate, and
even spoken ones were insufficient, without physical symbols" (*From Memory to Written
Record*, 260). In my opinion, this argument, while enormously influential, doesn't really
do credit to Bracton's understanding of documentary culture.

or accessory to his will, the making of fact into act. In this way, the very thing that makes charters probative – that they attest to the will of the donor – makes them, in the absence of the donor, almost foundational. For example, if the donor is away during the transfer of his land, and if he has appointed a human agent to transfer it for him, that transfer will work only if "the charter of the gift and the letters of procuration are read in public before neighbors specially called together for the purpose."[11] An agent or lawyer may formally transfer the land for the donor, but only the charter may express the donor's will to do so.

In fact, as Bracton implies in another place, the very language of charters can be interpreted as the rhetorical transformation of will into act and *vice versa*. The official clauses that comprise the narratives of charters typically begin something like "Let all present and future know that I, N of M . . . have given and granted and with this present charter of mine confirmed" ("Sciant presentes et futuri quod ego, N de M . . . dedi et concessi et hac presenti carta mea confirmaui"). The ostensible function of these and other clauses is to describe the details of the act (its actors, conditions, nature, and *modus*), so that the act will be confirmed by those present and "remembered" by future generations. According to Bracton, however, these clauses are not simply descriptive or memorable details but direct expressions of the donor's will, and as such, they are nearly indistinguishable from the founding of the act:

> When [the donor] says [in his charter], "I have given" [*dedi*], he makes clear his intention [*vult quod*] that the thing given be made the property of the donee. From the words, "I have granted" [*concessi*] it may be inferred that he gave his consent to the gift, for there is no great difference between "I have granted" [*concessi*] and "I have consented" [*consensi*] . . . And when he says, "to such a one" [*talis*, i.e., "so-and-so"] he indicates the person to whom the gift is made and names him specifically. (111)[12]

---

[11] Text and translation in Bracton, *De legibus*, vol. 2, trans. Thorne, 124 (hereafter cited in the main text by page number; translation is Thorne's, unless otherwise indicated). "Ita quod carta donationis et litterae procuratoriae coram vicinis ad hoc specialiter convocatis legentur in publico."

[12] "Et per hoc quod dicit, *dedi*, vult quod res data fiat accipientis. Et per hoc quod dicit, *concessi*, perpendi poterit ex hoc quod donationi consensum praebuit, quia non multum differt dicere *consessi* quam dire *consensi* . . . Item per hoc quod dicit, *tali*, vult quod certa persona exprimatur cui fit donatio." I have translated this passage slightly differently from Thorne in order to emphasize the slippage between granting and consenting.

Notice how Bracton deploys a curious semantic slipperiness in this passage in order to make the point that act and will are inseparable within documentary rhetoric: to grant (*concedere*) is in effect to consent to the grant (*consentire*). Or to put it another way, the very moment that the donor names himself in relation to an action or its recipient (*vult quod*), he associates the intent to act with the act itself. The document, moreover, is the rhetorical site where the donor's will is codified as a legal act, and, conversely, where the legal act is understood to originate in the will of the donor. As Bracton explains in a different section of *De legibus*, the legal document, merely by articulating the will of the donor, might serve as the grounds for a different legal action outside of the instructions that it contains. For example, if a man is accused of being a serf, he may prove his free status within his lord's realm with a charter of manumission. The charter makes him free insofar as it represents the will of the lord to free him, and correspondingly, when the lord is absent, the man must present the charter to prove that freedom. Yet even if the man's charter does not explicitly offer freedom from serfdom but does imply free status (for example, if it contains formulas such as "to have and to hold freely"), the man technically may be said to be free (115).[13] In this way, charter formulas, because they rhetorically conflate the moment of will with the moment of act, cause the donor's will to speak even to actions outside of the purview of the document itself.[14]

As Bracton goes on to explain a few sections later, the job of the document to express the donor's will extends to its material form, as well as to its official formulas, and indeed it is this strange interdependence of material and written form that makes the document an instrument of dominion within a given transaction. The charter simultaneously declares in official clauses the donor's will and the gift being willed, and materially extends that will as a textual object. For example, the

---

[13] Luciana Duranti points out that in medieval law partial acts are often oral, and therefore the simple mention in a document of related partial acts in oral form was sufficient proof of their existence (Duranti, *Diplomatics: New Uses for an Old Science*, 79).

[14] According to Duranti (following Raffel), the conflation of written record and juridical act is an effect of bureaucratization: "the world came to be seen as a series of witnessable and extractable facts which, transported into the record became identical with the record" (*Diplomatics*, 71).

testamentary clause and the seal (the most distinctive physical feature of a medieval document) together indicate the will of the donor not only to give a gift but also to establish materially the expression of his own will. As Bracton explains,

> Since credence would not be given to a writing of this kind unless some sign appeared that the gift and writing proceeded from the understanding and agreement [*a conscientia et voluntate*] of the donor, therefore, in testimony and in proof of the transaction let the donor affix such a sign, by adding to the charter of gift this clause, "That it may be secure" or "in testimony whereof I have set my seal to this writing." (119)[15]

Likewise, says Bracton, with the clause, " 'by my present charter I have confirmed,' [the donor] intimates that his will [*vult quod voluntas sua*], by which the thing is transferred to the donee and which must be firm, be confirmed by the present charter authenticated by his seal, for to confirm is but to reaffirm [i.e., to make firm again] what before was firm"(111).[16]

Bracton's rationalization of diplomatic procedure may seem tentative, but it suggests at least three important points about the way that legal documents might be thought to represent as material texts, and why they might mistakenly be ascribed agency in excess of livery (Bracton's initial concern). First, the whole document or textual object, both the official formulas that indicate the material presence of the document ("I have set my seal," "by my present charter"), and the material document itself (the seal, the whole charter sealed), together indicate the donor's will ("a conscientia et voluntate donatoris" [119]). Thorne translates this last phrase as "the understanding and agreement of the donor," but it is important to see that Bracton is not only referring to the donor's

---

[15] "Et quoniam huiusmodi scripturae non esset fides adhibenda nisi signum interveniret, quod talis donatio et scriptura a conscientia et voluntate donatoris emanaret, ideo in testimonium et approbationem rei gestae apponit donator signum adiciendo in carta donationis clausulam istam, *Quod ut ratum sit* etcetera. Vel sic, *In cuius rei testimonium huic scripto sigillum meum apposui.*"

[16] "Item per hoc quod dicit, praesenti carta mea confirmavi, per hoc innuit quod vult quod voluntas sua, per quam res transfertur ad donatarium, et quae firma esse debet, praesenti carta sigilli sui munimine confirmetur. Est enim confirmare id quod prius firmum fuit simul firmare."

comprehension or approval of the transaction but also to the ways that documentary formulas collapse consent and agency. Where the formulas encode or, in a legal sense, personify will – you might say that they confect legal subjectivity – the physical appearance of the charter serves as a material sign of that encoding or personifying. Second, the charter's double character as material form and written text semantically blurs its relation to the legal act. The will of the donor establishes or makes firm the legal act recorded in the charter ("what must be firm," "what before was firm" [III]), but the written record as legal instrument further expresses the donor's desire to make firm, substantiate, or even reify his own founding will. Thus, in the case of the charter, to confirm is to bear witness to or give evidence for the donor's will that a certain action take place, but, at the same time, to confirm is also to make firm once again, to reestablish the will of the donor by anchoring it to a material text ("be confirmed by this present charter authenticated by his seal, for to confirm is but to reaffirm what before was firm" [III]). Third, and perhaps most significantly, the documentary codification of will into a material text makes the absence of the donor a fundamental legal principle rather than just an unfortunate exception to customary practice. The very possibility of the donor's absence makes the legal document appear to be animated by will, to work independently of human agents and real action, because *its very existence depends upon the legal fiction of absence.*

Bracton makes one final point about documentary practice: it is the dual process of hearing and seeing the charter that converts the will of the author into a legal act. In other words, because the charter is *both* the narrative of the donor's will *and* the material sign of that will, in the case of the donor's absence, it must be heard and seen by the community in order for the legal act to be properly authorized and implemented. (It is as if what is rhetorically personified in the text must be dramatically impersonated to achieve its desired effects.) In this way, the material charter efficiently correlates rhetorical conventions and ritual performance. And in doing so, it becomes a profoundly social form of signification, because it is in the absence of the donor that it comes to represent the whole legal act. In the case of the donor's absence, for example, the donor's agent must read the text of the charter aloud *and* exhibit it to an audience: "In that case let the letters and charter be shown, that it may be said [the agent] had writ and charter, [or] in English, *he hadde bothe writ and charter*" (124–5).[17] Bracton's striking insertion of the English idiom here underlines the public performance of the charter, with the phrase "he hadde bothe writ and chartre" simultaneously invoking legal convention and public rumor.

The directive that the donor's agent exhibit both his charter and his writ suggests, moreover, that written records have two complementary functions in the transfer of land: they articulate will (the charter) and authorize the human agency of that will (the writ), thus mediating between the author of the act and his deputies. Bracton explains that even if the donor is present, witnesses should also be called in while the charter is being made, so that "they may verify what was done if required to do so, and [have] their names included in the charter" (119).[18] If it is impossible to find witnesses to the making of the charter, he continues, the charter should later be read, exhibited, and corrected in the presence of witnesses, and preferably in a very public place such as the hundred court, "so that if the gift is denied it may more readily be proved" (119–20).[19] This procedure of making and proclaiming the charter in public has the effect of recruiting more oral witnesses to the transaction, should the transaction be questioned at a later date, but it also guarantees that the charter truly represents the donor's will to make a gift in the first place. Notably, the guarantee depends not merely on the validity of the charter, whether it correctly transcribes the will of the donor into official formulas, but on the very manufacturing of will into written record, the physical making of absence into material written presence. Hence witnesses are needed to attest to that manufacturing process because, says Bracton, "If there were no witnesses present and no such ceremony was performed and a doubt arises as to the seal and the charter, if the witnesses, when asked, say they know nothing of the matter, the charter (though genuine and valid) may then fail because of lack of proof, for

---

[17] "Et in quo casu ostendantur litterae et carta ut dici poterit talis habuit breve et cartam, secundum quod Anglice dicitur, *He hadde bothe writ and charter.*"

[18] "ut veritatem dicere possint si inde fuerint requisti, et eorum nomina debent in carta comprehendi."

[19] "in locis publicis, sicut in comitatui hundredo, ut facilius probari posit si forte fuerit dedicta."

proof may fail though there is no absence of right" (120).[20] Witnesses are needed to corroborate the authenticity of the charter, not because the charter is a flimsy form of proof, inferior to oral testimony, but because it is nearly on a par with the gift itself. It is, in the donor's absence, the primary site of legal action.

PERSONIFICATION ALLEGORY AND LEGAL WILL: THE CASE OF DEGUILEVILLE

Bracton's purpose in *De legibus* is, on the surface, fairly straightforward: he wants to define dominion and, in the process, de-emphasize the role of the charter, relegating it from the dispositive to the probative. Yet by emphasizing the relations of dominion, and by conceding the complex role of the charter within those relations, he ends up producing a carefully nuanced theory of documentary practice which compromises his original purpose. He makes it clear that documents bear a special signifying relationship to legal will and thus to the transformation of subjectivity into legal action. In doing so, he shows how, in the absence of the donor, written text and material form are interdependent in the process of substantiating and confirming legal will. Finally, he shows that the making of the legal document into a material sign is necessarily a group effort: it is through the ritual performance of the document that the principle of absence is realized. Likewise, it is the ritual performance that completes the process by which the document becomes a site of legal action.

What significance, then, might Bracton's analysis of documentary practice have for our reading of fourteenth-century literary texts, and what might the peculiar status of the document as a material text have to do with certain forms of poetic representation? We have seen that Bracton, in his capacity as a legal theorist, makes legal documents co-extensive with the ethical subject by expounding the relationship between material documents and legal subjectivity. As we will see in this

[20] "Si autem testes praesentes non fuerint nec talis solemnitas adhibita, si de signo et carta oriatur dubitatio, si cum testes fuerint requisti dicant se nihil inde scire, ita deficere poterit carta quamvis vera et bona, propter defectum probationis, deficere enim poterit probation quamvis ius non deficiat."

chapter and the next, later medieval vernacular writers, without citing Bracton specifically, recognized the profound implications of such a relation for certain kinds of literary projects, and especially for experiments in personification allegory and lyric poetry. Key to the invention of this documentary poetics is Guillaume de Deguileville's *Pèlerinage* trilogy (1330–55) – *Le pèlerinage de la vie humaine, Le pèlerinage de l'âme,* and *Le pèlerinage de Jesu Christ* – which survives in eighty-six manuscripts and nearly every Western European language. The trilogy, enormously influential in late medieval England, tells the story of a pilgrim who experiences a dream-vision in which he encounters personifications offering various opinions on penance and salvation. The most memorable feature of Deguileville's otherwise rather conventional rendering of personification allegory is its number of legal instruments: Charity presents Moses with the last testament of Christ, Tribulation proves her authority to the pilgrim with commissions from God and Satan, the Devil records a confession from the Worm of Conscience, Mercy obtains a charter of pardon from Christ, Reason shows her divine commission to Rude Understanding, and so forth. Bracton's *De legibus* allows us to focus on what these documents reveal about literary form, rather than what they reveal about literary representation, and conversely, how documents in literature theorize legal relations. In doing so, moreover, it shows how the formal concerns of documentary poetics are profoundly social. Bracton's treatise and Deguileville's poem together call attention to the ways that textuality is negotiated through dominion, status, community, and performance.

Deguileville's trilogy, although originally composed in French, made up a significant part of the Middle English poetic corpus and had a remarkable effect on English notions of vernacular religious poetry. At the very least, it appealed to the tastes of the Francophilic, allegory-loving English aristocracy and to the poets who enjoyed their patronage and compensated for their deficiencies in French. Clearly by 1368, when Chaucer was translating into English Deguileville's ABC hymn to the Virgin, the first book in the trilogy, the *Le pèlerinage de la vie humaine* was already well-known in England, mostly likely as an anonymous English prose version of the poem's first redaction, the *Pilgrimage of the Lyfe of the Manhode*, which survives in six manuscripts from the early fifteenth century (two of them sumptuously illustrated).[21] By 1426 John Lydgate had adapted into English verse Deguileville's second redaction of the *Le pèlerinage de la vie humaine* as the *Pilgrimage of the Life of Man*, which Lydgate dedicated to Thomas Montacute, Earl of Salisbury and husband of Alice Chaucer. He also incorporated into his adaptation Chaucer's translation of the Marian hymn.[22] Sometime around 1413 Thomas Hoccleve, the Privy Seal clerk and Chaucerian enthusiast, may have been responsible for translating into English the second book of the trilogy, *Le pèlerinage de l'âme* (*The Pilgrimage of the Soul*). It has been more conclusively established that he translated one of the *Soul's* lyrics, notably a fictive charter of Christ, for Joan FitzAlan, Henry IV's mother-in-law (d. 1419).[23] Clearly, too, the trilogy provided a model for William Langland's *Piers Plowman*, as will become clearer in subsequent chapters of this book.

The popularity of the *Pèlerinage* trilogy, especially in England, was largely due to its ability to capitalize on the international success of the thirteenth-century personification allegory, *Le roman de la rose*. The dreamer-narrator of *Pèlerinage de la vie humaine*, like Chaucer's narrator in the *Book of the Duchess,* falls asleep after reading the "faire romaunce of þe Rose,"[24] and indeed the trilogy as a whole, which the prose translator slyly calls the "Romance of the Monk," advertises itself as an adaptation of personification allegory from courtly (and academic) literature to penitential literature.[25] The two allegories clearly played complementary

---

[21] Henry, "The Illuminations in the Two Illustrated Middle English Manuscripts of the Prose *Pilgrimage of the Lyfe of the Manhode*."

[22] Lydgate's translation survives in three manuscripts. For a description of the manuscripts, see Walls's article, "Did Lydgate Translate the *Pèlerinage de la vie humaine?*"; and Green's response, "Lydgate and Deguileville Once More."

[23] For the authorship of the *Pilgrimage of the Soul*, see the introduction to *The Pilgrimage of the Soul*, ed. McGerr, xxv–xxix. See also Furnivall's comments in the introduction to *Hoccleve's Works*. Burrow contests Hoccleve's authorship of the *Soul* in *Thomas Hoccleve*, 24.

[24] Text in *The Pilgrimage of the Lyfe of the Manhode* [*Lyfe*], ed. Henry, line 6 (hereafter cited in the main text by line number).

[25] Camille argues that the illustrations that most influenced the ones in manuscripts of the *Pèlerinage de la vie humaine* were from the earlier section of the *Roman de la Rose* written by Guillaume de Lorris, suggesting that Deguileville was writing the *Vie* at the same time that the *Roman de la Rose* "had developed a ubiquitous system of illustration, which by the second quarter of the fourteenth century already showed great variety." See "The Illustrated Manuscripts of Guillaume de Deguileville's '*Pèlerinages*', 1330–1426," 10.

roles in the literary education of the French duke Charles d'Orléans (1394–1465), an exemplary prisoner of war who lived in England for over twenty years. In his *magnum opus*, the courtly allegorical narrative *Fortunes Stabilnes*, the duke's lover-narrator negotiates terms of vassalage with the God of Love, but like Deguileville's narrator, he does so with a battery of versified missives, commissions, indentures, and pardons.[26] Both Deguileville and Charles d'Orléans were, technically speaking, French authors, but in a certain sense the translation of Deguileville's documentary poetics into the duke's literary enterprise was made possible by the translatability of Deguileville's trilogy into English allegorical dream-visions. Deguileville and Charles d'Orléans thus attest to a century of cross-channel elaboration of the *Roman de la rose:* Deguileville turned Jean de Meun's secular allegory into a spiritual pilgrimage exceedingly attractive to English readers; Charles d'Orléans returned the *Pèlerinages* to secular allegory, by way of English letters and documentary culture.

In many ways, the *Pilgrimage* trilogy is a supremely ordinary medieval allegory, so much so as to elude the taste of most modern readers, one of whom, C. S. Lewis, dismissed its personifications as "monstrous." In the last few decades, however, a few critics have tried to recuperate Deguileville, pointing out that what Lewis calls monstrous – Memory placing her eyes in her ears, and so forth – is, in fact, a flamboyant troping of personification allegory, and as such passes for a treatise on dream-vision, even as it remains a serious penitential narrative. J. Stephen Russell argues, for example, that Deguileville's monstrosities show that allegory is "a language rather than a spectacle," while Susan Hagen argues that Lydgate's *Pilgrimage of the Life of Man* is a sophisticated exposition of the arts of memory.[27] As I shall demonstrate here, Deguileville's exploration of personification allegory is remarkable because it is predicated on a remarkable innovation: fictive legal documents. These documents are remarkable because they are, properly speaking, neither symbolic nor literal accoutrements, as one might find in a typical allegorical dream-vision or miracle story. Rather, they serve as commentary on the operations and limitations of personification while, at the same time,

---

[26] See Charles d'Orléans, *Fortunes Stabilnes*, ed. Arn.
[27] Russell, "Allegorical Monstrosity: the Case of Deguileville"; Hagen, *Allegorical Remembrance*.

helping to make personification "work" within the narrative fiction of the pilgrimage.

Two scenes from the trilogy illustrate this innovation especially well: in the first, Mercy obtains a charter of pardon from Christ; in the second, Reason displays her commission from Grace Dieu. In the first scene, taken from the *Pilgrimage of the Soul*, the pilgrim has died and arrived at St. Michael's courtroom for final judgment.[28] His angel-warden has testified to his good faith and intent, but the devil and his loathsome sidekick "sotil Synderesis" (the Worm of Conscience) submit to the court a damning report of the pilgrim's sins. The pilgrim protests that the devil goaded him to sin and is therefore an unacceptable notary scribe, but the stern ladies of the court, Truth and Justice, maintain that the pilgrim had every opportunity to resist the devil's snares. Justice produces a set of scales, weighs the pilgrim's good deeds against "Sathanasses bill," and finds them insufficient. The pilgrim is on the verge of going to hell when Mercy suddenly halts the proceedings to purchase a charter of pardon from heaven. When she returns to the court, she opens her "skypet," her document-box, and displays Christ's pardon to the court, which turns out to be a beautiful charter sealed with a golden seal: "'And so haue I here of þe Lordes graunte a chartre of pardoun,'" she proclaims, "'which I shal rede tofore ʒow, wherof whoso wole shal haue the copye.' Thanne toke she forth a fair charter enseled with golde and radde it openly worde by word" (*Soul*, 49, ll. 23–8).

At this point, the pilgrim-narrator stops to invite his readers to inspect the charter as well ("wherof this is the sentence"), which turns out to be a fourteen-stanza poem in rhyme royal, the first few lines of which imitate the salutation of royal patents: "Ihesu, kyng of high heuene aboue,/Vnto Michael, my chief lieutenaunt,/And alle thyn assessours, which I loue... My gretyng; and vpon the peyne of drede/Vnto this present chartre taketh hede" (*Soul*, 49, ll. 30–2, 35–6). Christ decrees in his charter that those who sincerely repent before they die shall not be condemned to hell, even if their bad deeds outweigh their good ones. The superabundant grace of Christ's Passion, and of Mary and the saints, will be put in the balance against the devil's part. But Christ

---

[28] Text in *The Pilgrimage of the Soul, A Critical Edition of the Middle English Dream Vision,* [*Soul*] ed. McGerr (hereafter cited in the main text by page and line number).

warns that this charter excepts those who are complaisant, or who stubbornly refuse to repent until the very last moment: "Therfore out of this
chartre I excepte/Tho alle hwiche, vnto her lyues ende,/Haue euermore
in cursed synnes slepte…" (*Soul*, 51, ll. 13–15). After some deliberation,
St. Michael decides to add the charter to the pilgrim's side of the balance,
which happily sinks with the weight of God's grace. The pilgrim thus
narrowly avoids hell but must do time in purgatory before proceeding to
heaven.

What is immediately arresting about this scene is that the document –
Christ's charter – records an act of mercy, rather than justice; it is not,
as might be expected, an oppressively literate incarnation of the supernatural legal system.[29] But this scene shows further that Deguileville has
exploited the material textuality of legal documents to make a larger
point about personification. He demonstrates in this scene how personification allegory within a *penitential romance* might do more than offer
a set of mnemonic devices, which together make up an instructive or
entertaining narrative; it might constitute an authoritative and redemptive act in itself. Generally speaking, medieval personification allegory,
whether it uses personification proper or other materializations, draws
explicitly and dramatically upon two processes, seeing and hearing. We
see the material sign of an abstract quality (the beautiful lady Mercy,
the scales of Justice, Penance's broom), and we hear the explanation,
either from the narrator or from the personifications themselves, of
how the sign and its accessories illustrate that quality. The distinctive
material form of the legal document means that it too may serve as a
memorable iconographic accoutrement conjoined to a personification –
here, it represents pardon linked to Mercy, the very promise of the
Atonement. Indeed, illustrations of this pardon almost always depict
the characteristic single leaf of a patent with at least one hanging seal.
We are also told some concrete details about Mercy's pardon: she takes
it out of a box and holds it up for all to see, and the pilgrim tells us that
it has a golden seal, an indicator, presumably, of its divine origins.

In this sense, the material form of charters, like other instances of
personification in the *Pèlerinages*, exemplifies the necessity of visual

---

[29] For a very different interpretation of this scene, and for diabolical writing more generally, see Camille, "The Devil's Writing" and "The Language of Images in Medieval
England."

signs for processing abstract concepts – a charter of pardon would not be accepted as a grant, for example, without its authorizing seal. But as we saw in Bracton's *De legibus et consuetudinibus Angliae*, the form of a charter, *unlike* other visual signs, unfolds into a readable text, the purpose of which is to confirm and be confirmed by the material form. It is in these mutually affirming roles as readable text and material object, moreover, that Deguileville's charter exceeds the visual actualization of an abstract concept (as one might see in the allegorical narratives of Jean de Meun or Alain de Lille) and begins to unpack the entire operations of seeing and hearing central to personification allegory. It does so, first of all, by authorizing itself. It describes the history of the abstract quality – pardon – that the parchment with the gold seal nominally represents. It describes the grantor and recipients of pardon, the thing to be granted, the circumstances in which it was granted, and the conditions for its implementation. Just as the visual sign of the charter would not represent a grant of pardon if it did not have an open format and a hanging seal, so it would not represent Christ's intention to pardon if it did not contain this information and if that information were not expressed in official formulas. The charter is a sign that signifies a quality (pardon), and as such it participates in a larger allegorical narrative. It also, however, contains its own narrative within itself; it signifies authority as well as pardon because it authenticates itself.

As we saw with Bracton, moreover, the text of Mercy's charter further authorizes the material sign by narrating the voice of the absent grantor, Christ, as opposed to the voice of a personified character within the narrative, such as Mercy or the pilgrim. In doing so, the charter presents personification ideally as a legal fiction, as well as a literary fiction. Like *prosopopeia*, the case of the absent or imaginary speaker, the charter makes the intangible tangible and makes the material human. The visible layout of the charter materializes or substantiates the donor's will that an action take place (the golden seal), while at the same time the text of the charter speaks for the absent donor ("I, Christ," etc.). Importantly, the charter personifies in the sense of creating legal persons through narrative fictions: it is the making of legal personhood that permits an action to take place, even in the absence of the donor. As we saw with Bracton, too, the donor's will (here Christ's will), when encoded as an act within documentary formulas, becomes an entity with rights and privileges.[30] Likewise, the addressees, agents, purveyors, and beneficiaries named in the document (St. Michael, Mary, Mercy, the contrite pilgrim) are realized as actors within the legal drama of the text. What I am suggesting, then, by calling attention to the documentary poetics of this scene, is that Mercy's charter showcases a personification allegory in miniature, whose signifying claims exemplify and authorize the mechanisms central to all personification.

We might go even further, however, and say that Mercy's charter, by using documentary practice to unpack the signifying claims of person-ification allegory, shows how allegory performs, rather than symbolizes or illustrates, the penitential life. In other words, if Mercy's charter is the site at which the will of the donor (Christ) is encoded materially and rhetorically as a legal act (the granting of pardon), it suggests ways that personification allegory, at least in Deguileville's version of it, might be a redemptive process and a series of foundational moments. Generally speaking, iconographic appendages such as Penance's broom or Justice's scales are contiguous with the personification – they are emblems of the quality that the personified character represents. But Mercy's charter goes beyond the metonymic to represent the whole process by which pardon is authorized and disseminated through the mercy of Christ. To see and to hear this document is not simply to learn the significance of pardon but also to witness and participate in the process by which pardon is continuously established and made available as a material text. It is, we might say, performative inside and outside the literary fiction – it "outweighs" the devil's testimony by transacting salvation both with the pilgrim and with all of Deguileville's readers.

The scene of Mercy's pardon shows how documentary culture might be used to theorize the relationship between allegory, textuality, and redemption. But whereas that scene posits documents as unquestion-able *loci* of authority, authorizing both redemptive action within the allegorical fiction and the larger project of reading personification alle-gory, the scene of Reason's commission questions the method by which documents authenticate persons and, by extension, the various ways in which personification may be received, recognized, and named. More

---

[30] Although the author is personified as an actor the moment he takes a justified legal action, the charter is the written record of his personification. On this point, see Duranti, *Diplomatics*, 81–97.

specifically, Deguileville uses legal documents in this second example to show how the making of meaning within personification allegory is shaped as much by social conflict as it is by semantic and interpretative ambiguity. This is not to say that Deguileville is anticipating the trajectory of the modern, the "movement of the sign as material to the signifying process itself."[31] It is to say, rather, that he is interested in rationalizing the signifying process by calling attention to the material textualities of the sign, as well as the social dynamics in which that sign is produced.

At the beginning of Book 2 of the *Pilgrimage of the Lyfe of the Man-hode,* the pilgrim encounters a nasty churl with a churl's stereotypical features – "euele shapen, grete [browed] and frounced" – wielding a menacing staff (*Lyfe,* 2772–3). The churl accosts the pilgrim, threatening to take away his satchel and walking stick, and accusing him of breaking the king's – Christ's – law. This "law," which the churl insists upon interpreting literally, orders all men to leave at home their stick and satchel (from Luke 9.3: "Carry nothing with you, neither stick, nor bread, nor money, nor should you have two tunics"). The pilgrim is cowed into silence but is soon rescued by a noble lady named Reason, who has been sent by Grace Dieu to serve as the pilgrim's advocate. She loftily challenges the churl with a series of questions: whom does he serve, what does he do for a living, and what is his name? ("Cherl, sey me, now God keepe þee, wherof þow seruest and whi þou seemest so diuers? Art þou a repere or a mowere, or an espyour of weyfereres? How hattest þou, and where gaderedest and tooke þi grete staf?" [*Lyfe,* 2808–11]). She observes, moreover, that a staff is not a becoming prop for a good man. The feisty churl returns her challenge in kind, asking her whether she thinks she is some kind of "mayoress" or "enqueress" and demanding to see her commission, without which he will not believe that she has the authority to intervene. "Shewe þi commissioun," he says, "at þe leste þi name I shal wite, and þe grete powere þat þou hast, þat bi semblaunt þou shewest me: for if I were not suer þerof, I wolde to þee answere nothing" (*Lyfe,* 2814–17).

Reason promptly reaches into a pocket or small sack ("speyer") in her bosom and produces a box from which she draws forth her commission (Figures 2 and 3). She commands the churl to examine it so that he might

---

[31] Stewart, *On Longing: Narratives of the Miniature, the Gigantic, the Souvenir, the Collection,* 5.

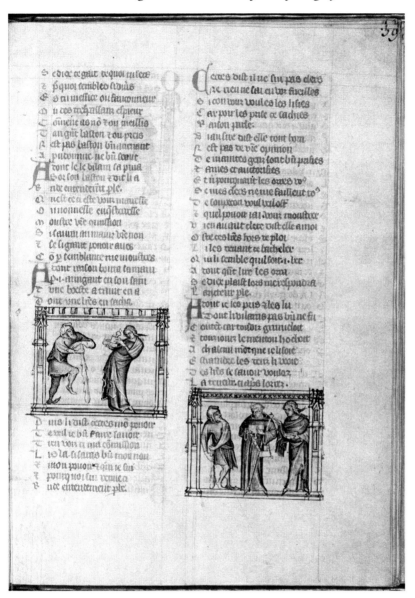

Figure 2 The pilgrim reads Reason's commission to Rude Entendement. From Guillaume de Deguileville, *Le pèlerinage de la vie humaine*. New York. The Pierpont Morgan Library MS. M.772, fol. 39. (fourteenth century). (With permission of The Pierpont Morgan Library).

Figure 3 Reason presents her commission to Rude Entendement. From Guillaume de Deguileville, *Le pèlerinage de la vie humaine*. Oxford. Bodleian Library MS. Douce 300, fol. 46v. (ca. 1390–1400). (With permission of the Bodleian Library).

"know" her: "Serteyn my poowere I wole wel do þe to wite. Hold, see heere my commissioun: rede it, and þou shalt wel wite my name and my power, and who I am, and whi I am come hider" (*Lyfe*, 2819–22).[32] The churl grumbles that he is no clerk and can't read anything in her leaves, and even if he could, he would find little to praise in them. Reason subsequently commands the pilgrim to assume the role of a clerk, to unfold the commission and to read it to the churl: "'Come forth clerk,' quod she to me: 'vndoo þese lettreres out of plyt, rede hem bifore þis bachelere þat weeneth he be a lord. Whan he heereth hem red, if God wole he shal answere me'" (*Lyfe*, 2828–31).[33] The narrator invites the reader to hear the commission as well, reproducing it within the text:

> Grace Dieu (bi whom gouernen hem þei seyn þe kynges, and reg-nen) to Resoun oure goode louede freend, and in alle goode dedes wel proued, gretinge: and of þat we sende, dooth pleyn execucioun. Of neewe we haue vnderstonde (wherof us is not [fair]) þat a cherl shrewede, prowd and daungerous, þat bi his name maketh clepe him and nempne him Rude Entendement, hath maad him an espyour of weyes, and a waytere of pilgrimes, and wole bineme hem here burdouns and vnscrippe here scrippes, bigylinge hem with lyinge wo-ordes. And for he wolde be þe more dred, he hath borwed of Orgoill his wikkede and cruelle staf, þat men clepen Obstinacioun (þe whiche michel more displeseth me þan doth þe frouncede cherl): for þe which thing, maundement we yiven you nouht in comaundinge, þat ye go þiderward, and amoneste þilke musard þat his staf he ley [doun], and þat he cesse of the surpluis. And if anything he withstond, oþerwole not abeye, yiueth him day competent at þe assyses of jugement. Of þis pleyn power we yiven yow and maken you commissarye. Yiven in oure yeer þat eche wiht clepeth MCCCXXXI. (*Lyfe*, 2836–55)

The commission, issued by Grace Dieu to Reason, describes the abuses of an ugly churl named Rude Understanding ("Rude Entendement") who is hostile and shrewd, and who is known for hindering pilgrims,

---

[32] The French original supplies a more detailed account of this process: "A donc Raison bouta sa main/ Par un amigaunt en son sain/ Et une boiste ataint en a/Dont une letres hors sacha" ("Then Reason put her hand into a slit in her belt and produced a box from which she extracted her letters"). (*Le pèlerinage de vie humaine de Guillaume de Deguileville*, ed. Stürzinger, ll. 5103–6).

[33] For further discussion of the peculiar social dynamic in this passage, see chapter 5 of this book.

depriving them of their satchels and walking sticks, and terrifying them with his large staff called Obstinacy. The commission entrusts Reason with the "pleyn power" to warn Rude Understanding to lay down his stick and, should he refuse, to assign him a day at which to stand at the assizes of judgment. It is dated to the year 1331, the date of the poem's first publication, thus bringing to the narrative both a sense of spiritual immediacy and authorial self-promotion (*Lyfe*, 2854–5).[34]

The churl, who is, of course, the same Rude Understanding mentioned in the commission, insists that he still has no idea who Reason is. He has heard her commission many times before, he says, but he cannot reconcile the description of Reason in the document with the name "Reason" because he has heard that name defamed at the mill (peasants sardonically call the grain measures "raison" because they are unfairly weighted). That name represents for him a deceptive practice rather than the abstract virtue that the personification who calls herself Reason claims to represent. Reason explains to Rude Understanding that he needs to differentiate between a name and a thing, to recognize when a vice is masquerading behind the "couerture" of honest virtue, or when a name doesn't correctly signify an object or quality: "Betwixe name and beeinge I wole wel make difference. Oon thing is to be Resoun, and anoother thing haue his name" (*Lyfe*, 2874–5). Conversely, it is incumbent upon him to recognize when a sign really does signify the thing, when it bears a natural fitness to the thing signified. Rude Understanding, true to his name, stubbornly rejects these explanations, retorting that when he hears the name "cat" he doesn't picture a calf, and, by the same flawed logic, something which calls itself Reason must either be deceitful or else it is not Reason at all. Reason quickly turns the table on the churl, asking him *his* name. Annoyed, he exclaims, you have my name in your document, why should you ask it? ("Thou hast my name in thi leues, and askest it!" [*Lyfe*, 2907–8]). "Aa!" exults Resoun, "Art þou þilke þat art set in my leues? þe name withinne wel I wiste, but þee knew I not" (*Lyfe*, 2910–12).

---

[34] Interestingly enough, Lydgate's translation of the second recension of the *Pèlerinage de la vie humaine* preserves the original date, while acknowledging that it is no longer immediate: "The daate countyd, a thowsand yer,/thre hundryd over, thrytty & on,/Wryte & asselyd nat yore agon." Text in *The Pilgrimage of the Life of Man* [Lydgate], ed. Furnivall, ll. 10555–7.

The debate between Reason and Rude Understanding obviously raises some difficult questions for personification allegory. To interpret it correctly is to recognize the right relationship between the name "Reason," the personification, and the abstract quality that the personification claims to represent. In the case of an allegorical fiction, the correct interpretation of which is also the cultivation of a proper spiritual attitude, the stakes are extremely high both for the author and reader. To interpret the allegory incorrectly is to jeopardize one's salvation. In general, personification allegory promises in a very concrete way to correlate a name to a quality. It fulfills this promise in part through the discourse of the personified character, which both establishes the correlation of name to quality, and attests to it. The pilgrim notes, for example, that Reason instantly gives herself away by her decorous and judicious speech, "for she wole nothing sey but sittingeliche and wel ordeyned" (*Lyfe*, 2801–2). The correlation of name to quality is further accomplished through the personification's physical appearance, which is meant to be a literal conformation of image to virtue – it should ideally illustrate *and* authorize. Thus Rude Understanding's challenge to Reason is ludicrous because it is almost impossible to read Reason incorrectly, judging from her appearance. If he were not so boorish he would see, as the pilgrim does, that the personification called Reason is a highborn and well-mannered lady, indicating both her natural relationship to virtue and her authority to define and implement it. In the same way Rude Understanding's churlishness – his rumpled eyebrows, wrinkled cheeks, and scary staff – assures us that he is a vice, and an unauthorized, incompetent, and literal reader to boot. He too is known by his speech. After he identifies himself in the commission, for example, Reason confesses that she knew it was him all along: "I wot bi þi wordes þat þou propirliche art Rude Entendement" (2918–19). Interestingly, in Lydgate's version, the churl interrupts his argument with Reason by breaking the meter into a puerile hopscotch chant: "I knowe kanvas/I knowe sylk,/I knowe the flye dreynt in the mylk," etc. (Lydgate, 10677–8). These lines prove that the quality of knowing – whether one knows only the rhythm of names (in the French *Vie*, "connaise") or, more profoundly, how they signify (in the French *Vie* "savoisse") – is circumscribed by the discourse of character.

As the exchange between Reason and the churl suggests, however, the relationship between the personification – the visual sign – and the abstract virtue that it claims to represent is always in danger of being mis-named or mis-recognized, despite the best efforts of the author. In his example of the millstones, for example, the churl disingenuously takes the discrepancies inherent in irony to be the literal truth: the peasants who call the false measures "raison" are alluding as much to a real virtue as they are to its corruption in specific contexts. (Indeed, for the peasants, the irony of "raison" works precisely in opposition to personification allegory: where Reason is an abstract concept personified as a lady, "raison" is a concrete object renamed as an abstract concept). The problem of naming is presented here, in other words, as a problem of character, of social status as well as pedagogy: the moral gap between the signifier and signified, in the absence of sacramentality, can only be transcended by honorable intention and social superiority, neither of which is stable. Thus the millstone example is an especially revealing illustration of semantic displacement and proliferation, since the kind of collusion between miller and landlord to which Rude Understanding is surely referring was one of the major causes of peasant outbreak in fourteenth-century England and France. In effect, by bringing up the example of the millstones, the churl undoes himself twice: he refuses to hear Reason because he is socially invested in misunderstanding signification, and he compromises his own class interests by missing the irony of "raison."[35]

Ultimately, however, Reason's commission posits an ideal relationship between the visual sign and the abstract quality that it illustrates. It is able to do this not because the document is, in this instance, an unexamined symbol of aristocratic authority, nor because it is a transcendental signifier, but rather because it makes a substantial case for personification allegory *at the same time* that it makes a case for relations of dominion. Reason mocks Rude Understanding's staff (Obstinacy) because it is indecorous, and he in his turn demands to see and tries to reject her commission. Clearly, however, the staff and the commission are not commensurate visual signs. Whereas the staff symbolically

---

[35] In "Acts of Vagrancy," Middleton persuasively argues that the *Piers Plowman* C. 5 "autobiographical passage" dramatizes the Statute of Laborers (1351), and particularly its legislative aftermath, which attempted to control wage hikes by punishing itinerancy and fixing wages. Although Deguileville's poem was written before the Statute of Laborers was put into effect, it's nevertheless clear in this passage how Deguileville anticipates Langland's portrayal of the dreamer as pilgrim and vagrant.

testifies to the violent literalness of bad reading – it is contiguous with Rude Understanding – Reason's commission does not represent Reason directly but rather Grace Dieu's will that Reason overcome Rude Understanding. Like Mercy's charter, then, it serves as an embodiment of and commentary on the personification ideal. It does this in one way through the exhibition of the material document; as we saw with Bracton, the public manufacture of will into act occurs through the legal procedure of hearing and seeing. Here the churl demands to see it, Reason produces it, the narrator reads it aloud, the churl confirms it (Figures 2 and 3). This is, in effect, the goal of a penitential text: to subordinate and interpellate at the same time that it shows how something rhetorical might be performative, or really, how divine authority might be successfully manifested through language.

More importantly, perhaps, Reason's commission elaborates on the personification ideal by means of the documentary fictions that corroborate the material sign. By narrating the story of the quality called Reason, by naming in official formulas the grantor, recipient, date, condition, and mode of her appointment, date, etc., the commission offers incontrovertible evidence for the integrity of the visual sign within personification allegory (Reason's hermeneutic triumph) and, by extension, for the mastery of Reason over bad scriptural reading (the pilgrim's penitential goal). Because the churl admits to recognizing himself in the document through his reluctant witnessing (says the narrator, "at euery woord I redde, I sygh his teeth grynte" [*Lyfe*, 2834–5]), so he is also forced to confess two other truths: first, that the lady standing before him is the true personification of Reason, and second, that Reason is a virtue and not the false weights at the mill. Reason claims that she didn't know the churl because, by alienating the name from the thing named, he had given her reason not to know herself. Her self-identification thus depends on the witnessing practices of others: "I heeld an oppinyoun *þat I and my name is not oon*: for with my name may appare him eche þeef that goth to stele, and þerfore I wende soo of þee, for hadde I not yit lerned þat þou and Rude Entendement *weren oon [ioyngtliche]* – but now I see wel withoute suspecioun þat *ye ben oon withoute distinctioun*" (*Lyfe*, 2912–17, emphases mine). But once Rude Understanding is duped into identifying himself in Reason's document, thus linking name to appearance, so too might she identify him by his rude behavior, also described in her document. In this way, Reason's commission becomes a symbol of aristocratic authority insofar as it establishes hermeneutic sovereignty: it establishes Reason's dominion over the churl at the same time that it forces the churl to concede his position on semantic "diversity," and bridge the unseemly gap between name and thing.

Reason's commission also defends personification allegory by suggesting that it might be authenticated through the legal fiction of person, in which natural persons (real people) acquire legal status at the moment that the will of the author is translated into documentary formulas: e.g., "Grace Dieu (bi whom gouernen hem þei seyn þe kynges, and regnen) to Resoun oure goode louede freend, and in alle goode dedes well proued, gretinge and of þat we sende, dooth pleyn execucioun... þat a cherl shrewede, prowd and daungerous, þat bi his name maketh clepe him and nempne him Rude Entendement, hath maad him an espyour of weyes, and a waytere of pilgrimes... Of þis pleyn power we yiven yow and maken you commissarye," etc. (*Lyfe*, 2837–43, 2853–4). The commission names so effectively, in other words, because it demonstrates the ways that personification might take part in the human at the same time that it acquires within the narrative fiction "a specially structured agency, insofar as the ability of one human being to act or intend is in many or all of its capacities transferred to another."[36] Elizabeth Fowler astutely points out that legal personhood names human beings (and corporations) as legal actors by incorporating them into fictions of social relations – the roles that people assign to each other (friend, assailant, commissary, wife), as opposed to those which they represent themselves. Taken together, then, Bracton and Deguileville help us to see how a natural (real) person acquires legal personhood *textually* by means of the rhetorical relations stipulated by diplomatic practice, and consequently, how documentary formulas might stand in for the work of personification allegory. Indeed, it is the textual acquisition of legal person in Reason's commission that makes it a primary site of meaning. It is, moreover, the commission's naming of actors within social relations – the narrative of legal person – that informs and finally resolves the interpretative contest between Reason and Rude Understanding. As Reason sarcastically informs the churl, "'sithe I woot þi name, gret

[36] Fowler, "Civil Death and the Maiden," 768–70.

44

neede haue I nought to aske more of þe remenaunt: in my letteres it is al cleer, for an espyour þou art of weyes, and an assaylour of pilgrims'" (*Lyfe*, 2929–31).

In this scene, then, Reason's commission offers an ideal of personification allegory in which name and visual image are inexorably linked. It is an ideal, too, in which penitential discourse itself becomes a socially-contingent and efficacious practice through the making of documentary fictions.[37] Most importantly, however, the commission becomes the instrument with which "bad reading" may be overcome and the reader may reconcile reason and grace. By articulating the will of the grantor that Reason overcome Rude Understanding, the commission effects that very act, not because it possesses supernatural powers (it does), but rather because it defends the signifying claims of personification allegory within a penitential narrative, and discloses the true identities of Rude Understanding and Reason. Moreover, the pilgrim, by identifying Rude Understanding as a stubborn criminal and by accepting Reason for who she is, may finally make the critical leap from reading personification allegory correctly to reading scripture correctly. The churl first confronts the narrator with a very literal reading of Luke, a reading that threatens to discourage the narrator from his pilgrimage path. But by witnessing the document, by naming and subduing his "inward churl," the pilgrim is able to overcome his spiritual and hermeneutic obstinacy by accepting the "natural" relationship between visual sign and abstract virtue. It allows him, in other words, to perform two kinds of penitential reading simultaneously: first, to recognize the literal truth of personification allegory; and second, to transcend the churl's literal reading of Luke to justify the use of allegory within the penitential experience. The whole point of personification allegory is that it literalizes that which is not meant to be taken literally – in a certain way, it works counter to the logic of biblical hermeneutics. Yet Reason's commission effectively reconciles allegoresis and hermeneutics: it proves that the pilgrim in a personification allegory-*cum*-psychomachia may literally carry stick and satchel because Luke is meant to be read allegorically.

---

[37] Interestingly enough, in Lydgate's version, Rude Understanding tells Reason, "a *replicacion*/I wyl make vp-on thy name," a word that evokes simultaneously the semiotic duplication of meaning and the response of a legal plaintiff (ll. 10584–5, emphasis mine).

To use Bracton's language, the material written record provides the dispositive grace needed to read allegory well.

We have seen that Deguileville's documentary poetics enabled him to negotiate the place of allegory in penitential narratives. It also enabled him to differentiate his project from the semiotic preoccupations of the much more famous dream-vision, the *Roman de la rose*. As Kevin Brownlee has pointed out, each character in the *Roman de la rose* embodies "a different discursive practice, a different poetics," and likewise "the very identities of these characters are defined by – are coterminous with – their discourse."[38] In fact, argues Brownlee, it is the limitation of discourse to character that foregrounds the status of language in that poem. Nowhere is this idea more germane than in that famous scene from the *Roman de la rose* where Reason and the Lover discuss whether language, and particularly its capacity to name, properly functions as a veil for allegorical truth or as a mask for courtly vices (whether, for example, one should say "coilles" for testicles or something more delicate). This scene is an obvious counterpart to the language dispute between Reason and Rude Understanding in the *Pilgrimage of the Lyfe of the Manhode*. In that scene, theories of naming have everything to do with the discursive limitations of character. Reason and Rude Understanding *as characters* can't help but argue about interpretation and will forever be at odds because they can only speak as they are. The problem with limiting discourse to character, however, is that the ability to name correctly, to argue convincingly for one mode of interpretation, has serious implications for the penitential reading of both scriptural text and allegorical fiction. Ultimately, however, Reason's commission transcends the discursive limitations of personification advertised in the *Roman de la rose* by justifying the poetic integrity of allegory, and reconciling it to the *Pilgrimage*'s larger penitential project.

[38] Brownlee, "The Problem of Faux Semblant," 253.

2

Lyric, genre, and the material text

In the last chapter we saw that medieval legal documents differ from other kinds of writing because they embody a singular relation of material form to written text. It is precisely this singular relation that occupied a jurist like Henry de Bracton, who was anxious to establish the priority of livery of seisin (the formal transfer of land), and who hoped to prove that documents are no substitute either for seisin or, even more importantly, for the donor's founding will. But Bracton finally develops an extraordinary theory of documentary signification in the process of defining other customs and principles. He shows that, although the donor's will technically founds a legal action, in the absence of the donor, the document personifies the donor's will, and in doing so transforms legal will ("I want") into legal act ("I give"). The documentary transformation of will into act is crucially realized, moreover, through the interrelation of text and material text. Where the clauses of the charter confirm the donor's will that an action take place, the material charter further substantiates the donor's will by equating verification and reification, because, says Bracton, "to confirm is but to reaffirm [i.e., to make firm again] what before was firm."[1]

The relationship between materiality and textuality described by Bracton informs what I have been calling a documentary poetics, a poetic practice and theory which reached its full flowering in fourteenth-century English literature, and which, in so many ways, defined that literature's understanding of itself. This documentary poetics was

---

[1] Bracton, *De legibus et consuetudinibus Angliae*, vol. 2, trans. Thorne, III. "Item per hoc quod dicit, praesenti carta mea confirmavi, per hoc innuit quod vult quod voluntas sua, per quam res transfertur ad donatarium, et quae firma esse debet, praesenti carta sigilli sui munimine confirmetur. Est enim confirmare id quod prius firmum fuit simul firmare."

absolutely central to writing in English from 1350 to about 1425. This is not to say, however, that documentary poetics originated in English or was restricted to England. We have already seen, for example, that the French monk Guillaume de Deguileville capitalized on the intersections between documentary culture and literary form to justify the role of allegory in penitential literature. For Deguileville, documentary poetics offered not simply a reflexive mode but also a socially-inflected literary theory with which to measure the operations of allegory. Importantly, too, this documentary poetics was not a poetics defined *against* Latin or French, but rather it emerged through English poets' need to examine the conditions of their own literary making. In fact, literary documents do appear in Anglo-Latin and Anglo-French literature of the late thirteenth and early fourteenth centuries, but usually in the form of academic satires or legal parodies. These satires and parodies are certainly fictive, but like forgeries, they aren't explicitly interested in fiction, *per se*. By contrast, poets writing in English in the second half of the fourteenth century regarded documentary culture as a means of articulating the strategies and ambitions of their own literary making. Their citations of legal documents are dizzyingly extravagant but nearly always serious. They exceed rather than undercut institutional forms, they exult in diplomatic formulas, and in many cases, they extend Bractonian principles of materiality and textuality, rhetoric and subjectivity, and absence and presence far beyond anything that Bracton himself could possibly imagine. Most significantly, perhaps, it is the *translation* of documentary practice into English poetry and of legal formulas into literary forms which produced a documentary poetics capable of describing the literary conditions of late fourteenth-century England. From this perspective, the making of an English documentary poetics was the making of English documentary culture as well.

The popularity of Deguileville's *Pèlerinages* in late medieval England gives us some sense of just how strong the English taste for documentary culture really was. Take, for example, Chaucer's translation of Deguileville's ABC hymn to the Virgin (before 1372), for which Lydgate left a space in his adaptation, *The Pilgrimage of the Life of Man* (ca. 1426). Deguileville's version simply states that Christ took on human form in order to ally himself with humanity and offer mercy to the faithful: "Homme voult par sa plaisance/Devenir, pour aliance/Avoir a humain lignage." Chaucer, on the other hand, draws upon the image of Christ's charter to express the same idea: "He vouched sauf, tel him, as was his wille,/Bicome a man, to have our alliaunce,/And with his precious blood he wroot the bille/Up-on the crois, as general ac-quitaunce/To every penitent in ful creaunce."[2] A quittance was a semi-official pardon or written release issued to someone who owed a financial debt. By calling Christ's Passion a quittance, Chaucer is suggesting first that Christ's sacrifice forgave the debt of original sin, and second that that transaction was at once deeply personal and universally applicable. Christ made a special concession to all humanity by absorbing the debt owed to him.[3] Certainly, by alluding to a document of Christ, Chaucer may have simply been redistributing another of Deguileville's fictive documents, yet by referring to Christ's bloody pardon, he was probably catering to an English predilection not just for the law but also for the law's particular mode of textuality.

Like Chaucer, Lydgate enthusiastically exaggerates documentary forms in places where Deguileville's poem is merely suggestive. In the scene of Charity's last will and testament, for example, where Deguileville only evokes the testament form, Lydgate closely follows the format of real wills in which the testator disposes of his soul, corpse, and goods.[4] His Christ leaves his soul to his father, his corpse to the sepulcher, his heart to all faithful Christians, his five wounds to those who contend with the devil, his ordinance as protection for souls de-fending themselves in the heavenly courts, and so forth (Lydgate, 4773–872). Lydgate's innovations, the graphic distribution of Christ's body and greater adherence to documentary forms, generally recall Passion "complaint" poetry and, more specifically, the corpus of popular English

---

[2] Deguileville's and Chaucer's versions are printed in Skeat, ed., *The Complete Works of Geoffrey Chaucer*, vol. I, 264.

[3] Hall, *Select Formulas of English Historical Documents*, 130, #141.

[4] In a typical fourteenth-century will, a widow from Lincoln distributes her body and goods in the following fashion: "First, I bequeath my soul to Almighty God and Blessed Mary and all Saints, and my body to buried in the church of St. Cuthbert in Lincoln . . . and with my body I bequeath to the said church my best super tunic . . . to Alice wife of William de Hull in Lincoln one robe of cloth mixed of brown colour" (*Lincoln Wills*, vol. I, ed. and trans. Foster, 5).

lyrics called the *Charters of Christ*, circulated in England between 1350 and 1500.[5] The *Charters of Christ* are allegories of salvation by means of two elaborate conceits: Christ's crucified body as a legal document, and salvation history as the issuing and completion of a land grant. In the earliest of these lyrics, the *Long Charter* (ca. 1350–80), Christ reports that he wanted to grant heaven to humankind and so followed proper legal procedure by a livery of seisin: the formal transfer and occupation of the heritable property (forty weeks in Mary's womb). Because the devil has tried repeatedly to force him off his property, however, Christ has now decided to draw up a charter of feoffment so that humankind might be secure in its heritage of heaven. He has decided, moreover, that he should draw up the charter on his own skin for greater durability. This charter is the crucified body of Christ and the contract of the Atonement: the stretching of the parchment is the nailing of his body to the cross; the pen is the scourge; and the ink the spit of his tormenters. Christ reads this charter-body aloud to all passersby ("*Sciant presentes & futuri,* /wite ӡe þat are and schal be-tyde,/þat Jhesu crist wiþ blodi syde..." [ll. 98a–100]), naming himself as author of the act, humankind as the *destinarius*, heaven as the gift freely given ("ffre to haue, and fre to holde,/wiþ al þe purtynaunce to wolde" [ll. 115–16]), and the conditions of the gift, that men and women continue to keep Christ's "love-deeds" in mind and pay a "rent" of true penance.[6] After describing his crucifixion, Christ recounts how he used his charter-body to harrow hell and left a copy of the charter (the Eucharist) with the priest so that future generations would remember and benefit from his sacrifice.

This extraordinary lyric tradition probably originated in Franciscan literature, such as the *Fasciculus morum* (ca. 1325), a Latin preaching handbook containing some English lyrics and surviving in twenty-eight manuscripts.[7] The *Fasciculus morum* also contains a fourteen-line fictive charter issued by Christ on the cross, which confirms that Christ has

---

[5] Helen Philips discusses Chaucer's redistribution of Deguileville's work in "Chaucer and Deguileville: The *ABC* in Context."

[6] Text in Furnivall and Horstmann, eds., *The Minor Poems of the Vernon Manuscript*, vol. 2, 637–57 (hereafter cited in the main text by line number). Spalding has also edited several manuscripts of the *Long Charter* in *The Middle English Charters of Christ*, 19–81.

[7] See Wenzel's introduction to his edition of the *Fasciculus morum: A Fourteenth-Century Preacher's Handbook* (hereafter cited in the main text by page and line number, translations are Wenzel's, unless otherwise indicated).

won back his rightful inheritance from the devil and now grants heaven eternally to his spiritual heirs. The charter adheres to conventional diplomatic formulas in spite of its unusual circumstances. It opens with the general inscription of a charter, "Let all present and future, all who are in heaven, on earth and in hell... know," along with the superscription identifying the author, "that I, Christ, Son of God the Father and of the Virgin Mary, true God and man... etc." Likewise it ends with a typical attestation: "in witness thereof I have written this present charter with my own blood," along with the place and date of execution: "Written, read, confirmed, and given to mankind on Good Friday, on Mount Calvary, publicly and openly, to last forever in the year 5232 after the Creation of the world" (146–7, ll. 84–5).[8] This document proves God's commitment to the salvation of humankind, narrates the circumstances that enabled such a contract to take place, and professes to be a material written record that anyone may read, witness, and display. One early fifteenth-century reader of the *Fasciculus morum* was apparently so fascinated by the charter that he copied it separately under the title *Carta Domini nostri Iesu Christi*.[9] The *Fasciculus morum* further depicts Christ's charter as a material record of the Passion inscribed on Christ's crucified body: "Just such a charter did Christ write for us on the cross when... he stretched out his blessed body, as a parchment-maker can be seen to spread a hide in the sun" (212–13, ll. 253–6),[10] and it frequently reuses the charter motif to conceptualize the bond between God and

---

[8] Transcript of the charter: "Sciant presentes et futuri, omnes qui sunt in celo et in terra ac in inferno, quod ego Christus, Filius Dei Patris et Marie Virginis, verus Deus et homo, pro hereditate mea iniuste et prodiciose a meis ablata diuque sub manu adversarii detenta teste toto mundo in stadio pugnavi, adversarium devici, victoriam optinui, et hereditatem meam iuste recuperavi, seisinam in Parasceves cum heredibus meis accepi, habendum et tenendum in longitudine et in latitudine in eternum secundum quod dispositum est a Patre libere et quiete, annuatim, et continue reddendo Deo Patri cor mundum et animam puram. In cuius rei testimonium hanc presentem cartam sanguine proprio conscripsi, legi, et per totum mundum publicavi, sigillumque divinitatis mee apposui, cum testimonio Patris et Filii et Spiritus Sancti; nam hii tres unum sunt qui testimonium dant in celo. Scripta, lecta, confirmata, et generi humano tradita feria sexta Parasceves supra montem Calvarie, publice et aperte, in eternum duratura, anno a creacione mundi 5(2)32" (*Fasciculus morum*, 146–7, ll. 84–98).

[9] In BL Additional 21253, fol. 168a, where it is followed by a Latin commentary. For a description and transcription of the fifteenth-century excerpt, see Spalding, ed. *Middle English Charters*, xiii, 95.

[10] "Set huiusmodi carta[m] scripsit nobis in cruce quando... corpus suum benedictum extendit, sicut pergamenarius ad solem pergamenum explicare videtur."

humanity. Faith itself "is a charter for Christians to have and hold the kingdom of heaven freely and in peace. If anyone holds in good faith a charter given to him rightfully by his lord... the lord is held to keep him and protect him from all others" (586–7, ll. 204–9).[11]

Just as the charter in the *Fasciculus morum* probably helped to give rise to the *Long Charter* lyrics, so the actual charter within the *Long Charter* seems to have been the most attractive part to late medieval readers. The slightly later and more economical *Short Charter* (ca. 1380–1400), a rhymed charter of approximately thirty-five lines, omits most of the narrative framework of the *Long Charter*, retaining only an expanded version of the charter read by Christ on the cross. Like the *Long Charter*, the *Short Charter* grants "heavens blisse withouten endinge" to all readers who repent and remain in charity with their neighbors, and like the *Long Charter* it is organized by Latin tags, which are subsequently translated very loosely into the vernacular as, for example the notification, "*Noverint universi presentes et futuri*/Weetis all that bee heere/Or that shall bee leife and deere," the disposition of the document, "*dedi et concessi*/I have geoven and doe graunt," and the attestation, "*cuius rei testimonium*/ffor furder witnes who list appeale/To my heere vnder-honged seale..."[12] The *Short Charter* also includes an impressive list of human and cosmological "witnesses" from Luke ("*his testibus:*/Witnesse the Earth that then did quake/And stonys great that in sunder brake... Witnesse my moder and St. Ihon,/And bystanders many a one"), with the evangelists serving as notaries (Spalding, 6–7, ll. 21–8). Two other versions of the *Short Charter* circulated in the late fourteenth century, the Latin *Carta libera* and the English *Carta Dei*, both of which imitate the standard charter form and profess to be issued by Christ on the cross. A prose "spin-off" of the *Charters of Christ* called the "Charter of Heaven" was also copied from the 1380s with the collection of vernacular religious tracts called *Pore Caitif*.[13]

---

[11] "[Fides] est carta Christianorum habendi et tenendi libere et quiete regnum celorum, quia sicut qui fideliter habet cartam alicuius domini sibi iuste concessam ... debite tenetur eum dominus salvare et warrantizare pro quibuscumque aliis."

[12] Text in Spalding, ed., *Middle English Charters*, 6–7, ll. 1–2, 7, 30–32 (hereafter quotations from the *Short Charter*, *Carta Dei*, and *Carta libera* will be from Spalding's edition and will be cited in the main text by page and line number).

[13] See Lagorio and Sargent, "Bibliography: English Mystical Writings," in *A Manual of the Writings in Middle English*, ed. Hartung, vol. 23, 3470–1, for a list and contents of *Pore*

It is obvious even from this brief overview that the literary appro-priation of documentary culture involved two different strategies. On the one hand, the official clauses of legal documents (e.g., "sciant pre-sentes et futuri") were associated with structures of institutional power, making them authenticating tags which, like scriptural and liturgical quotations, might be successfully incorporated into vernacular poetry. On the other hand, because these formulas were designed to accom-modate a variety of situations, and because, not unlike the liturgy, they rely upon formulaic narratives, they were easily adaptable to a variety of poetic contexts. The rest of this chapter investigates the ways in which late medieval English poets pressed the language of documentary culture into the service of vernacular piety. I first sketch out a short history of documentary culture in later medieval England, arguing that changes in languages of record, bureaucratic careers, and the university curriculum made the written record ripe for literary consumption and vernacular transformation. I then argue that the *Charters of Christ* lyrics constitute a particularly fascinating experiment in English documentary poetics, the goal of which was to reframe the aspirations of the Middle English religious lyric. As we will see, these charter-lyrics try to negotiate the textuality of the Passion and the operations of the lyric by situating both within the context of documentary culture. In doing so, they posit theories not only of poetic form, but also of the invention of genre itself.

ENGLISH BUREAUCRACIES AND THE RHETORICAL TRADITION

By the thirteenth century, Italians were copying legal treatises and formularies in the vernacular, but the English bureaucracy did not follow suit until the early fifteenth century, well after the advent of vernacular poetry.[14] From the eleventh to the thirteenth century, the

---

Caitif manuscripts. As we will see in chapter 3, this dramatization of the Atonement as a bloody charter was ultimately derived from Augustinian exegesis of Colossians 2:14–15, a passage cryptically stating that Christ blotted out the handwriting of a decree ("chirogra-phum decreti") against us and defeated the "principals and powers" by nailing the bond to the cross: "Delens quod adversus nos erat chirographum decreti, quod erat contrarium nobis, et ipsum tulit de medio, affigens illud cruci; et expolians principatus et potestates traduxit confidenter palam triumphans illos in semetipso."

[14] Camargo, *Ars dictaminis, Ars dictandi*, 41.

post-Conquest aristocracy conducted its diplomatic and cultural affairs in Anglo-Norman, while Latin soon overtook Old English as the language of royal correspondence and of the judicial system generally. From the mid-thirteenth through the fourteenth century, as Anglo-Norman was declining as a language of personal and literary expression, its bureaucratic incarnation, law French – really, a specialized lexicon – began to replace Latin in letters of retaining, parliamentary petitions, pleading, and business.[15] Latin, of course, would remain for centuries the language of ecclesiastical business and of solemn royal documents. There were never firm distinctions, however, in the uses of French, Latin, and English, and all three languages might have been used side by side in the law courts and in public proclamations. As Clanchy explains, "A statement made in court in English or French...might be written down in Latin, or conversely a Latin charter might be read out in English or French."[16] The Magna Carta, for example, was periodically proclaimed in English (possibly four times a year),[17] and the sole royal document preserved in English before the fifteenth century, Henry III's Confirmation of the Provisions of Oxford (1258), was similarly issued in Latin, French, and English, presumably for the purpose of public proclamation.[18]

By the last quarter of the fourteenth century, however, English had begun to compete with French and Latin as England's first language of literature and record. In 1356, the mayor of London ordered proceedings in the sheriffs' courts to be conducted in English, and, in 1362, Parliament issued the Statute of Pleading, which ordered all lawsuits to be conducted in English and subsequently recorded in Latin. The first English wills date from the 1370s, and the first English petitions

---

[15] This shift to "law French" was anticipated by the gallicized entries in the Domesday Book, and brought into focus by Henry III, whose 1258 confirmation of the privileges of Oxford was drawn up in French and English, as well as Latin. By the reign of Edward I, however, a professional class of lawyers conducted all their legal pleadings in Anglo-Norman which, around the same time, also became the language of record for the *Statutes of the Realm*, the *Rotuli Parliamentorum*, and some town and guild records. See Rothwell, "Language and Government in Medieval England," and "The Legacy of Anglo-French."

[16] Clanchy, *From Memory to Written Record*, 206.

[17] On reading the Magna Carta aloud, see chapter 5.

[18] Clanchy, *From Memory to Written Record*, 265; Hall, *Select Formulas of English Historical Documents*, 60, 73.

to parliament date from the 1380s.[19] It is telling that by the late fourteenth century, the Oxford master Thomas Sampson (fl. 1350s–90s) had to write a French grammar to help his students compose model letters and documents; some translation of those documents into English must have taken place in his classroom.[20] After 1417, Henry V conducted in English nearly all his correspondence with royal and urban governments, and the London guilds soon followed suit. It may be that Henry's decision to use English in official letters was premeditated and strategic: he hoped to legitimize the Lancastrian coup by associating his dynasty with a national language and literature.[21] But the *Charters of Christ*, developed from Franciscan preaching around 1350, and Deguileville's *Pèlerinages*, translated into English well before 1400, anticipate this process of reshaping official discourse into what was becoming the *lingua franca* of aristocratic patrons, parliamentarians, and their clerks.

The vernacular appropriation and transformation of documentary culture was no doubt assisted, in part, by the influx of diplomats, lawyers, and clerks into burgeoning royal and ecclesiastical bureaucracies, several of whom wrote the poetry that would be the template for Chancery English.[22] Whether these clerk-poets were educated in the royal household, on a baronial estate, at grammar school or university, or in a Chancery apprenticeship, their training most likely included reading and writing legal documents.[23] Chaucer, as controller of the wool custom, processed about one thousand export documents yearly. He was later permitted to farm out these onerous duties to a deputy, but for five years he was supposed to execute all paperwork in his own hand.[24] Thomas Hoccleve spent most of his career, apparently with some regret, in the office of the Privy Seal, and Thomas Usk, a professional scrivener,

---

[19] Baugh and Cable, *History of the English Language*, 145. On the stagnation and decline of Anglo-Norman in England, see Crane, "Anglo-Norman Cultures in England," 35–60.

[20] Camargo, ed., *Medieval Rhetorics of Prose Composition*, 151.

[21] Fisher, *The Emergence of Standard English*, 26–35.

[22] See Tout's classic essay on the subject, "Literature and Learning in the English Civil Service in the Fourteenth Century," esp. 368.

[23] Orme suggests that some apprentices might have learned the composing of letters and deeds from scriveners, "those professional exponents of the art" (*English Schools in the Middle Ages*, 78).

[24] "Ita quod idem Galfridus rotulos suos dictum officium tangentes manu sua propria scribat." Text in *Chaucer Life-Records*, ed. Crow and Olson, 158. On Chaucer's education, see Green, *Poets and Princepleasers*, 71–2; and Pearsall, *The Life of Geoffrey Chaucer*, 99.

would also have required knowledge of "testamentz, chartes, et toutz autres choses touchantz la dite mystier [the trade of scrivener]," as affirmed by his written "Appeal" of Northampton in 1385.[25] Langland's education and career can only be inferred from his poem and have been debated for decades. Lister Matheson, using genealogical data, has hypothesized that Langland served as a legal clerk in London and Worcestershire, while Kathryn Kerby-Fulton and Steven Justice, using scribal and codicological evidence, have traced Langland's activities to the community of letters that sprang up around the law courts of London.[26] It is perhaps sufficient to say that a fourteenth-century Londoner with enough literate skills to compose a poem would likely have had some familiarity with the composition of legal instruments.

In the thirteenth and fourteenth centuries, moreover, documentary rhetoric increasingly played a role in education, as Oxford University began to cater to students seeking posts in law and administration, just as Italian universities had begun to do at least a century earlier. This development coincided with the production of *dictamen* (composition) books and formularies in England from at least the middle of the thirteenth century. Celebrated rhetoricians such as John of Garland (ca. 1195–1260) and Thomas Merke (d. 1409) wrote textbooks on prose and verse composition which offered examples from a variety of genres, from samples of historical prose and devotional poetry to ecclesiastical correspondence, charters, and indentures.[27] In England, however, the *ars dictaminis* was never central to the university arts curriculum and rhetorical handbooks on the Italian model were sparsely produced. Latin letter-writing was mainly taught through the apprentice system of the royal chancery, and most English administrators were content to

---

[25] Usk also seems to have been a "jack-of-all-legal-trades" and later jeopardized career and life as clerk for the rival Brembre and Northampton factions (Strohm, *Hochon's Arrow: The Social Imagination of Fourteenth-Century Texts*, 147–53).

[26] Matheson, "William Langland: Social, Political and Geographical Backgrounds"; Kerby-Fulton and Justice, "Langlandian Reading Circles and the Civil Service in London and Dublin, 1380–1427," 59–83. Modern scholars have speculated that Langland was a clerk in minor orders who served as a chantry-priest, an itinerant hermit, or even an Oxford master. Important recent studies include Galloway, "*Piers Plowman* and the Schools"; Alford, "Langland's Learning"; and the essay collection, *Written Work: Langland, Labor, Authorship*, ed. Justice.

[27] Examples can be found in *The Parisiana Poetria of John of Garland*, ed. and trans. Lawler, 142–59.

use practical formularies and Registers of Writs, rather than continental-style rhetorical handbooks.[28] Even at Oxford the *ars dictaminis* was often taught, not by university grammar masters, but by "rogue academics on the precarious fringes" of university life, who catered to students planning to take up junior posts in estate administration.[29] In this way, *dictamen* at Oxford brought together "the learning of the universities and teaching of practical administration and legal skills," associated not with the *ars notaria* but with basic clerical skills.[30] By the late fourteenth century, for example, vocationally-minded students could skip the arts course altogether and sign up with Thomas Sampson and his associate, the scrivener William Kingsmill. The centerpiece of their course was Sampson's extremely influential *Cartulariae*, a formulary of model deeds and records, which attracted a substantial readership outside the university as well.[31] As administrative and diplomatic positions opened to the mercantile and artisan classes, grammar schools also altered their curriculum accordingly. By the late fourteenth century, they were teaching prose composition, a subject that usually included the study of model letters and documents in Latin and in business French.[32]

Yet English *dictamen* studies, however practically-minded, were never entirely opposed to what Usk calls "poysy mater." Even in "business school," the legal document was considered something of a literary exercise, and grammar textbooks from this period recommend the same rhetorical devices for official correspondence as they do for verse and personal letters, the only difference being that more attention is given to the physical preparation of the documents.[33] Like other rhetorical exercises, moreover, *dictamen* handbooks often display highly fictional situations and allegorical characters as, for example, in a model writ issued

---

[28] Richardson, "The Fading Influence of the Medieval *Ars dictaminis* in England after 1400," 226–7.

[29] Ibid., 228.

[30] Evans, "The Number, Origins and Careers of Scholars." In *The History of Oxford*, vol. 2, ed. Catto and Evans, 523–5.

[31] Richardson, "Business Training in Medieval Oxford," 270.

[32] See Orme, *English Schools in the Middle Ages*, 77; Griffiths, "Public and Private Bureaucracies in England and Wales in the Fifteenth Century," 119–20; and Bennett, "Careerism in Late Medieval England," 26–30. For an excellent account of the late medieval Oxford curriculum see Coleman, "The Science of Politics and Late Medieval Academic Debate."

[33] Camargo, *Ars Dictaminis, Ars Dictandi*, 28.

from Discretion to the King of Christmas in an All Souls manuscript.[34]
The model document also provided *dictatores* with a vehicle for autobiography as well as for pedagogy, and consequently it is often difficult to
distinguish "real" copies of official documents from fictional. Master
Sampson, for example, intended his course to be workmanlike but
nonetheless introduced a personal and often self-promoting character
to his model documents. In his *Modus dictandi*, he has wittily inserted
his name into a number of salutations and social situations: "Thomas
Sampson, abbot of the monastery of Saint S. of R. . . . sends greetings,"
or "Thomas Sampson, lord of W., sends greetings to our beloved N.,"
or closer to the truth, perhaps, "Thomas Sampson, deputy of Oxford,
bailiff of the freehold of Morton sends greetings." Likewise, he might
sign it, "Given under my seal on Thursday, on the feast of the blessed
Bishop Sampson," or "dated on Monday on the feast of the blessed
Sampson."[35] He probably intended these playful and widely-circulated
"autobiographical" documents to sell his course, copyright his book, and
amuse his students. Yet his documents also demonstrate the capability
of official formulas to accommodate new, even imaginary situations,
as well as to express the authorial subject. This fictionalizing character
of dictaminal exercises hardly begins with medieval England – it goes
back to Italian models from as early as the twelfth century. Sampson's
handbook suggests that dictaminal subjectivities were increasingly available to writers in later medieval England, and further, that they were
circulated outside of the university arts curriculum as well.

If Sampson's book shows how formularies could serve as vehicles
for instruction, authorship, and even entertainment, practicing clerks
and administrators used them in even more explicitly literary contexts. The aforementioned Richard of Bury (1287–1345), who was re-
cruited from Oxford to pursue a distinguished career as King's Clerk,
bishop of Durham, and eventually Lord Chancellor, channeled his vast
administrative experience into a popular formulary, the *Liber epistolaris*

---

[34] Taylor, *English Historical Literature*, 221–2.
[35] Camargo, *Medieval Rhetorics of Prose Composition*, 161, line 298; 162, line 304; 163,
ll. 349–50, 357. "Thomas Sampson, abbas monasterii sancti S. de R., dilecto filio dompno
Willelmo S., commonacho nostro, salutem in amplexibus Filii virginis gloriose . . .
Thomas Sampson, dominus de W., dilecto nobis N., salutem . . . Thomas Sampson, vice-
dominus Oxonie, balliuo libertatis de Morton, salutem . . . Datum sub sigillo meo die
Jouis in festo sancti Sampsonis episcopi . . . Datum die lune in festo sancti Sampsonis."

(compiled ca. 1324–25), which is made up of over fifteen hundred examples of letters and charters chosen more for their literary than historical value. These include authentic royal pardons, papal bulls, and Italian letter collections documenting adultery, naughty students, and anxious fathers.[36] At the end of his life, he wrote his confession of bibliophilism, *Philobiblon*, and, amazingly enough, he introduces the entire confession as an official ecclesiastical document: "To all the faithful in Christ to whom the tenor of the present writing may come, Richard of Bury... [wishes] eternal salvation in the Lord and [wishes] to present continually a pious memorial of himself before God, both during his life and after his death."[37] Whereas Sampson's formulary teaches the application and composition of legal documents through fictive illustrations of the authorial life, Bury's confession shows how a life constituted by books might be expressed through the fictions of the written record. John Burrow, writing about Hoccleve, argues that the autobiographical aspects of medieval poetry are not the less referential because they rely on conventional expressions of petition and address. Because medieval self-writing ostensibly had practical functions, such as confession or consolation, it did not justify the creation of an individual or fictional voice.[38] Julia Boffey argues in the same vein that the testament (from which Bury also draws) offered fifteenth-century poets the opportunity of "creating a text around an authenticating impulse similar to that built

[36] Denholm-Young, "Richard de Bury, 1287–1345," in *Collected Papers on Mediaeval Subjects*, 20; see also Denholm-Young's edition of Bury's formulary, *The Liber Epistolaris of Richard de Bury*.
[37] Bury, *Philobiblon*, ed. Thomas, 6–7. "Vniversis Christi fidelibus ad quos tenor praesentis scripturae pervenerit, Richardus de Bury, miseratione divina Dunelmensis episcopus, salutem in Domino sempiternam, piamque ipsius praesentare memoriam iugiter coram Deo in vita pariter et post fata." In 1343 Bury's chancery used an identical formula, for example, in a letter of arrangements for Alverton Hospital (*Richard D'Aungerville of Bury, Fragments of His Register and Other Documents*, ed. Dean of Durham, 169). For more on documentary self-writing, see my discussion of William Thorpe in chapter 6.
[38] Burrow, "Autobiographical Poetry in the Middle Ages: The Case of Thomas Hoccleve." Hoccleve complained about his job at the Privy Seal, but at the end of his life, while reaping the benefits of the royal pension plan, he, like Bury, assembled an immense French and Latin formulary. In "Bureaucratic Identity and the Construction of the Self," Ethan Knapp calls attention to the formulary's autobiographical elements, suggesting that the formulary was not just a reference book but an example of the "petitioning subject" that Hoccleve so assiduously cultivates in his poetry.

into the literary complaint or epistle: a testator, like a plaintiff or a correspondent, has some ostensible justification for generating a written document."[39] Likewise, A. C. Spearing argues that Charles d'Orléans composed his allegorical narrative *Fortunes Stabilnes* as a series of verse epistles and legal documents because, as a prisoner of the English aristocracy, he was cut off from his realm; the conventional diplomatic formulas expressed his absence and his authority simultaneously.[40] Similarly, in the *Philobiblon*, written over fifty years earlier, Bury's conventional salutation works simultaneously as a learned mode of literary presentation and a proper occasion for "mapping out" or "stretching forth the life" of its clerkly author.

Certainly, in some sense all letters were thought metaphorically to make their makers present because they pretend to transmit the author's voice and authority. Troilus, for example, imagines that he is holding his estranged Criseide when he rereads her old letters:

> The lettres ek that she of olde tyme
> Hadde hym ysent, he wolde allone rede
> An hondred sithe atwixen noon and prime.
> Refiguring hire shap, hire wommanhede
> Withinne his herte, and every word or dede.[41]

By bearing in hand Criseide's brief letters, Troilus reanimates her voice, and "refigures" her shape. In the famous line at the end of the *Troilus*, Chaucer affectionately sends forth his book to brave the world and its *auctores*: "go litel bok, go, litel myn tragedye . . . and kis the steppes," etc. (1786). He speaks of his poem, that is, as his offspring but not as a double for himself. By contrast, a fifteenth-century poet, echoing Chaucer, imagines that his letter will impersonate him to his lady: "Go! little bill, and do me recommende/Unto my lady with godely countenaunce . . . I will her love and never mo,/Go! little bill, and sey her so."[42] The crux of the difference between these two examples is not the word "bok," which in Middle English can refer to any kind of text, but the word

---

[39] Boffey, "Lydgate, Henryson, and the Literary Testament," 41.
[40] Spearing, "Prison, Writing, Absence: Representing the Subject in the English Poems of Charles D'Orléans."
[41] *Troilus and Criseide*, 5: 470–5, in Benson, ed. *The Riverside Chaucer*.
[42] Davies, ed., *Middle English Lyrics*, #105, ll. 1–2, 13–14.

"bill" ("letter" or "petition"). For medieval poets, poems were progeny, but letters, metaphorically speaking, were extensions of the self.

In the end, neither Bury nor Sampson makes hard and fast distinctions between legal documents and letters. It was, after all, the nature of rhetorical handbooks and collections to blur distinctions between historical documents and epistolary belles-lettres, as well as between the institutional making of experience (template, handbook, formulary) and its subjective expression (confession, anonymity, conventionality). Yet, legal documents, by virtue of their peculiar claims to agency, subjectivity, and materiality, might bring into focus the literary strategies of English penitential literature, in ways that no other texts could. For some English writers, in fact, documentary culture provided a kind of literary theory with which to explore the temporal, historical, and performative modes of Passion lyrics. The *Charters of Christ* manuscripts suggest, moreover, that the legal document served as a generic model for the Passion lyric, a genre classified as much by its material form as by its rhetorical effects. In "On Lyric Poetry and Society," Adorno writes that "we can speak of the social dimension of the lyric not in terms of the author's objectives or relations" but only if "the social element in them is shown to reveal something essential about the basis of their quality."[43] I am suggesting that the authors of these *Charters of Christ* lyrics were deeply invested in recovering the social dimension of the lyric, which they located not just in the practices of the law but in the law's textual apparatus, in the formal and material processes by which legal documents come into being.

THE *CHARTERS OF CHRIST* AND THE LYRICAL SELF

Of the many varieties of Middle English religious lyric, the most moving is surely the "complaint from the cross." In these poems, Christ typically addresses the audience, urging its members to compare his suffering to others' and rebuking them for their ingratitude. In one such lyric taken from Friar Grimestone's Commonplace Book (ca. 1370), Christ says,

[43] Adorno, "On Lyric Poetry and Society," *Notes to Literature*, vol. 2, ed. Tiedemann, trans. Nicholsen, 38–9.

Ye that pasen by the weye,
Abidet a litel stounde,
Beholdet, al mi felawes
Yef any me lik is founde.
To the tre with nailes thre
Wol fast I hange bounde;
With a spere al thorou my side
To mine herte is mad a wounde.[44]

This lyric speaks right from the heart of late medieval piety, merging as it does the liturgical reproaches of Good Friday, "O vos omnes qui transitis per viam attendite et videte si est dolor sicut dolor meus" (O you who pass by the way look and see if there is any sorrow like my sorrow) (Lamentations 1.12), with the homiletic call to penitence: who among you is worthy of the incomparable sacrifice of Christ? Its distinctive address is inherently dramatic. It imagines a crowd of people indifferent to and complicit in Christ's torture, and in doing so, it identifies the lyric's audience typologically with the gospel's original crowd. The York *Play of the Crucifixion*, to take another example, proposes the lyrical-liturgical address to be the very essence of the dramatic mode. Christ speaks only twice in this play, each time reciting a version of the traditional remonstrance, "Al men þat walkis by waye or strete,/Takes tente 3e schalle no travayle tyne./Byholdes Myn heede, Myn handis, and My feete…"[45] As this last example suggests, moreover, Christ's lament might serve as penitential instruction. His exhortation to the audience ("Beholdet, al mi felawes") doubles as an iconographic guide to the suffered-Christ ("Byholdes Myn heede, Myn handis, and My feete") and consequently as a step toward the contrition that the rebuke is meant to encourage. It was this heady combination of the dramatic and the iconographic that made these poems so attractive to fourteenth-century preachers. For example, the author of the Latin sermon handbook, the *Fasciculus morum*, quotes English Passion lyrics to teach the meaning of charity, attributing the following verses to Christ on the cross: "I honge on cros for loue of þe./Lef þy synne for loue of me./Mercy aske, amende þe sone/And I for3yf þe þat is mysdone" (212, ll. 275–9).[46] A few lines later, the writer

---

[44] Davies, ed., *Middle English Lyrics*, #46, ll. 1–8.
[45] Walker, ed., *Medieval Drama: An Anthology*, 140, ll. 253–5.
[46] For more information about these English lyrics, see Wenzel, *Verses in Sermons: "Fasciculus morum" and its Middle English Poems*, 26, 47.

again invokes Christ's lament from the cross, this time citing the traditional liturgical reproach: "A, 3e men þat by me wendenn,/Abydes a while and loke on me,/3ef 3e fyndenn in any ende/Suche sorow as here 3e se on me" (216, ll. 36–9). These poems are supposed to convince their audiences of the promise of the Atonement and the exigency of penance by cultivating an affective response within each listener. And they accomplish this, I am arguing, largely through their characteristic forms of address: they enfold the liturgical into the lyrical complaint, juxtaposing public ritual in its prescribed form with the personal expression of public ritual endured.

Interestingly enough, the English Passion lyrics collected in the *Fasciculus morum* are encased within an extended metaphor of Christ's charter, initially inspired by the Latin charter described at the beginning of this chapter: "Let all present and future know, who are in heaven and earth and hell, that I Christ, son of God the Father and of the Virgin Mary, truly God and man..." (146–7, ll. 84–5).[47] Referring to the debt of original sin, for example, the sermon-writer declares, "but truly Christ canceled this servitude totally when he left his whole body for us as a charter. For Christ says..." At this point he inserts the first lyric fragment quoted above ("I honge on cros for loue of þe/ Lef þy synne for loue of me"). Likewise, in the next section on the Passion ("to have a firmer understanding of this matter we will...show on what day this charter was written, in what fashion and in what place...With respect to the manner of his suffering and of the making of this charter... we now show in what hour, age, and season he confirmed this charter through his Passion" [215, ll. 1–2; 215–17, ll. 18–19; 219, ll. 1–2]),[48] the sermon-writer introduces the second lyric quoted above ("A, ye men þat by me wendenn/Abydes a while and loke on me"), followed by a similar lyric in both Latin and English ("Byholde, mon, what I dree,/Whech is my payne, qwech is my woo/To the I clepe now I shal dye" etc. [216–17, ll. 51–3]). It is true that much of the *Fasciculus morum* is sprinkled with English lyrics, not just this section, many of which have to do

---

47 "Sciant presentes et futuri, omnes qui sunt in celo et in terra ac in inferno, quod ego Christus, Filius Dei Patris et Marie Virginis, verus Deus et homo." See note 8 above.

48 "[Ad] maiorem autem huius (rei) securitatem habendam, de confectione huius carte ostendit secundo quo die fuit scripta, quo modo, et in quo loco...(C)irca modum autem passionis sue et istius carte confeccionis...iam ostenditur qua hora, qua etate, et quo tempore hanc cartam per suam passionem confirmavit..."

with Christ. This section gives the appearance, however, that the lyrical complaint from the cross, with its vacillation between lament and reproach, aporia and invocation, somehow proceeds from or seeks resolution in documentary forms. It is as if a lyric spoken by Christ, while originating in the liturgy, acquires a different agency and context in conjunction with the material document. For example, the lyric might assume the evidentiary character of direct quotation ("for Christ says . . ."), at the same time that the written record is transformed into an allegorical narrative: e.g., "to have a firmer understanding [*securitatem*] of this matter," "with respect to the manner of his suffering and the making of this charter," "he confirmed the charter with his Passion." Or perhaps, the lyric aspires in this instance to a documentary relationship between the lyrical speaker (Christ) and material form (Christ's charter-body), to a relationship, in other words, in which the crucified Christ becomes a sacramental body through documentary forms of address.

The mutual affirmation of these two discourses, the lyric and the charter, is much more flamboyantly realized in the *Charters of Christ* lyrics, which participate in the "complaint from the cross" tradition but which identify Christ's first-person superscription in the charter with his lyrical address. The result is a giddy amalgamation of lyric, liturgy, and diplomatics:

> To shewen on alle my loue-dede,
> Mi-self I wole this chartre rede.
> 3e Men þat gon bi þis waye,
> A-bydeþ a luytel, I 3ow preye,
> And redeþ alle on þis parchemyn,
> 3if eny serwe beo lyk to myn.
> *O [v]os omnes qui transitis per viam, attendite et vidite, etc.*
> Stondeþ and hereþ þis chartre red,
> whi I am woundet and al for-bled.
> *Carta: Sciant presentes & futuri,*
> wite 3e þat are and schal be-tyde,
> þat Jhesu crist wiþ blodi syde,
> þat was boren in Bedleem
> And offred in to Jerusalem,
> þe Kynges sone of heuene aboue,
> With mi ffadres wille and loue
> Made a sesyng whon I was born,

To þe, Monkynde, þat was forlorn.
Wiþ my chart[r]e here present
I make nou a confirmament:
þat I haue graunted and ȝiuen
To þe, Monkynde, wiþ me to liuen
In my Rewme of heuene- blis,
To hauen and to holden wiþ-outen mis. (ll. 91–112)

This passage, which appears near the middle of the *Long Charter*, cleverly assimilates liturgical-lyrical reproach ("O vos omnes qui transitis per viam") to documentary invocation ("Sciant presentes et futuri"). Even more remarkably, it does so through three highly experimental vernacular "translations". The Latin tag ("O vos omnes qui transitis per viam") identifies Christ's first lyric address ("ȝe men that gon bi this weye/A-bydeþ a luytel, I ȝow preye") directly with the Good Friday Mass. But the second lyrical address, "Stondeþ and hereþ þis chartre red, /whi I am woundet and al for-bled" shifts the terms of liturgical address by turning the sorrowing speaker into a legal actor. Like the typical lyric speaker, Christ impersonates himself to arouse sympathy or guilt, "stondeþ and hereþ" thus capturing the general sense of the liturgical *attendite et vidite* (stand and see) immediately preceding. At the same time his lament summons into being the contractual relations of the Atonement, "stondeth and hereth this chartre red" thus capturing the general sense of the charter notification immediately following ("Sciant presentes et futuri"). In this way, the verse "stondeþ and hereþ þis chartre red" imagines the lyrical address as a hybrid or transitional state between the liturgical and the documentary. Finally, the third English address, "wite ȝe þat are and schal be-tyde,/þat Jhesu crist wiþ blodi syde", completes the process by which the lyric speaker is transformed from liturgical to legal actor. These lines reiterate the ritualized abjection of the first two addresses – they invite the gaze of passersby, they refer to Christ's wounded body ("þat Jhesu crist wiþ blodi syde") – at the same time that they redefine abjection as legal principle. The documentary Christ turns the exhortative into the proclamatory, just as it turns the pathetic self (the lack of will) into legal subject (the will to act).

As we saw with Bracton, moreover, the moment that the authorial will is transcribed into documentary formulas it becomes indistinguishable from the action that it wills. Documentary formulas effectively collapse action and will: to grant (*concedere*) is to consent to the grant (*consentire*). As a result, the document becomes the rhetorical (and material) site where the grantor's will is codified as a legal act, and, conversely, where the legal act is understood to originate in the grantor's will. The *Charters of Christ* lyrics eagerly deploy conventional formulas of address in order to transform Christ's complaint into the will to act:

> *Noverint Universi Presentes et Futuri*
> Witt all that now bene here
> And aftir sall be both leue and dere
> That I Ihesus of Nazareth
> Ffor loue of man has suffred deth
> Vpon the rode with woundes fyve
> Whilest I was man on earth alive
> *Dedi et concessi*
> I have geoven and doe graunt
> To all that aske in faith repentaunt
> Heavens blisse withouten endinge (6, ll. 1–9)

This passage, taken from the *Short Charter*, shows how official charter formulas convert lyrical complaint into legal notification and, by extension, into legal action. Likewise, they convert the historical circumstances that produce a lyric self – death, heartbreak, exile – into the historical circumstances in which a legal grant is made ("*Dedi et concessi*/I have geoven and doe graunt"). Another English charter lyric, the *Carta Dei*, makes this relation of lament to legal will especially clear: "Knowyn alle men that are & shuln ben/that I Jhc' of Nazaren/Wyt myn wyl and herte good/For myn handwerk and for my blod/Have grantyd, 3ovyn and confermyd is" (97, ll. 1–5). Here Christ's will to suffer is the very confirmation of his intention to grant. In all of these poems, moreover, the passage from liturgical to diplomatic address helps to reconcile the paradox implicit in every Passion lyric: how is it that Christ's voice is at once the prescribed formula of public ritual, the lament of the self that repeatedly suffers through the ritual reenactment of death, but is at the same time the performative Word, the Author of ritual himself?

Alain Boureau has argued that the incorporation of the Pauline epistles and canonical legislation into the liturgy had the effect of placing the medieval epistolary corpus "at the meeting point between the divine and the human, between the Good News (the Gospel) and the jurisdiction of the papacy."⁴⁹ Following Boureau, we might argue that the *Charters of Christ* lyrics expose this institutionalization of address within the liturgy – the collusion between the liturgical and the bureaucratic. As a result they attempt to re-form the institutional "o vos omnes qui transitis" into vernacular scripture – a radical alternative. From a different perspective, however, the *Charters of Christ*, by adapting documentary forms to Passion poetry, demonstrate the supreme interchangeability of speakers within the lyric. Documents, as we have seen, constitute a poetic theory situated both inside and outside the lyric. They also call attention to the ways that poetic form emerges from – or is revealed by – the interplay of discourses. Rather than being irreducible signs transparent with meaning, medieval documents are sites of discursive and formal experimentation which help to clarify what a lyric does in the first place. Judson Boyce Allen once argued that the first-person pronoun of medieval lyrics was easily "plagiarized" because medieval authors presumed that "certain kinds of statements which include the first person pronoun may be validly made by anyone, not because they are true statements about any possible world or situation, but because they are the kind of true statements because of which any given speaker, by attaching himself to them, becomes himself true."⁵⁰ Indeed, the *Charters of Christ*, by Englishing legal and liturgical tags, call attention to the truth-claims of the documentary "I," and to the ways that the appropriation of the first-person formula authenticates speakers by making the speaking voice adaptable to different discourses.

The *Charters of Christ* further manipulate documentary fictions to theorize the relationship between memory and salvation. Medieval writers thought of memorization as a moral exercise and tended to privilege the construction of self through memory, the storing of the lives of others in "þe coffre of þin herte," over new and individual experiences.⁵¹ Remembering the Passion was consequently a penitential imperative: by conforming to the "suffered-Christ," by picturing the number of his

⁴⁹ Boureau, "The Letter-Writing Norm, A Mediaeval Invention," 30.
⁵⁰ Allen,"Grammar, Poetic Form, and the Lyric Ego: A Medieval *A Priori*," 205. See also, Leo Spitzer's classic 1946 essay, "A Note on the Poetic and Empirical 'I' in Medieval Authors." Spitzer writes, "In the Middle Ages the poetic 'I' had more freedom and more breadth than it has today; at the time the concept of intellectual property did not exist because literature dealt not with the individual but with mankind" (45).
⁵¹ Carruthers, *The Book of Memory*, 179–83.

wounds and recalling the words uttered from the cross, the penitent might internalize Christ's experience, realize the magnitude of his love, and begin to reciprocate.[52]

The *Charters of Christ* participate in the commemorative character of late medieval piety, but they do so in very specific ways: they recognize that legal instruments are appropriate vehicles of moral memory, not simply because they are evidentiary – they help us recall past transactions – but rather because they are the textual means by which memory (witnessing) might bring about legal action. It is true that, by virtue of their standardized formulas ("to have and to hold," "witnessed by," "dated"), documents were thought to preserve knowledge of historical events as the chroniclers' phrase, "munimenta et memorium" (in law French, "registers et rolles de remembrauncez") suggests.[53] Fictive documents, such as the one in the *Charter of the Abbey of the Holy Ghost*, often use these formulas for biblical instruction, to encode Christ's true identity, the nature and beneficiaries of his grant, and the context in which the grant was made: e.g., "*Hijs testibus*: Of þis bereþ witness aungel & man, heuene & erþe, sone & mone & al þe sterris... *Explicit carta. Memorandum quod primo die incarnacionis hominis &c.*" (338–9).

Yet by allegorizing Christ's crucified body as a charter, the *Charters of Christ* lyrics also show how remembering the Passion is the same thing as witnessing the conditions of salvation and participating in the charter's grant of heaven, pardon, or peace. To remember the liturgical-lyrical Christ is to be complicit in his suffering, to reproduce his plaintive voice and gawk at his tortured body. It is simultaneously to will oneself into the scriptural past and to dehistoricize Christ's lament by placing it within a ritual context. To remember the documentary Christ, however, is to witness a continual proclamation, and thus to re-inscribe the lyric speaker and his audience into an altogether different set of social and

---

[52] This cultivation of moral memory fell heavily to the duty of Franciscan affective literature, which achieves its effects through lyrical invocation and graphic bodily metaphor: the speaker (Christ, a priest, or a fellow penitent) exhorts the reader to remember Christ's suffering and then guides the reader through the Passion, making suffering visible by translating the poetic present into the historical past. See Jeffrey's excellent discussion of this process in *The Early English Lyric & Franciscan Spirituality*, 43–72.

[53] Latham, *Revised Medieval Latin Word-List from British and Irish Sources*, s. v. "munimenta."

historical relations. We saw that by translating the liturgical complaint of Christ on the cross into the conventional invocation of charters, the *Long Charter* draws a likeness between lyrical speaker and legal actor. Additionally, by translating the historically past but liturgically present "omnes qui transitis per viam" into the "presentes et futuri" addressed by the conventional charter, the *Long Charter* suggests that the audience of the charter-body, merely by reading it, may become contemporary witnesses to and beneficiaries of the event: Christ's charter-body. The transition from the English lines directly before the charter invocation, "Stondeþ and hereþ þis chartre red,/whi I am woundet and al for-bled" (ll. 97–8), to the lines directly after the invocation, "Wite ʒe þat are and schal be-tyde,/þat Jhesu crist wiþ blodi syde" (ll. 99–100), shifts the emphasis from the spectator/torturer to the witness/recipient. In the first set of lines, the audience is provoked into an affective response (guilt by typological association), whereas in the second, the audience is called upon to attest to the visual appearance of the charter.

Christ's body also changes in these lines from being the object of the affective gaze ("whi I am woundet and al for-bled") to being the descriptive detail ("þat Jhesu crist wiþ blodi syde") that permits a legal audience to confirm the author's identity and the charter's authenticity. The poem suggests, in other words, that the very practice of witnessing, of seeing and hearing the material written document, converts affective memory to legal memory, just as it transforms the suffering body of Christ into an efficacious one. In a similar fashion, the *Long Charter* exploits the temporal fictions of charters to show how Christ's sacramental body transcends history to effect the salvation of those present and future. In his charter Christ recites the conventional formula "hac presenti carta confirmasse" ("with this present charter [I have] confirmed") but conspicuously alters it from past to present tense: "Wiþ my chartre here present/I *make nou* confirmament" (107–8, emphasis mine). By using the present tense of "confirm," the charter becomes the embodiment of historical continuity and perpetual memory.

In the *Long Charter*, moreover, the reader of the charter not only participates in the divine contract by witnessing the material text but actually manufactures the Atonement through the act of memory. By reading his charter-body aloud to all who pass by, Christ simultaneously retells and re-enacts the story of his Passion: "And þis I made for Monkynde,/my loue-dedes to haue in mynde...To shewen on alle my loue-dede,/Miself I wole þis chartre rede" (60–1, 91–2). The charter is an instructive guide to the Passion because it is itself graphic testimony to Christ's sacrifice and indelibly records the events that formed it. Conversely, Christ's Passion is reenacted the moment that the charter's terms are remembered: Christ promises, "In my Rewme of heuene- blis,/To haue and to holden wiþ-outen mis,/In a condicioun ȝif þou be kynde/And my loue-dedes haue in Mynde" (111–14), and he warns that "þeose þat beoþ of rente be-hynde,/And þeose dedes haue not in mynde,/Fful sore may þei ben a-dred/Whon þis chartre schal be red" (225–8). (The pun on "deed," meaning both physical action and written record, is critical to all of these passages; it would only make sense to English-speaking audiences after about 1300.)[54] The audience of the poem, by witnessing and remembering Christ's charter, helps to turn Christ's corporeal deeds into a written deed, and *vice versa*, by remembering the terms of the contract, it helps to confect Christ's crucified body. The "Charter of Heaven" juxtaposes memory and contract in a similar way: "Euery wise man þat cleymeþ his eritage eiþir askeþ gret pardoun, kepeþ bisili & haþ often mynde vppon þe chartre of his calenge [i.e., his "challenge," a claim to a right or property] & þerfore eche man lerne to liue vertuously & kepe & haue mynde vppon þe chartre of heuene blisse," and a few lines later, "þere weren vppon þe blessid bodi of crist open woundes...þis is þe noumbre of lettres wiþ which oure chartre was written, bi which we moun cleyme oure eritage if we liven riȝtli & kepe þis chartre stidfastly in mynde."[55]

The shift from liturgical to documentary address in the *Charters of Christ* lyrics is further accompanied by the shift in the relation of the speaking Christ to his suffering body, a relationship that draws upon the materials as well as rhetorical conventions of documentary practice. What Christ's charter reveals, in other words, is not simply the appropriability and agency of the lyrical "I," but the elusive relationship between lyric and metaphor in medieval Passion poetry. It shows, for example, exactly how metaphor underwrites lyric subjectivity, and more specifically, it explains the relationship between pathos and agency.

---

[54] *Middle English Dictionary*, s. v. "dede"
[55] Text in Spalding, ed. *Middle English Charters*, 100–01 (hereafter cited in the main text by page number).

Textual vulnerability was a powerful metaphor in a manuscript society where the creation of the text literally testified to the death of a creature, and the *Charters of Christ* typically portray Christ in ways evocative of manuscript culture. Not only is he symbolically the *Agnus Dei*, but as a piece of parchment he resembles the skin of a spotless sheep or calf killed, flayed, and stretched for manuscript production. The "Charter of Heaven," explains it this way: "þe parchemyn of þis heuenli chartre is neiþir of scheep ne of calf: but it is þe bodi & þe blessid skyn of oure lord ihesu loomb... & was þere neuere skyn of scheep neiþir of calfe so sore & so hard streined on þe teynture eiþir harewe of eny parchemyn makere as was þe blessid bodi & skyn of oure lord ihesu crist" (100). From this perspective, Christ's charter resembles any number of penitential book tropes, as discussed at the beginning of Chapter 1, not to mention the huge corpus of lyrics enumerating the physical sufferings of Christ (e.g., Christ's body as a beehive or Swiss cheese). Christ's charter exemplifies here the "outrageous inversion of interiority and exteriority" characteristic of Passion poetry:[56] it is the sacramental word made flesh allegorized as the flesh made word.

At stake, however, in the metaphor of Christ as a charter is not simply the graphic visualization of the suffering Christ, but also the paradoxical relationship between abjection and performance that other texts, which are not identified by their material form, simply cannot sustain. As a generic material text, as a "book," Christ's wounded body produces penitential empathy and iconographic information, but as a legal document, that body may be understood as a redemptive textual object, which simultaneously attests to and implements the conditions of the New Law. A few lines after the passage from the "Charter of Heaven" quoted above, for example, the speaker marvels at this transformation: "þis scripture is oure lord Ihesu Christ! þe charter & bull of oure eritage of heuene... þorouȝ vertu of hise chartre þou schalt haue þine heritage of bliss duringe wiþouten ende" (Spalding, 102). The *Carta Dei* likewise depends upon the relationship between agency and textuality to describe the paradoxical agency of suffering: "knowyn alle men that are & shuln ben/That I Jhc' of Nazaren... Haue grantyn, govyn and confermyd is/To christenemen in erthe I wys/Throurch my chartre that

---

[56] Beckwith, *Christ's Body: Identity, Culture, and Society in Late Medieval Writings*, 61.

the mon se/my body that heng on the tre" (Spalding, 97, ll. 1–2, 5–8).
It calls attention to agency through documentary procedure – Christ's
very lament is collapsed into the performative voice of the charter – and
then it immediately reveals that charter to be a textually vulnerable body.
By comparing Christ to a charter, these poems show how Christ is at
once victim and savior of humanity, casualty and guarantor of the New
Law. In this way, the material subjectivities of the charter unravel the
paradox of the granting and suffering body of Christ.

The substitution of Christ's charter for a generic material text further
suggests ways that textuality itself might provide a crucial link between
lyric (*o vos omnes*) and metaphor (Christ's bloody charter), or, to put it
differently, between the narrative of the absent self (temporal presence),
on the one hand, and the immediacy of figurative expression on the
other (visual presence). Legal documents, as we saw with Bracton, mediate between absence and presence as a matter of principle. Technically
speaking, they record a past act already spoken and performed – they
are evidentiary, they help us to recall and prove events. Yet, as Bracton's
De legibus suggests, the very absence of the author and belatedness of
the written record make charters instruments of legal action in their
own right. As proxies of will, documents claim to be written transcripts
and material extensions of the donor's legal subjectivity; consequently
in recording the will of the absent author, they perform him rhetorically
and materially. Importantly, the documentary performance of will is
gestured to by documentary formulas themselves. As Bracton says, the
clause "by my present charter I have confirmed" means that the donor
intimates that "his will [*vult quod voluntas sua*], by which the thing is
transferred to the donee and which must be firm, be confirmed by the
present charter authenticated by his seal, for to confirm is but to reaffirm
[i.e., to make firm again] what before was firm."[57]

What is so interesting about the *Charters of Christ* lyrics is that they
exploit documentary relations of absence and presence to dramatize the
continual availability of the word made flesh. They are aided in this
endeavor by the execution clause of letters patent, *in cuius rei testimonium has litteras nostras fieri fecimus patentes* (in witness thereof we have
had our letters made open). This clause, along with the attestation of

---

[57] See chapter 1 note 16 above.

all solemn royal documents under the great seal, *teste me ipso* (witnessed by myself), seems to have given rise to the fiction that the king had personally, and therefore physically, invested himself in the document's agency and authenticity. By using this clause, the king makes firm in the material text his intention to confirm the act. And because he wants the document to be watertight and long-lasting, he has, in effect, become part of the material text himself: the open letters, the matrix of the seal, and the bloody ink. A precedent for this fiction is the English translation of Henry III's 1258 Confirmation of the Provisions of Oxford, which translates the standard *in cuius rei testimonium, etc.*, as "for thaet we willen thaet this beo stedefaest and lestinde, we senden ȝew this writ open, iseined with ure seel, to halden a manges ȝew ine hord. Witnesse us seluen...".[58] The English version of this clause differs from the Latin standard by insisting upon a causal relationship between the king's intentions and the physical layout of the document. It expresses his personal desire to strengthen the document – he sends it open so that it will be "stedefaest and lestinde" – and it stresses the document's intrinsic value as a material object – it is worthy of keeping in a treasure chest ("to halden a manges ȝew ine hord"). Thus the English translation interprets the form of the legal document (open letters) as a literal confirmation of the author's intention to make the act firm.[59] The conditions of the medieval archive probably reinforced this interchange between intention and material form: important documents were stowed in treasure chests along with relics and precious jewels, and some relics were "sealed" to prove their authenticity.[60]

The *Charters of Christ* lyrics borrow these patent clauses to describe Christ's physical investment in the written record of the Atonement; in doing so, they transform personal intention (Christ's love for humanity) into corporeality (Christ's charter-body), and lyrical presence into

---

[58] Hall, *Select Formulas of English Historical Documents*, 73, #70b. The French version reads "et pur ce ke nus colons ke ceste chose seit ferme et estale, now enveons nos Lettres Overtes seelees de nostre seel en chescun Cunte a demorer la en tresur" (#70a).

[59] From 1240 to the end of the Middle Ages all royal letters under the great seal were personally attested to by the king, perhaps adding to the fiction that any document that had once been in the presence of the king was doubly confirmed. In 1272, Henry III was still claiming that a patent was forged if it bore a place and date that conflicted with his itinerary. See Chaplais, "English Diplomatic Documents to the End of Edward III's Reign," 24–9; and *English Royal Documents*, 18.

[60] Clanchy, *From Memory to Written Record*, 52.

metaphorical presence. To that purpose they employ what is called, in a very different context, "diplomatic criticism," to establish a textual relationship between lyric and metaphor. For example, in the *Fasciculus morum*, Christ uses the patent execution clause to emphasize his personal commitment to the truth of the charter, and to equate two different kinds of security – intention and material form: "In witness thereof [*in cuius rei testimonium*] I have written this present charter with my own blood...and sealed it with the seal of my divinity" (146–7, ll. 92–3).[61] The sermon-writer later observes about Christ's charter, "On that exchange he left a most reliable (*firmissimam*) charter for us. Notice that a charter that is written in blood carries with it extreme reliability (*securitatem*) and produces much admiration" (212–13, ll. 251–3).[62] By punning on patent clauses, these lines identify the sacrifice of the Atonement with the intentions of its author, showing in the process how the documentary "I" elides the distinction between personal attestation (*securitatem*) and physical confirmation (*firmissimam*). Similarly, the *Carta Dei* writes Christ's physical commitment to the Atonement into its patent execution clause. Christ says, "In wytnesse of thys thing/My syde was opned in selying./To thys chartre trewe and good/I have set my sel, myn herthe blood" (Spalding, 97, ll. 25–9). These lines manipulate patent formulas ("my syde was opned in selying", "I have set my sel, myn herthe blood") in order to conflate the speaker's intention with his desire for perpetual physical confirmation. As a result, they "discover" a vernacular poetics of sacramental presence within institutional forms. In much the same way, the *Short Charter* translates the self-attestation "in cuius rei testimonium" (in witness thereof) in such a way as to locate the intention of the lyric speaker within the bodily presence of the Passion metaphor: "ffor furder witness who list appeale/To my heere under-honged seale/ffor the more stable surenesse/this wounde in my hearte the seale is" (Spalding, 7, ll. 29–32). Importantly, these poems are not particularly interested in the talismanic properties of fictive documents, despite the fact that they describe the incursion of the divine into the physical world. It is true that seals were often treated with excessive reverence, and large

---

[61] "In cuius rei testimonium hanc presentem cartam sanguine proprio conscripti... sigillumque divinitatis mee apposui."
[62] "Super quod cartam firmissimam nobis requit. Et nota quod carta conscripta sanguine vehementer solet importare securitatem et magnam generare admiracione."

solemn documents, the legitimacy of which depended on the intactness of their seal, were often laid flat or folded in storage drawers, their seals carefully attached to their documents and preserved in little leather or cloth bags, or wrapped in cuts of old vestments.[63] Yet the *Charters of Christ* lyrics are attracted much more to the ways that lyric subjectivity is materially articulated through documentary practice than they are to the fetishization of written artifacts.

MATERIAL GENRES

What does it take for a lyric to be a charter? I have argued throughout this chapter that documentary culture served as a mode of textuality eminently suitable for exploring the fictions of devotional poetry. Documentary culture provided medieval poets with a locus of institutional authority – Latin tags, feudal relations, and the like – with which to rehearse the requisites for salvation and dramatize the sovereignty of the Word. Yet, strangely enough, it was the creative Englishing of documentary practices that underlined, and sometimes even distorted, their signifying claims. Rather than counteracting institutional forms, English poets used those forms to arouse the pieties of their readers, while at the same time theorizing the operations of the religious lyric. Finally, the peculiar documentary relationship between materiality and textuality allowed fourteenth-century poets to conceptualize the work of the Passion – both the work of the Passion itself and the translation of that work into lyric poetry.

By way of conclusion, I would like to suggest that, just as the document as a distinctive material text was used to explore the operations of the lyric, so it also gave shape to the lyric as a genre. I have already explained that the symbolic quality of the legal document, unlike other medieval texts, is indistinguishable from its functional quality. Whereas a medieval codex arranges but doesn't classify the texts it contains, the integrity of the documentary text depends upon the appearance of its material form: the layout of the text on the (single) page but also the shape of that page, the way it is folded, sealed, and so forth. The material form of a document classifies it symbolically – when we hear "document"

---

[63] On the maintenance of seals, see Sayers, "The Medieval Care and Custody of the Archbishop of Canterbury's Archives."

we picture a particular shape – but it also classifies it functionally – the formulas of a document work very differently when they are enrolled in a cartulary than when they are issued as a single page. In that way, we might say that the *genre* of a legal document is expressed through its material form, which represents, in this case, the relationship between style and function, rather than the relationship between style and content. For the scribes of the *Charters of Christ* lyrics, this interdependence between materiality and textuality was important for thinking through the genre of the Passion lyric precisely because these lyrics advertise the interchangeability of content and function, the slippage between the trope of Christ's charter and the performativity of the Passion. To put this idea a different way, the *Charters of Christ* scribes were interested in formulating a theory about genre in a literary culture that had no theory of genre, as we know it. They found in documentary culture, and in the *Charters of Christ* lyrics, a way of tracing out the boundaries of genre, thereby constructing a meaningful relationship between poetic making and poetic use.

The *Long* and *Short Charters* enjoyed a long production life and were continually modified to accommodate a diverse readership. The *Long Charters* probably originated in penitential contexts ranging from preachers' miscellanies to lay books of penance. One early *Long Charter*, for example, was copied into a manuscript (Bodley 89) containing other items of pastoral interest, including Jerome's *Tractates on the Catholic Faith*, a bilingual *Speculum Christiani*, and a rhymed English conversation among the seven sins followed by a Latin commentary.[64] The earliest extant copy (ca. 1350) appears in the midst of a thick collection of rhymed vernacular prayers followed by the *Prick of Conscience* (BL Rawlinson poet. 175). Another early *Long Charter* is found in the Vernon manuscript (ca. 1380s–90s), a huge compilation of vernacular religious works probably commissioned by a wealthy patron for a religious house.[65] In the fifteenth century, we find the *Long Charter* bound in miscellanies with courtly poetry, travel narratives, and vernacular epics,

---

[64] The *Long Charter* was probably added at a later date; it is the last item in the collection and has been copied by a different, larger hand. For a description of the manuscript, see Homstedt, ed., *Speculum Christiani*, xxii–xxiii.

[65] For the patronage and audience of the Vernon manuscript see *Studies in the Vernon Manuscript*, ed. Pearsall.

as well as with pastoral or penitential texts. One later revised version was incorporated into a large collection of middle English metrical poems, such as the *Stations of Rome* and *Emare*, a second one appears in an early fifteenth-century manuscript with *Mandeville's Travels*, and a third was compiled with works by Lydgate and Chaucer.[66] Clearly, the *Long Charter* appealed to a broad spectrum of readers with different literary tastes and capabilities, who generally judged it to be a devotional poem appropriate for preaching, prayer, or even entertainment.

The compact *Short Charter*, by contrast, suggested a more iconic and practical application than it did a pastoral or meditative one. One late fifteenth-century scribe copied the *Short Charter* into a bundle of charms ("to haue a good onde"), medical prescriptions ("a playster ffor sore yne"), and recipes for dying silk, implying perhaps that the *Short Charter* was meant to serve some immediately curative effect.[67] Several *Short Charters* are "sealed" with illustrations of Christ's seal, the matrix of which is adorned with popular religious motifs such as a pelican piercing its own breast or a wounded heart.[68] According to one sixteenth-century hand, a version of the *Short Charter* was originally carved into a late fourteenth-century gravestone in Kent (Figure 4). These varied receptions of the *Short Charter* anticipated the indulgence craze in the late fifteenth and early sixteenth centuries, when print would astronomically increase the number of indulgences in circulation, making them available to the lay collector. Not only were indulgences sometimes believed to clear the sinner of both *poena* and *culpa* (as the *Charters of Christ* lyrics seem to do by awarding heaven), but they were also thought to ward off devils in this life and the next. Some late medieval wills stipulate, for example, that the pardons collected by the deceased be displayed on or near his grave, either to impress the mourners, to frighten devils, or to expedite proceedings in the heavenly court.[69] Certainly, there are outward affinities between a charter of Christ and a papal indulgence (although as we shall see in subsequent chapters, the

---

[66] BL Cotton Caligula A. II; Bodleian Additional C. 280; BL Harley 2382.

[67] Cambridge St. John's College B. 15, fol. 14.

[68] The pelican, a eucharistic symbol, was a popular design on anonymous personal seals of the fourteenth century. See Harvey and McGuiness, *A Guide to British Medieval Seals*, 91, fig. 85.

[69] Duffy, *The Stripping of the Altars*, 288.

Figure 4 *Short Charter* depicted with a hanging seal. London. The British Library MS Sloane 3292, fol. 2v. (sixteenth century). (With permission of the British Library).

former was often used to point up the failures of the latter), and some later readers tried to eliminate the discrepancies. One late fifteenth-century scribe, for example, doctored up his *Short Charter* into a generous indulgence awarding 26,030 years and 11 days' relief from purgatory.[70] Apparently, some readers thought to transform it from what it says it is – Christ's freely-given contract drawn up on the cross – into what it could potentially be – a passport to heaven, which one need only flash at the purgatorial guards in order to avoid centuries of punishment.

We owe the survival of most of the extant copies of the *Short Charters* to the usual cast of antiquarian characters: Sloane, Harley, Stowe, Dodsworth, and Cotton. Their interest in these poems is beyond the scope of this study; one thing that could be said about them, however, is that they were especially concerned to add or reproduce any illustration that would make the *Charter of Christ* lyrics resemble real documents. For example, BL Additional Charter 5960 (Figure 5), copied in an early sixteenth-century hand, depicts a *Short Charter* laid out as a charter on a rectangular piece of parchment with parchment tongues, lists of witnesses and notaries at the end of the text, and, where its seal should be, a quotation from the Psalms.[71] Likewise in BL Stowe 620, fol. 12a (Figure 6) an antiquarian hand has framed the late medieval copy, originally transcribed in long columns, into an open document with a hanging seal; the same thing has been done to the *Short Charter* in BL Sloane 3292 (Figure 4). Perhaps these early modern collectors thought to trivialize medieval practice in the service of Protestant antiquarianism. Or perhaps they thought they were endorsing their materials by making them documents of English history, much like they would aristocratic genealogies or heraldic charts, with which several of the *Short Charters* are compiled. It is clear, however, they were following the lead of medieval scribes, who, I propose, were trying to figure out how to classify the lyric through the materialities of documentary form.[72]

---

[70] Spalding, ed., *Middle English Charters*, xiii–xxxv.

[71] A near-exact copy of this charter is compiled in BL Harley 6848, Ar. 36, fol. 221.

[72] Unlike the *Charters of Christ* manuscripts, the illustrations of the documents in Deguileville's *Pèlerinages*, as for example, Mercy's charter, Charity's last will and testament, and Reason's commission, are always executed as captions outside of the documentary texts that they depict. They call attention to the material integrity of the documentary text by drawing in a seal, or in some illustrations the box or sack in which the document

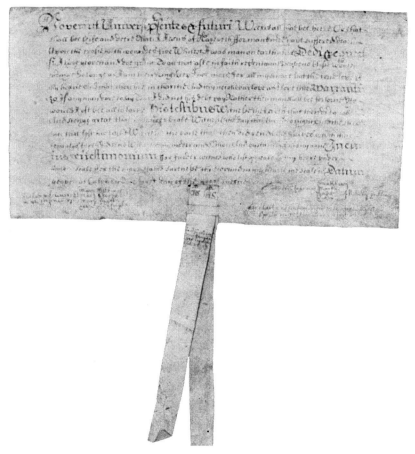

Figure 5 *Short Charter* drawn up as a charter. London. The British Library
MS Additional Charter 5960 (early sixteenth century). (With permission of
the British Library).

One example of the way that documentary culture enabled medieval
poets to define the lyric as a material genre is a version of the *Short Charter*
called the *Carta redemptionis human[e]*, written in the empty ruled lines
at the end of CUL Additional 6686 (Figure 7). The manuscript, copied
down between 1400 and 1450, is a miscellany of vernacular devotional
works such as the *Mirror of the Blessed Life of Christ* and two treatises

is transported (Figures 2–4), but they do not contain the document as it appears within
the narrative, nor is the document within the text set off differently on the page.

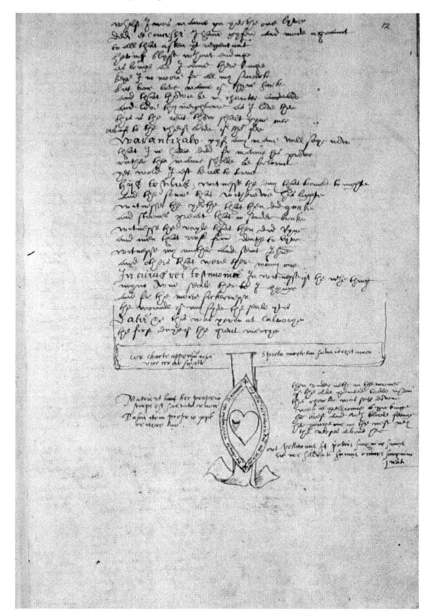

Figure 6 *Short Charter* depicted with a hanging seal. London. The British Library MS Stowe 620, fol. 12v. (sixteenth century). (With permission of the British Library).

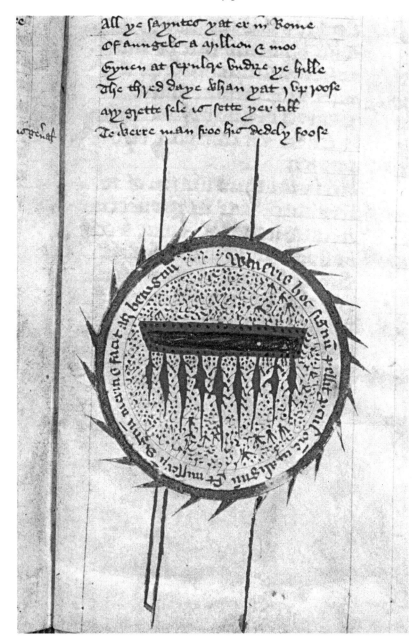

Figure 7 *Short Charter* depicted with a hanging seal. Cambridge University Library MS Additional 6686, p. 271 (ca. 1400–50). (With permission of Cambridge University Library).

attributed to Richard Rolle. In the original version of this poem, Christ grants heaven to humankind through the Atonement in exchange for a "rent" of two-fold charity. The charter is said to be granted on Calvary on the first day of the "great mercy," thirty-three years after Christ's birth. Additional 6686 begins with this original charter of feoffment, but the charter has oddly proliferated: the scribe has tacked two more fictive documents onto the original, each with its own rubricated title. In the first of these two additional documents, a writ of attorney or letter of procuration, Christ names John the evangelist as his proxy and charges him with the livery of seisin (the formal occupation of the land) to all those who adhere to the terms of the original charter: "To liver siesine to all þaase/þat hede to my wordes taase/Eftir þe tenor of my dede/þerof mad for mannes nede" (43–6). John's writ is witnessed by the other three evangelists and the Virgin Mary. In the second additional document, Christ issues from the sepulcher a general charter of pardon: "Ihesu of Nazarth...To all þat er both ying & olde/Be þis presentes his grace renewes/and gretis mankynd a þousand folde" (56–9). This pardon is witnessed by the early Church fathers, Ambrose, Jerome, Augustine, and Gregory, and grants pardon to those who have enthralled themselves in sin but have repented before death ("To all that oute of synne wil ryse/Of thair trespas full repentaunte/And soberly sewe to my servise/General pardon I thame graunte/Be their trespase neuer so greete/Be their houre neuer so late" [72–7]).

Clearly, the scribe of Additional 6686 understood the legal document to be a versatile form with which to narrate the multiple acts of the Atonement: the forgiveness of original sin, the transmission of the Word through the gospels, and a general pardon for those who sufficiently repent for accumulated sin. The legal document, by its very method of organization, the information that it contains, and the iterability of its formulas, lends itself to the proliferation of stanzas and variations on a theme. Because it is formally consistent, it can also accommodate infinite legal arrangements. Thus the scribes of other *Charters of Christ* might attribute all sorts of functions to Christ's charter, as suggested by the various titles that they chose to give them: *feoffment ihesi, magna carta libertatis et remissionis,* and *testamentum christi.*[73] In

---

[73] This last title may refer to the bequest that follows the charter (Christ leaves his mother to St. John), but more likely to Christ's complaint, a popular literary form of which

Additional 6686, however, it is not just that the one document serves as a template for several experiences of the law, but rather that the lyric presents itself as a compound act or series of documents: it contains all the partial acts that culminate in the final act (pardon for sins). In this way, the poem demonstrates how a narrative of the self (Christ, the penitential subject) might be refashioned, through the appropriation of legal formulas and practices, into a narrative of contractual relations and into a genre of redemptive action. The *Long Charter* also allegorizes salvation history as a series of legal acts (e.g., the Incarnation is the livery of seisin, the Crucifixion is the execution of the charter, the Eucharist is the indentured copy of the charter) of which the charter is the most meaningful, as it is the literal confirmation of the others and their perpetual record. Yet the legal acts in Additional 6686 are meaningful *insofar* as they are documentary: they take into account the continual transmission of the contract of salvation, while at the same time glossing with additional documents the central act of the Atonement. In this way the lyric, through the citation and iteration of documentary formulas, and through the collection of written evidence, becomes a genre of the Atonement. It begins, that is, to imitate its subject: the efficacious and continuous performance of the Word.

The *Short Charter* in Additional 6686 is a self-consciously literary event: it is concerned with the communicability of the lyric, the relationship between lyric and narrative, and the performativity of genre. But the graphic image at the bottom of the third column would seem to belie its literariness: a large pendant seal wreathed by a green crown of thorns, the matrix of which depicts a large gaping wound, presumably the wound in Christ's side. The seal, which hangs by two red strings painted onto the end of the poem, illustrates the execution clause (*in cuius rei testimonium*) that makes up the last few lines of the original *Short Charter* (the feoffment of heaven): "In testimone of whilk thinge/ myn owene sele ther to I hynge/And for the more sikkernesse/The wound in my side the sele it is." The last two lines of the third document in Additional 6686, the charter of pardon, from which the seal literally

the *Charters of Christ* are a part. Similarly, the "Charter of Heaven" pronounces Christ's charter to be both a charter of feoffment and a pardon: "vndirstonde wel þat þe chartre of his eritage, & þe bulle of his euerlastinge pardoun: is oure lord ihesu crist" (Spalding, ed., *Middle English Charters*, 100).

84

seems to hang, rephrases the execution clause of the first document: "my grette sele is sette þertill/to were [caution] man froo his dedely foose." The legend of the seal, while difficult to make out, is clearly a Latin couplet, and a benediction of sorts: "Vulneris hoc signum pellit [per cuius orem] malignum/Et misserum dignum meritis facit atque benignum" (This sign of the wound drives away evil [through its mouth]/And makes the wretched kind and worthy of merit).

I suggest that this illustration of the seal, like the proliferation of documents within the text itself, is not, as we might first suspect, a crude attempt at a talisman or charm, but rather an experiment in genre within the context of Atonement theology. As such it helps to reshape lyric textuality into material form, inventing for the lyric a genre already advertised within the lyric itself and located in documentary practice. One way that it remakes lyric into a material genre is the way that it responds to the extended metaphor of the *Short Charter*: Christ's sacramental body as a bloody charter. The lyric, by continually displacing the literary onto the textual and the textual onto the material, reverses – really collapses – tenor and vehicle. Or, to put it another way, the lyric compares Christ's crucified body to a written charter, but in doing so, it tends to equate sacramentality and documentality: it maps the word made flesh onto the flesh made word in such a way as to obscure the boundaries between the signifier and the signified. The *Short Charter*, perhaps as a result of such ambiguity, also tends to replace lyrical with documentary conventions, as seen in the transition from the *Long Charter* to the *Short Charter* (in which the 300-line lyrical narrative is reduced to a 36-line fictive charter), but more pointedly in the expanded *Short Charter* of Additional 6686, in which the charter literally multiplies. And just as the vehicle (the charter) seems almost to take precedence over the tenor (the sacramental efficacy of the Word), so the materiality of documentary practice takes precedence over its textuality. The charter becomes the classifying function or material determinant of the lyric (its genre, but also its historical precedent) rather than simply its governing metaphor. Another example of this externalization of metaphor into material genre is the illustrated *Short Charter* in London BL Additional 37049 (Figure 8). In the illustration, Christ's mid-section is unfurled into a charter, which appears to be nailed to his hands and feet like a broadside, and which is inscribed with the verses of the *Short Charter*. Christ's

Figure 8 Christ's crucified body depicted as a charter and inscribed with the text of the *Short Charter*. London. British Library MS Additional 37049, fol. 23r. (ca. 1400–50). (With permission of the British Library).

wounded heart hanging from the bottom of the cross is further made to look like a seal hanging from a parchment tag, thus illustrating the last few lines of the original text, already quoted several times above: "ffor furder witnes who list appeale/To my heere vnder-honged seale/ffor the more stable surenesse/this wound in my hearte the seale is" (Spalding, 7, ll. 29–32). In this illustration, as in Additional 6686, the vehicle of the metaphor, by virtue of its peculiar claims to material textuality, has stretched the lyric into a legal document.

The curious seal painted onto Additional 6686 also helps classify the lyric as a material genre through the notion of hanging or extension, which the scribe presents simultaneously as a rhetorical and material device. We saw that this poem inverts trope into genre by adding more documents onto the first, as if in doing so it might add successive glosses onto the original charter of feoffment, glosses which depend textually and legally upon that original charter but also extend it into a redemptive narrative. In this way documentary practice extends lyric into narrative by increasing the number of chronologically progressive and legally interdependent acts. The illustrated seal (painted in the same hand as the rubrication) literalizes this idea of extension by suggesting that the whole lyric depends upon its material reification – the hanging of the pendant seal – to become a redemptive genre. Thus the seal quite literally hangs on the last verses of the poem ("my grette sele is sette þertill/ to were man froo his dedely foose"), which in turn reiterates the execution clause of the original charter of feoffment ("In testimone of whilk þinge/ Myn owene sele þer to I hynge, etc."). The painted seal, in other words, is not simply an illustration of the themes of the poem, but a theorizing of the relationship between genre and material form, a relationship contained within the last few lines of the poem itself (the documentary execution clause).

An elegantly rhymed Latin version of the *Short Charter*, the *Carta libera*, makes a similar point about the classificatory functions of legal documents. Like the English *Short Charter*, it ends with an execution or "hanging" clause, rendered into Latin verse in such a way as to emphasize Christ's bloody presence: "In cuius rei testimonium requiei ut stet tranquillum proprium cor pono sigillum" (In witness of this thing of repose, I have placed my own heart as the seal so as to make it secure)

Figure 9a *Carta Dei* inscribed on the dorse of a charter. Oxford. Bodleian Library MS Kent Charter 233 (ca. 1400). (With permission of the Bodleian Library).

Figure 9b

(Spalding, 97, ll. 33–4).[74] A second scribe from approximately the same period has added another execution clause to the end of the poem, reinforcing the conceit that Christ has written the charter in his own blood and sealed it with his heart: "Sanguine tamen puro cartam, frater, tibi scripsi/Et pro securo proprium cor penditur ipsi, amen"

[74] This manuscript was probably commissioned by a wealthy religious patron or academic community and was compiled in a beautifully illuminated manuscript containing other Latin religious texts such as the *Meditationes Vitae Christi* attributed to Bonaventure and Latin tractates on the festivals and the seven deadly sins (Cambridge. St. John's College D. 8, fol. 174b and Cambridge St. John's College E. 224, fol. 22a).

(I have yet written this charter for you, brother, in spotless blood/And in order to safeguard this thing my own heart has been hung on it [as the seal], amen) (Spalding, 97, ll. 37–8). What was so compelling for the second scribe, I am suggesting, was the possibility of using the "hanging" clause simultaneously as a literary device and a documentary practice. He saw the possibility of extending the lyric rhetorically by making his own verses dependent on the original, while at the same time transforming the whole lyric into a material genre by appealing to the interrelation of text and body within the execution clause of the legal document ("my own heart has been hung on it [as the seal], amen").

Two other *Charters of Christ* manuscripts suggest a similar reciprocity between material genre and vernacular lyric: the *Carta Dei* (ca. 1400), inscribed on the dorse of an official charter, Bodleian Kent Charter 233 (Figure 9) and a *Long Charter* found on the back of a presentment made in King's Court, Oxford (1412) in protest against a new window that the university had installed in Blakehall, St. Peter's Parish.[75] We may guess that for the educated and litigious authors of these documents, the lyric had two, mutually illuminating literary "personalities": it was at once a religious lyric and an efficacious text that strengthened the official document through its very resemblance to that document. The document classified the lyric at the same time that the lyric enforced the document. If genres, as Fredric Jameson puts it, are "essentially literary *institutions*, or social contracts between a writer and a specific public, whose function is to specify the proper use of a particular cultural artifact," for these medieval writers the legal document classified the lyric as a genre by making it quite literally a social contract, one drawn up within specific materialities of documentary practice.[76]

[75] Spalding, ed., *Middle English Charters*, xxxii.
[76] Jameson, *The Political Unconscious*, 106.

PART II

Langland's documents

3

Piers Plowman and the archive of salvation

Brian Stock writes, in *Listening for the Text,*

> Societies may be chartered by myths that we call literature, but no
> society is ever motivated by more than a small part of its heritage
> at a given time or place. Action is normally based on small units –
> scripts, scenarios, and parts of bigger narratives. The historian or
> ethnographer must read a whole society's archive, but he or she must
> also listen carefully for those key texts.[1]

Piers Plowman has always accommodated a wide variety of readers: reformers, historians, poets, and perhaps most importantly, penitents. To
read *Piers Plowman* as a penitent is also, however, to do the work of a
notary scribe, chancery clerk, or monastic chronicler: to witness, transcribe, and justify a number of disordered legal instruments. Medieval
and modern readers alike have been struck by the poem's preoccupation
with legality, and its numerous written instruments – Mede's charter,
Truth's Pardon, Piers's testament, Hawkyn's quittance, Moses's maundement, and Peace's patent – can be understood as particularly legible
moments in its dramatization and critique of the law. Yet the poem
presents these same documents as "key texts" in the construction of
salvation history, as those small scripts that enact the heritage of a given
society. More specifically, *Piers Plowman* reveals the conditions of God's
contract with humanity as the unpacking or unfolding of an *archive*
of redeeming texts. By *archive* I don't mean postmodern theory's figurative "collection of discourses," abstracted from the materialities and
genres of preservation. Rather, I mean the two definitions that Foucault

---

[1] Stock, *Listening for the Text: On the Uses of the Past,* 14.

eloquently describes and eventually discards: first, "the sum of all those texts that a culture has kept on its person as documents attesting to its own past, or as evidence of a continuing identity," and second, "the institutions, which, in a given society, make it possible to record and preserve those discourses that one wishes to remember and keep in circulation."[2]

This chapter argues that Langland's documents are key texts both because they are the foundational texts for salvation history – the way that that history can be meaningfully encountered as *text* – and because they are the material and legal instantiations of that history within the life of the penitential reader. As the first part of this chapter argues, *Piers Plowman* presents salvation history, the continual proclamation and witnessing of the Redemption, as a collection of documents in a number of institutional forms (the archive), which must be sorted and annotated into a justifying narrative (the cartulary or chronicle). The poem, in other words, depicts the penitential writing of history, the relentless outlining of the societal onto the redemptive, as both a repository of legal instruments attesting to origins and as the processing and enrolling of the same. This kind of clerical work, the documenting of the Redemption, shows how a culture's key texts become recognizable at the moments when its scriptural history is written into the materialities of contemporary practice. This kind of clerical work also demonstrates something about Langland's historical method. It shows that his documenting of salvation history effectively integrates two strains of medieval historiography: the chronicle and the romance. By writing salvation history as documentary history, Langland shows how the pilgrimage of the self, the heroic search for transparent and supremely authorized moments of reading, is bound up in documentary procedure and the kind of narratives that it engenders. As we will see, moreover, Langland's historical method invokes a medieval tradition reaching all the way back to Augustine, in which legal documents serve as the fundamental unit of historical writing at the same time that they serve as the central trope of penitential experience.

If Langland's documents represent the penitential writing of salvation history, they also register the shock of the historical encounter. As the

2 Foucault, "The Historical *A Priori* and the Archive," in *The Archeology of Knowledge*, trans. Smith, 129.

second part of this chapter argues, the documents in *Piers Plowman*, and especially the tearing of Truth's Pardon, dramatize what it means to realize history textually but also what it means to confront a larger historical narrative than that which is normally experienced individually. As with legal documents, the shock of Truth's Pardon is historical, but it is also, importantly, contractual: it demonstrates what it means to perform history as legal text. As we will see, moreover, it is once again Augustine who helps us to describe what we already see in the Pardon episode: it is through documentary practice that we explode the difference between social satire (one's generation, one's self) and soteriology (generation after generation). Likewise, it is documentary practice that allows us to explode the difference between history and allegory. Indeed, by presenting salvation history as a series of documentary encounters, *Piers Plowman* suggests ways that poetry itself constitutes a puncturing through to history.

CHIROGRAPHUM DEI: EXEGESIS AND THE ARCHIVE

Medieval historical writing was developed in large part by monks who had archives at their disposal and pressing reasons to record the claims of institution, nation, or world. Documented histories proliferated rapidly in the two centuries after the Norman Conquest; as Andrew Galloway explains, the immediate impetus for this proliferation was an increase in the production of charters, from two thousand before the Conquest to tens of thousands in the centuries following.[3] As a result, later medieval cartularies are often nearly indistinguishable from monastic chronicles, as in the case of the chronicle of Battle Abbey or the chronicle of Matthew Paris (1200–59), the latter of which circulated with a companion volume of all the letters, writs, and decrees discussed in the chronicle. It is not so surprising, then, that medieval royal biographies and universal histories often interweave romance and chronicle. Even a "popular history" such as the *Brut* sometimes included documents in its fourteenth-century continuations.[4] Nor is it surprising that saints' lives and legal documents

---

[3] Galloway goes on to argue that deeper causes included "maintaining or redefining social and economic rights in the face of massive political dislocation" ("Writing History in England," 257–9).

[4] Taylor, *English Historical Literature*, 52; see also, Gransden, *Historical Writing in England*.

co-exist in even the most strictly annalistic of chronicles. Thomas Walsingham, for example, in his chronicle of the monastery of St. Alban's, transcribes all sorts of legal instruments recording the abbey's privileges, concessions, and properties, or the revocation or confirmation of the same. His chronicle is, in a sense, the gloss that binds these documents together – the "writing out" from small units of historical writing. But, interestingly enough, the St. Alban's chronicle attests as much to the capacity of documentary practice to generate a romance of origins as it does to its capacity to generate the primary texts of evidentiary histories. Walsingham reports that during the 1381 revolt, the villagers of St. Alban's were trying to force the abbot to draw up a new charter of liberties, when a minor miracle occurred: the abbot's seal, engraved with the likeness of Saint Alban, could not be extracted from the wax until the third try. Walsingham concludes that the saint did not wish the villagers to be lords over him but wished to hold sway over them, as he had done up to that time.[5] Both the charter itself and the story of its making address the material relationship between possession and identity. But whereas the charter attests to that relationship – it is concerned with the text of the grant and its legal viability – the story of its making recounts the charter's near-miraculous origins.

In terms of historical writing, then, we may think of the legal document as a key text, first, in the sense of being a foundational text, which can be either stored in a drawer or a pot, or transcribed, glossed, and kept on one's person as evidence; and, second, in the sense of being part of a larger institutional practice from which different types of historical narrative may be drawn. As we will see, the dual function of the document as both the legal *evidence* for individual possession or institutional liberties, and the narrative *process* by which a story of origins comes into being, takes on a curiously redemptive character in *Piers Plowman*. Before turning to *Piers Plowman*, however, it is illuminating to take a brief look at another penitential allegory, the prose treatise called the

---

[5] Walsingham, *Gesta abbatum monasterii Sancti Albans*, ed. Riley, 323. "Ubi mirabile illud contigit: Cum charta de libertate villae, vel villanorum, sigillari debuisset, quod cum omni cautela et diligentia cera apposita a scientibus sigillo communi fuisset, in quo vetustissimo opere imago gloriosi Protomartyris Britannorum, Albani, figuratur, tenens in manu palam, nulla potuit arte per tres vices avelli vel removeri de sigillo; praenosticans proculdubio Martyrem nolle eos fore dominos sed velle dominari, ut hactenus super eos."

Charter of the Abbey of the Holy Ghost (ca. 1380), designed to accompany the *Abbey of the Holy Ghost*.[6] In the *Charter of the Abbey*, the narrator explains that God the Father is the founder of the abbey (the soul), and the Holy Ghost its warden, but the abbey can never be truly safe without charters to guarantee and protect its properties from the devil ("goode dedis & charteres of here places where-þorou þei mowe kepen here londis, rentys & fraunchises, oftensiþes per auenture þei schulden ben mysserued & suffren mochel persecucion of here enemyes & of false men").[7] The devil once invaded the abbey (the Fall) and stole its charter, but the narrator proposes to write a "book," a charter that will reconfirm the grant and protect it from further attacks by recording the original grant made at Creation: "þerfore y make here a book þat shal be clepid 'þe Chartre of þe abbeye of þe holy gost,' In whiche I schal tellen first whan & where & of whom þis abbeye was first I-foundid..." In the lengthy charter that follows, God perpetually grants to Adam and Eve the territory of Conscience ("*Sciant presentes & futuri &c.* Wetiþ ȝe þat ben now here, & þei þat schulen comen after ȝou, þat almiȝti god in trinite, fader & sone & holy gost, haþ gouen & graunted & wiþ his owne word conformed, to Adam, þe first man þat euere was, & to Eue his wyf, & to here heyres, a lytel preciouse place þat is clepid Conscience"), on which site God has built the abbey of the Holy Ghost (the human soul) populated by "gostly" nuns (the virtues). All creation witnessed this charter ("*Hijs testibus*: Of þis bereþ witness aungel & man, heuene & erþe, sone & mone & al þe sterris..."), which was drawn up in Paradise on the day that God created man ("*Explicit carta. Memorandum quod primo die incarnacionis hominis &c.*") (338–9).

The charter of the abbey thus grants conscience to Adam and all his heirs, so that they might enjoy perpetual "ioye and blisse." After

---

[6] The *Abbey of the Holy Ghost* is a short meditative treatise probably composed originally for French aristocratic women but translated into English in the late fourteenth century to meet the needs of the "spiritually ambitious" English bourgeoisie. See Nicole Rice, "Spiritual Ambition and the Translation of the Cloister: *The Abbey* and *Charter of the Holy Ghost*." Hussey suggests that the text was possibly commissioned for a female religious house ("Implication of Choice and Arrangement of Texts in Part 4"). Significantly enough, the *Charter of the Abbey*, which accompanies the *Abbey of the Holy Ghost* in eighteen manuscripts, is an entirely English innovation.

[7] Text in *Yorkshire Writers: Richard Rolle of Hampole, An English Father of the Church and His Followers*, vol. 1, ed. Horstmann, 338–40 (hereafter cited in the main text by page number).

the devil broke into the abbey and snatched away its charter, however, neither Adam, nor Eve, nor any of their heirs had the right "to chalenge þe lordschip of þis world ne þe blisse of heuene, but onlyche in þe mersy of god" (341). The charter continues, however, to provide a temporal hinge between the Fall and the Atonement, and between the history of the redemption and the salvation of the individual soul. God once endowed ("haþ gouen & graunted") Adam, Eve, and their heirs with the moral faculties to discriminate between good and evil. Adam and Eve subsequently lost their charter and Paradise in the bargain, but Christ restored the faculties of the soul and refortified it against the devil (as perhaps implied in the charter by the phrase, "& wiþ his owne word confermed," and by the *explicit* quoted above, which simultaneously alludes to Creation and the Incarnation). Consequently, the charter remains present and effective (*habendum et tenendum*) for all present and future souls (*sciant presentes & futuri*) who wish to attain heaven.

Anne Middleton, writing about the manuscript history of *Piers Plowman*, observes that "for a significant part of its early audience whose testimony survives, *Piers* belonged among works in which the quest for salvation and the examination of the foundations of possession and authority were mutually metonymic," and she names the *Charter of the Abbey* as one of those works.[8] Significantly, like *Piers Plowman*, the *Charter of the Abbey*'s primary purpose is the textual reconstruction of salvation history. It is as if the *Charter of the Abbey* has been appended to the *Abbey of the Holy Ghost* in order to show how salvation history, the "foundations of possession and authority," is continually made relevant as documentary text. The charter, first of all, mediates between documentary and romance histories. It is, on the one hand, the founding text that protects and authorizes the institution (the soul). It preserves chronology – it was granted on the first day of the incarnation of man – and therefore it must be historically preserved as the foundational text of heavenly bliss. On the other hand, the charter is also the very process by which a redemptive narrative may be continually spun out, regardless of chronology: God granted the charter, the devil stole it away, Christ restored the possession, and the narrator rewrites the charter for his medieval readers. This charter is simultaneously the confirmation

---

[8] Middleton, "The Audience and Public of *Piers Plowman*," 110.

of possession granted, and the never-ending story of its adventuresome loss and gain. In writing these two kinds of history, then, the charter effectively mediates between the soteriological and the penitential: it is the textual site at which the soteriological past may be read and copied by the penitential reader, and it is also the means by which salvation is made written history within an allegorical romance. It is evidence for a past contract but also the very narrative that continually confirms that contract, making it efficacious for new readers (the heirs) as well as for its historical actors (Adam and Eve).

I would like to make a similar argument about *Piers Plowman*. It is tempting to think of Langland's documents as separate instances of literacy or legality, together adding up to a cultural critique or theological doctrine. I would like to suggest, however, that the fraught relationship in the poem between literacy and spirituality is bound up in the realization of salvation history within the fiction of the poem. It is, moreover, the poem's portrayal of contemporary documentary culture – the issuing of charters, patents, seals, and the like – that makes such a realization possible. Or to put this idea a different way, the documents in *Piers Plowman* do add up to a coherent vision, but that vision has less to do with a *mentality* than it does with the historical *procedure* of writing salvation through material legal documents. Langland's documents appear in the B-text's two "historical" sections: the first seven passus or *Visio* of contemporary society, and Passus 17–19, the retelling of biblical history from Adam to Christ. Each of these sections dramatizes the immanence of the divine in the human condition by mapping legal documents onto master narratives of Augustinian exegesis, and by obliging the clerkly reader to compare and contrast them – to arrange them but also to choose between them. Further, by making legal documents the key texts of salvation history, these two sections together integrate two genres of historical writing: the cartulary-chronicle (the writing out from legal documents) and the romance of pilgrimage (the legal document encountered within the action of the narrative). And it is by integrating these two genres that the poem finally models the penitential process: what it means to chronicle the past while at the same time experiencing the past as present.

To see how Langland writes salvation history as documentary practice, it is necessary to examine two exegetical master narratives that grew up around Colossians 2:14–15, a passage that plays a part in nearly every medieval discussion of the Atonement. This passage cryptically states that Christ blotted out the handwriting of a decree ("chirographum decreti") against us and defeated the "principals and powers" by nailing the bond to the cross: "Delens quod adversus nos erat chirographum decreti, quod erat contrarium nobis, et ipsum tulit de medio, affigens illud cruci; et expolians principatus et potestates traduxit confidenter palam triumphans illos in semetipso." Nearly every patristic and medieval exegete of this passage interprets the "chirograph" as a record of original sin in the form of a written contract drawn up between humanity and the devil. Augustine was particularly taken with the idea of a diabolical chirograph, and the two lines from Colossians surface repeatedly in his *Confessiones, Contra Iulianum,* and *Enarrationes in Psalmos,* among his other works. He writes, for example, that Christ "redeemed the guilty from captivity, in which we were detained by the devil ... and in this exchange for us, with his own blood, [and deleted] the chirograph in which we were held to be debtors."[9] Likewise, in his commentary on Psalm 103, sermon 4, he tells us that Christ shed his own blood, erased humanity's debt ("deleat chirographum nostrum") and reconciled God and humanity.[10]

Later exegetes generally followed Augustine's interpretation of the Colossians passage. Rabanus Maurus (d. 856) wrote, for example, that Christ poured forth his blood to delete the chirograph of damnation ("chirographum maledictiones") drawn up between Adam and the devil.[11] In *Cur Deus homo,* Anselm of Canterbury (d. 1109) tried to counter the "devil's rights" advocates – those who argued that Christ had to compensate the devil for the redemption of man – by explaining that the chirograph of original sin was drawn up not between man

---

[9] "Redemit nocentes a captiuitate, in qua detinebamur a diabolo ... et ipse pretio nostro sanguine suo delens chirographum quo debitores tenebamur." *Enarrationes in Psalmos* 138:1, ll. 5–9. Text in *Enarrationes in Psalmos,* CCSL 38–40. Psalm numbers refer to the Latin Vulgate. See also *Confessiones,* V. 9, 41; VII. 21, 20–5; IX. 13, 34–7 (CCSL 27) and *Contra Iulianum,* I: 2, 4; I: 6, 26 (PL 44: 641–2).

[10] "Fundat sanguinem suum, deleat chirographum nostrum, componat inter nos et Deum, nostram voluntatem corrigens ad iustitiam, illius sententiam flectens ad misericordiam" (*Enarrationes in Psalmos,* 8. 27–30).

[11] "'Aspersione sanguinis mei, uem pro totius mundi funda redemptione': delens chirographum malectictiones, quod Adam meruit in paradiso transgressione praecept, quod contra humanum genus scriptum erat" (*Homiliae in Evangelia et Epistolas,* 84.4 [PL, 110: 310]).

and the devil but rather between man and God.[12] Despite Anselm's efforts, however, later medieval theologians continued to interpret the chirograph as a diabolical record obliterated by Christ's sacrifice. Even the *Glossa ordinaria*, the interpretative guide for centuries of medieval scholars, includes diabolical readings of the chirograph: "Chirograph: that is, the 'memory of sin'; by decree: that is, 'by law.' For conscience and the devil brought that sin to mind in order to accuse us."[13] In the mid-thirteenth century, the popular hagiographer Jacobus de Voragine (ca. 1230–98) was still defining the chirograph as a usurious bond, drawn up between Eve and the devil:[14]

> This sort of debt the apostle calls a chirograph, a handwritten bill, which Christ took and nailed to the cross. Augustine says of this bill: "Eve borrowed sin from the devil and wrote a bill and provided a surety, and the interest of the debt was heaped upon posterity. She borrowed sin from the devil, when, going against God's command, she consented to his wicked order or suggestion. She wrote the bill when she reached out her hand to the forbidden apple. She gave a surety when she made Adam consent to the sin. And so the interest on the debt is posterity's burden."[15]

---

[12] *Cur Deus Homo*, Ch. 7, edited in *Opera omnia*, vol. 1, ed. Schmitt, 58. "At si obtenditur 'chirographum' illud 'decreti quod adversum nos' dicit apostolus fuisse et per mortem Christi deletum esse et putat aliquius per illud significari, quia diabolus quasi sub cuiusdam pacti chirographo ab homine iuste ante Christi passione peccatum, velut usuram primi peccati quod persuasit homini et poenam peccati exigeret, ut per hoc iustitiam suum super hominem probare videatur: nequaquam ita intelligendum puto... Decretum enim illud non erat diaboli, sed dei." On the relation of Anselm to his predecessors on the question of the devil's rights, see Marx, *The Devil's Rights and the Redemption in the Literature of Medieval England*.

[13] "Cyrographum: id est memoriam transgressionis quod erat ex decreto id est ex lege. Conscientia enim et diabolus ad accusandum erat memor illius transgressionis" (*Biblia Latina cum Glossa ordinaria: Facsimile Reprint of the Editio Princeps of Adolf Rusch of Strassburg [1480/1]*, fol. 391).

[14] Christopher Baswell cites an even earlier Latin literary reference to a chirograph written on Christ's forehead ("*Latinitas*," 148).

[15] *The Golden Legend*, vol. 1, ed. and trans. Ryan, 210. The Latin original is as follows: "Huiusmodi autem debitum apostolus uocat cyrographum, quod quidem christus tulit et cruci affixit. De quo cyrographo dicit Augustinus: Eua peccatum a dyabolo mutuauit, cyrographum scripsit, fideiussorem dedit et usura posteritati creuit. Tunc enim dyabolo peccatum mutuauit, quando contra preceptum dei sue praue suggestioni consensit, cyrographum scripsit, quando manum ad uetitum pomum porrexit, fideiussorem dedit quando Adam peccato consentire fecit et sic usura peccati posteritati creuit" (*Legenda aurea*, ed. Maggioni, 347, ll. 172–5). The Middle English translation of Voragine

The devil's record, with all its emphasis on diabolical cunning and self-inscription, continued to thrive in exempla literature well into the fifteenth century. The *Gesta Romanorum* (c. 1350), for example, a collection of morality tales about Roman emperors, explains that the history of our sins becomes in the devil's hands a charter of homage or debt: "Seven sithes in þe day fallith þe rightwise man; and [the devil] sealith þe chartre when he makith a man do synne, and so he alleggith in þe sight of god, þat þe soul is his."[16] In this passage, the failure to repent is rhetorically indistinguishable from the event of original sin; the charter relocates the salvation drama to a contemporary penitential context.[17] What was perhaps the most influential version of the devil's record, Rutebeuf's *Le miracle de Théophile* (ca. 1260), tells the story of a Faustian deacon who sells his soul to the devil in exchange for worldly goods and honor. Théophile confirms this transaction with a charter written in his own blood, but he subsequently repents and calls upon the intercession of the Virgin, who restores to him the incriminating charter.[18] The French and English popularizers of the Théophile legend probably had in mind the devil's record from contemporary exegesis of Colossians. An early author of the legend, Fulbert of Chartres, calls Théophile's charter a chirograph, as do several of the fifteenth-century English adapters of the story, one of whom reports that Théophile renounced his faith and "made hym a cyrographatt wretten, & seelid it with his awn ring."[19] In

---

explicitly traces its origins to Colossians 2:14: "this dette here thappostle calleth Cirographe or oblygacion the which Jesus Cryst bare & ttouchydit to the crosse" (*Short Title Catalogue of Books*, 24873, fols. xvi–xvii). Voragine's quotation from Augustine is actually a restatement of a passage in an anti-Pelagian tract attributed to Augustine: "Eva ergo peccatum a diabolo mutavit, Adam consensu cautionem fecit, usura posteritati crevit ... huius chirographi usurae sunt, illae malignissimae passiones, quibus tam majorum aetate quam parvulorum animae deprimuntur, a quibus liberari neminem posse nisi per Christum" (PL 45:1649).

16 The *Early English Versions of the Gesta Romanorum*, ed. Herrtage, 74–5.

17 In some English stories the devil's record is entirely replaced by the self-incriminating confession of a guilt-ridden cleric who is too traumatized to confess to a priest and consequently damns himself to hell or is saved by the miraculous erasure of the charter-confession. See, for example, the exempla compiled in a fourteenth-century manuscript, BL Cotton Vitellius, fol. 7, along with a French translation of the *Ancrene Wisse* (*The French Text of the Ancrene Riwle*, ed. Herbert, xi).

18 Rutebeuf, *Le miracle de Théophile*, ed. Dufournet.

19 From *An Alphabet of Tales*, ed. Banks, 318, ll. 28–30. The chirograph, which to early exegetes meant simply a handwritten bond, probably continued to be a compelling image

another, possibly related English version, Théophile implores the Virgin, "Swete ladi! mak me haue/that vnsely cirograue,/that the fend made me write/ffor elles of him am I not quyte."[20] All of these stories depict documentary practice as a penitential process insofar as it typifies the events of the Atonement itself: the production of a charter of sin, and the legal transformation of that charter. In all these stories, moreover, penitence entails the layering of exegetical metaphor onto contemporary documentary practice.

The exegetical narratives of the devil's record further inspired a number of social satires, probably in part because the conspiratorial nature of that record might easily be attributed to other malefactors, and in part because it was supposed to be issued primarily by the guilty party himself (Eve, Théophile, the sinner). From the late thirteenth century, for example, there survives a witty Anglo-Norman charter, probably written by the reforming archbishop John Pecham (d. 1292), in which the devil grants various vices to the rich and powerful in return for their allegiance. Sometime in the early fourteenth century, Nicholas Bozon (fl. 1300–30), a prolific Franciscan writer from the north of England, composed a versified Anglo-Norman patent from the emperor Pride. From the mid-fourteenth century survives an *Epistola Luciferi* (1359) in Latin and English, satirizing both possessioners and friars: "Lucifer, lord and prince of the depe donion of derknenes...to all our childryn of pryde, universall and singuler...helthe, welthe and gretyng," etc. And finally, at the turn of the fifteenth century, a Lollard writer tried his hand at a devil's record, the *Epistola Sathanae ad clericos*, in which the devil delivers to "alle the brethren of our ordre" a progress report on the corruption of the friars, and cautions his minions against the "lewid Lollers" who tell the common people about God's law.[21]

to later writers because of the association of chirographs with indentured contracts of maintenance drawn up between lords and retainers. For examples, see Jones and Walker, eds., "Private Indentures for Life Service in Peace and War, 1278–1476."

[20] From *The Story off Theofle*, ed. Kolbing, "Die jungere engliche fassung der Theophilussage," 52, ll. 577–80. Another version of "St. Theophilus," is found in the *South English Legendary*, vol. 1, ed. D'Evelyn and Miller, 221–37.

[21] Pecham's charter is printed in Jeffrey and Levy, ed. and trans., *The Anglo-Norman Lyric: An Anthology*, 137–9. Bozon's charter is printed in *Les contes moralisés de Nicole Bozon*, ed. Smith and Meyer, ii–iii. The *Epistola Luciferi* is printed in Raymo, ed., "A Middle English Version of the *Epistola Luciferi ad clericos*," 233–48. The Lollard charter is printed in Hudson, ed., *Selections from English Wycliffite Writings*, 89–93.

Significantly, however, in fourteenth-century sermons and lyrics, a "new" document of Christ, a *chirographum dei* drawn up on the cross, emerges from the exegetical past to confront the devil's record, either by pardoning the debt owed, or by granting heaven. The concept of a written bond roughly synonymous with Christ's body and the gospels had already circulated in patristic writings generated by Colossians 2:14–15. As early as the third century, for example, Novatian describes the Holy Spirit in Christ as a divine chirograph or bond: "He is the consecrator of a heavenly birth, a pledge of the promised inheritance, and a kind of chirograph, so to speak, of eternal salvation."[22] In his commentary on Psalm 118, Saint Ambrose (d. 397) also refers to the divine chirograph or bond, which he explicitly contrasts with the chirograph of sin: "we address you by means of your chirograph, you who have taken away our chirograph; we make a chirograph of death, you have written a chirograph of life."[23] As we will see later in this chapter, Augustine was also deeply interested in the *chirographum dei*, a divine bond equivalent to the Passion and to the gospels. For all of these authors, the idea is that one writes oneself into the *chirographum debiti* of original sin – the self-confessed record of one's own bad deeds – but one may subsequently confirm one's heavenly heritage by receiving or copying down the *chirographum dei*. The *chirographum dei* represents God's grant of heaven in the form of a handwritten bond, indicating Christ's personal investment and liability in the Atonement, as well as the supreme readability of his Word.

Despite the popularity of the devil's record among later medieval exegetes and sermon-writers, the divine bond was practically disregarded until the fourteenth century, when it was revived as an interpretation of the second verse of the Colossians passage, "and he has taken the

---

[22] *De Trinitate*, XXIX (PL 3:0944D). "Hic est qui operatur ex aquis secundam nativitatem, semen quoddam divini generis et consecrator caelestis nativitatis, pignus promissae hereditatis et quasi chirographum quoddam aeternae salutis." Paschasius Radbertus (ca. 786–860), an exegete popular with later medieval writers, refers to Novatian when he writes that "accepimus pignus promissae hereditatis nostrae et quasi quoddam cyrographum aeternae salutis" ([in Christ] we accept the token of our promised inheritance and the chirograph of eternal salvation)." *Expositio in Matheo libri XII*, 2.3547 (CCCM 56–56B.)

[23] "Tuo te chirographo contenimus, qui nostrum chirographum sustulisti. Fecimus chirographum mortis, tu scripsisti chirographum vitae." Ambrose, *Expositio in Psalmum* CXVIII (PL 15:1419B).

same out of the way, affixing it to the cross." The *Fasciculus morum*, for example, repeats the story of Eve's chirograph from Jacobus de Voragine but also imagines a different charter nailed to the cross, which confirms Christ's successful bargaining with the devil and restores humanity's inheritance of heaven. Eve sold herself for a mere apple, but Christ outbid the devil by offering his body as a charter of confirmation or feoffment:

> But Christ offered and gave more than the devil, not just an apple, but his body and soul all together...In this way Christ, when his hands and feet were nailed to the cross, offered his body like a charter to be written on. The nails in his hands were used as a quill, and his precious blood as ink. And thus, with this charter he restored to us our heritage that we had lost.[24]

The *Fasciculus morum* further describes Christ's charter as a quittance or revocation of record, borrowing the language of Colossians 2:14–25: Christ's charter not only records his victory (a redeeming charter) but also renders null and void the bond of original sin (the damning chirograph): "And there he certainly destroyed the contract [*dissolvit cyrographum*] that our first parents made with the devil...Christ canceled [*delevit*] this servitude totally when he left his whole body for us on the cross as a charter [*carta*]" (212–13, ll. 263–4, 269–70).[25] By 1400, the popular sermon-writer John Mirk could write,

> And yet forto by man out of þe deueles þraldam, [God] sende [Christ] into þis world, and wyth his owne hert-blod wrot [man] a chartur of fredome, and made hym fre for euer, but hit so be þat he forfet hys chartur. So whyle þat he loued God, he kepeth his chartur, for God asket no more of a man but loue.[26]

---

[24] "Set Christus plus optulit et dedit quam diabolus, quia non tantum unum pomum set simul et semel corpus et animam . . . Sic Christus manibus et pedibus in cruce affixus corpus suum ad cartam scribendam exposuit; clavos eciam in manibus habuit pro calamo, sanguinem preciosum pro encausto. Per hanc cartam hereditatem amissam nobis restituit." *Fasciculus morum: A Fourteenth-Century Preacher's Handbook*, ed. and trans. Wenzel 212–13, ll. 248–9, 256–9 (hereafter cited in the main text by page and line number). The text of this deed is discussed in chapter 1.

[25] "Et certe, tunc dissolvit cyrographum quod cum diabolo primi parentes pupigerunt . . . Christus istam servitutem omnino delevit quando in cruce totum copus suum pro carta nobis reliquit."

[26] Mirk, *Festial*, ed. Erbe, 172, ll. 15–19.

If we turn to *Piers Plowman* now, we can see that Langland dramatizes this tension between Christ's charter and the devil's record in Patience's sermon to Hawkyn (the personification of the active life). Patience warns Hawkyn that if he wants to clean his sin-stained coat, he must continually avail himself of the sacrament of penance: "Confession and knowlichynge [and] crauyng þi mercy/Shulde amenden vs as manye siþes as man wolde desire" (14. 187–8).[27] Lest Hawkyn despair in the efficacy of this process, however, Patience assures him that Christ has comforted all people with the contract of the Redemption. If the devil (the "pouke" or "queed") should overwhelm him with the memory of sins past, Hawkyn may defend himself with a divine quittance or pardon, a written proof of his release from debt. This document turns out to be Christ's loving Passion, which liberated all sinners from the devil's bond and continues to provide a model of behavior for humanity:

> A[c] if þe [pouke] wolde plede herayein, and punysshe vs in conscience,
> [We] sholde take þe Acquitaunce as quyk and to þe queed shewen it:
> *Pateat &c: Per passionem domini*,
> And putten of so þe pouke, and preuen vs vnder borwe.
> Ac þe parchemyn of þis patente of pouerte be moste,
> And of pure pacience and parfit bileue.
> Of pompe and of pride þe parchemyn decourreþ,
> And principalliche of al[l]e peple, but þei be poore of herte.
> (14. 189–95)

In this passage, the devil's plea is both the original debt of sin that implicated all humanity and the punishing conscience of the sinner that leads him to despair and ultimately to damnation. Conversely, Christ's quittance represents at once the historic release of the faithful from the devil's jurisdiction and the eternal contract between God and humanity to which any repentant sinner may appeal. To benefit from this document, however, to have one's conscience assuaged and erased, one must conform to Christ's personal example of patience, faith, and poverty, all of which make up the parchment of the patent. Christ has stood bail for all humanity (we "preuen us under borwe" [191]), but his pardon continues to be effective only for those who observe certain conditions for gaining heaven. Thus if Patience calls this patent a quittance, it is one only

---

[27] All citations of the poem are to *'Piers Plowman': The B Version*, ed. Kane and Donaldson, unless otherwise noted.

in the sense that it releases the recipient from the debt of original, not individual sin. The pardon is absolute in respect to the Atonement but only conditional or temporary in respect to the Last Judgment. Patience goes on to explain that the efficacy of other spiritual works depends upon the penitent recognizing the conditions of Christ's original contract, both its charity and its severity: "Ellis is al on ydel, al þat euere we [diden],/ Paternost[er] and penaunce and Pilgrymag[e] to Rome" (14.196–7).

The soteriological action summarized in Patience's sermon to Hawkyn unfolds on a grander scale in the *Visio*. In this larger drama, Mede's charter represents the devil's record and Truth's Pardon represents Christ's charter; together these two documents encompass the first sequence of documents in the poem. The scene of Mede's charter opens, like the Prologue, with throngs of people in attendance from different estates: "Of alle manere of men, þe meene and the riche"(2.56). Simony and Civil read aloud to this assembly an allegorical charter complete with Latin tags ("*sciant presentes et futuri*"), in which Favel proclaims that he has enfeoffed Mede and Fals with a countryside of vices and sealed his charter in the date of the devil: "In þe date of þe deuel þ[e] dede [is asseled]/By siȝte of sire Symonie and Cyuyles leeue" (2.113–15).[28] In fashioning this charter, Langland has enlisted two strains of the devil's record tradition. The first is clearly derived from the allegorical satires discussed above, which use the devil's record for social critique, upbraiding the wealthy who abuse the poor or parodying friars who cater to the nobility; society is implicated, in other words, by writing up a damning account of itself. If Mede's charter adheres more strictly to conventional formulas than other documents in *Piers Plowman*, it does so precisely because it follows in this comic reformist tradition.[29]

But the satirical framework of Mede's charter partly obscures the penitential aspect of documentary writing, as reflected in the *Théophile* stories or Deguileville's *Pèlerinage de l'âme*, in which a sinner writes

---

[28] As D. Vance Smith points out, the conventional beginning of the charter echoes the rush of the mob at the beginning of *Piers Plowman* itself (*The Book of the Incipit*, 144).

[29] Most of the literary criticism on Mede's charter has dealt with its sources. See Hughes, "The Feffment that Fals Hath Ymaked"; and Burton, "The Compact with the Devil in the Middle English Version of *Piers the Plowman*, B. II." For information on the relation of Mede's charter to contemporary documents recording the transfer of property rights, see Tavormina, *Kindly Similitude*, 20–25.

himself into his own damnation, abandons his soul to the devil, and loses faith in his redemption. For example, if the charter initially satirizes the aristocracy with mock toponyms such as the "Erldom of Enuye" and the "lordschipe of leccherie," by the time it reaches Gluttony and Sloth it no longer portrays the sins as aristocratic holdings. It becomes clear that the "dwellings" in question refer not merely to the seven deadly sins but to the very recesses of hell where the unredeemed sinner will live eternally. Mede's charter departs, in other words, from a static allegory of contemporary abuses to a more sympathetic narrative of an individual's alienation from grace and future suffering. The fluctuation of plural and singular pronouns in lines 99–102 further suggests that this charter records the fall of an Everyman who has entrenched himself in sin and succumbed to despair.[30] Sloth, the traditional enemy of penance, prevents the sinner from amending his soul in time ("Til Sleuþe and sleep sliken hise sydes" [2.99]), and he loses it to the devil forever:

> And þanne wanhope to awaken h[y]m so wiþ no wil to amende
> For he leueþ be lost, þis is [his] laste ende.

(The charter then returns to addressing Mede and Fals):

> And þei to haue and to holde, and hire heires after,
> A dwellynge wiþ þe deuel and dampned be for euere
> Wiþ alle þe [p]urtinaunces of Purgatorie into þe pyne of helle.
> Yeldynge for þis þing at one [yeres ende]
> Hire soules to Sathan, to suffre with hym peynes,
> And with hym to wonye [in] wo while god is in heuene.
>
> (2. 100–7)[31]

Like Théophile's chirograph, Mede's charter recounts the story of a sinner who has despaired of salvation and must yield his soul to the devil "at one yeres ende." As in those stories, moreover, Mede's charter, by using the formula for perpetual tenure ("to haue and to holde, and hire heires after"), gestures to a larger soteriological and eschatological

---

[30] This transformation from static allegory to confessional narrative is less pronounced in the A-text, which is missing B. 2.100–101. Not all of the B-manuscripts read "his" in line 101. Bodleian Laud Misc. 581, for example, reads "hir" ("their") (Kane and Donaldson, 261). Kane and Donaldson also place quotation marks before line 102 ("And þei to haue and to holde") to show where the charter picks up again. It is important to see, however, how easily the form of the document slips into a personal penitential narrative.

[31] See Derek Pearsall's note in *"Piers Plowman": An Edition of the C-Text*, 59, n. 104.

narrative. This formula is conventional for a land-grant, but in this context it also alludes to the burden of original sin that incriminated Adam and his descendents until the coming of Christ. Similarly line 107, "And with hym to wonye [in] wo while god is in heuene," looks backward to the Atonement and forward to the day of judgment when God will once again descend to judge the living and the dead. At this point, the charter re-enters the field of folk with witnesses drawn from the most satirized occupations of the third estate – a pardoner, beadle, reeve, and miller – suggesting that all the estates help to produce this universal damning charter, not just the aristocracy, the charter's ostensible subject. By drawing on both devil's record traditions – the satirical and the penitential – Mede's charter reflects the operations of the *Visio* as a whole. The charter, like the *Visio*, records the inescapable burden of sin that simultaneously hinders the proper functioning of society and condemns the unrepentant sinner to despair and hell. And by oscillating between the satirical and the penitential, the charter imbricates the making of salvation history in the poem with the poetic remaking of contemporary society; as a result, the debt of original sin becomes the very incrimination of the self.

I have been arguing so far that the poem depicts legal documents as key texts in the contract of the redemption by incorporating the figurative documents of biblical exegesis (the *chirographum debiti*) within the framework of contemporary practice (Mede's charter of feoffment). With the Pardon, Langland similarly writes exegetical discourse into contemporary documentary practice, demonstrating in the process how salvation history might be experienced as a series of documentary texts within the trajectory of the poem. Like Mede's charter, Truth's Pardon is a key text in the sense that it is the briefest, most compact unit of historical – and even allegorical – writing. It is the summary and evidence of salvation history, which may be transcribed and glossed into a redemptive narrative, at the same time that it attests to the ongoing life of the individual within society.

The Pardon enters the *Visio* in response to the corruption of society depicted by Mede's charter, or, more immediately, in answer to the narrator's plea at the end of B. 6. The narrator predicts disaster unless "god of his goodnesse graunte vs a trewe" (6. 330), and Truth immediately responds, "Treuþe herde telle herof … And purchaced [Piers] a pardoun

a pena & a culpa/For hym and for hise heires eueremoore after" (7. 1–4).
The narrator later contrasts Truth's Pardon with papal pardons, but it
would be a mistake to understand the Pardon purely in relation to contemporary indulgences. The Pardon, like other fictive documents, recalls
the original document of emancipation drawn up on the cross and may
therefore be understood to be an absolute pardon "a poena & a culpa,"
as indeed it claims to be. Like Hawkyn's quittance, this Pardon once liberated the patriarchs and prophets from the devil's prison and, by doing
so, counteracted the devil's record of original sin to which Paul refers in
Colossians 2:14–15. And like Hawkyn's quittance, the Pardon continues
to protect sinners from the devil's damning testimony or from their
own guilty consciences by offering the hope and promise of salvation.

From this perspective, Truth's Pardon serves as a corrective to Mede's
charter, just as Christ's charter (*chirographum dei*) serves as a corrective
to the devil's record (*chirographum debiti*) in exegetical and sermon
literature. From this perspective, the Pardon is at once a penitential event
and a historiographical or clerical exercise. The Pardon revokes Mede's
charter simultaneously by offering a blueprint for a better society and
a new contract for the individual soul. The actors in Mede's charter are
irredeemably damned, but according to the long version of the Pardon
(what may be taken to be the dreamer's commentary on the Pardon),
each estate and occupation of society may reform by performing deeds
of penance and charity and, consequently, may avoid despair in this
life and hell after death. For example, the lawyer who does *pro bono*
work and defends the innocent may escape the devil's testimony: "Shal
no deuel at his deeþ day deren hym a myte/That he ne worþ saaf
[sikerly], the Sauter bereþ witnesse" (7. 51–2). Likewise Truth sends
merchants a special letter under his "secret seal," explaining that they
may earn heaven through community service: endowing hospitals and
monasteries, funding dowries, repairing bridges, and so forth (7. 26–33).
In this letter, Truth promises to save the merchants from the despair
("wanhope") and devils that plagued the sinner in Mede's charter.

> And I shal sende myselue Seint Michel myn [a]ngel,
> That no deuel shal yow dere ne [in youre deying fere yow],
> And witen yow fro wanhope, if ye wol þus werche,
> And sende youre soules in saufte to my Seintes in Ioye.
>
> (7. 34–7)

This passage evokes Deguileville's description of Saint Michael's heavenly court, in which Mercy procures a divine charter of pardon to save the pilgrim from the devil's testimony. Mede's charter, like the devil's testimony in Deguileville, grants an eternal dwelling in hell to Mede, Fals, and all their progeny who ally themselves with the devil: "And þei to haue and to holde, and hire heires after,/A dwellynge wiþ the deuel, and dampned be for euere" (2. 102–3). Conversely, Truth's Pardon includes Piers and "hise heires for eueremoore after" (7. 4); in other words, those who amend their lives and perform their proper functions in society prove their lineage from Christ and inherit the kingdom of heaven. And just as Mede's charter charts the moral downfall of a society in which all estates are complicit, so the Pardon presents a comprehensive plan to renew the prospects of individual sinners and of the Christian community as a whole.

Of course the Pardon also exists in a second, disconcertingly shorter form, as Piers and the priest discover when they read it together. The two lines from the Athanasian Creed which make up the short Pardon, "Et qui bona egerunt ibunt in vitam eternam;/Qui vero mala in ignem eternum" (And those who do well will go to eternal life/Those who do evil, to eternal fire),[32] would appear to belie the roomy contract of the longer version by turning it into a rigid equation of reward and punishment. It doesn't seem to be much of a pardon after all, first, because it jettisons documentary literacy – the priest declares he can't find a pardon in the document, and Piers contemplates a different lifestyle altogether – and second, because it offers nothing beyond strict justice. Readers of the poem have long debated the problem of the two versions, and I hope to contribute more to that debate later in this chapter. I want only to point out here that, like Truth's Pardon, fictive charters in later medieval literature typically remind readers both of the currency of the Atonement and the exigency of doing penance: they are both divine gifts and legal contracts replete with stipulations and conditions. To this purpose, they use the same lines from the Creed alternatively to soothe and admonish

---

[32] Clause 41 of the Athanasian Creed was recited at prime in the Sarum Rite. Most of the Creed is devoted to explaining forth the doctrines of the Trinity, Incarnation, and Atonement, and it declares faith in those doctrines necessary for salvation. Only the last few lines of the Creed address the day of judgment and the necessity of good works for salvation (*New Catholic Encyclopedia*, s. v. "Athanasian Creed").

the reader. In the Middle English version of Deguileville's *Pèlerinage de l'âme*, discussed in some detail in chapter 1, the pilgrim, nearly at his wits' end with fear at the devil's testimony, confesses his sins and prays desperately for deliverance.[33] Mercy thereupon halts the proceedings, negotiates with Christ and the Virgin, and returns with a charter of pardon which serves as a "countirpeis a-gayn the fendis part" and offers heaven to those who sincerely and faithfully repent (in other words, the first half of the verse from the Creed):

> So that they han me "Ihesu, mercy!" cried,
> Er that the breth out of the body 3ede,
> And alle her wrecchede lustes han defyed
> In verray faith, as techeth hem th'Crede,
> So that 3e shal a3enst hem not procede,
> As for to iuggen hem to helle peyne.[34]

Similarly, in the *Long Charter* Christ explains that his charter, drawn up on the cross, grants humanity his "Rewme of heuene-blis" and continues to secure it against the ever-avenging devil: it will make people "more siker...a3eyn þi foos, ful of wrake."[35]

Like good confessors, however, these fictive charters threaten as well as comfort, and they impart strict terms for divine pardon and protection. In fact, the conditional nature of the contract is a pastoral imperative. The *Fasciculus morum* recommends that a preacher extract a true confession from the sinner "now by comforting him if he despairs, now by asking him about his sins if he is ashamed, now promising him life and forgiveness if he amends himself, now threatening him with unbearable punishment so that he does not commit mortal sin" (406–7, ll. 24–7).[36] Likewise Deguileville's charter of pardon includes sincere penitents but

---

[33] For discussions of Langland's reading of Deguileville's trilogy, see Woolf, *Art and Doctrine: Essays on Medieval Literature*, ed. O'Donoghue, 139; and Burrow, *Langland's Fictions*, 113–18.

[34] Text in *Pilgrimage of the Soul, A Critical Edition of the Middle English Dream Vision*, ed. McGerr, 50, ll. 26–31 (hereafter cited in the main text by page and line number).

[35] *Long Charter*, ll. 39–40, 113, printed in Furnivall, ed., *Minor Poems of the Vernon Manuscript*, 637–57 (hereafter cited in the main text by page and line number).

[36] "Nunc confortando peccatorem si desperet, nunc peccata inquirendo si erubescat, nunc vitam et veniam pollicendo si se corrigat, nunc penas intollerabiles comminando ne moraliter peccet."

excludes a long list of sinners, who "in mysgouernement" trust too much in the pardon, remain stubbornly unrepentant, despair of mercy, or repent too late (in other words, the second line from the Creed). This document is absolute but not universal, and it warns prospective sinners not to be overconfident:

> Wherefore no man so bolde ne hardy be,
> Trustynge vpon this present pardonaunce,
> To surfete or to synne in no degre,
> Vpon the trust of fynal repentaunce,
> Which is my ȝifte. (*Soul*, 51, ll. 27–31)

Similarly, at the end of the *Long Charter*, Christ restates the two lines from the Creed in no uncertain terms. He grants heaven to those who pay their rent (perfect shrift), and hell to those who don't: "þeose þat beoþ of rent be-hynde...fful sore may þei ben a-dred/whon þis cha[r]tre schal be red:/Alle þeose schul go to helle-pyne;/And with me to blys schul go alle myne" (ll. 225–30).

In all these fictive charters, salvation depends upon a delicate balancing act between the two lines from the Creed, just as medieval soteriology tries to balance justice with mercy. Significantly for *Piers Plowman*, however, many fourteenth-century writers imagined this credic balancing act to be a formal written contract, the textual confirmation of a theological event. Like these other fictive documents, Truth's Pardon is a charter of pardon that negotiates as well as pardons, and threatens as well as saves. The terms of this charter are, moreover, those of the Athanasian Creed, which remind the reader of the document's origin on the cross, its eschatological import, and its contractual nature. If anything, the Pardon, by existing in two versions, accounts more for the "absent middle" (Traugott Lawler's phrase) of the two lines from the Creed than any other literary text: it recommends intermediary acts such as prayer, purgatory, and penance and stresses the efficacy of good works. Neither Deguileville's charter of pardon nor the *Long Charter* mentions purgatory – the recipient is either saved or damned – but according to the long version of the Pardon, kings and knights who rule justly and protect the Church will "han pardon þoruȝ purgatorie to passen ful liȝtly" (7. 11). Only the truly destitute may avoid these measures altogether, having had "hir penaunce and hir Purgatorie [vp]on þis [pure] erþe" (7. 106).[37]

Taken together, Mede's charter and Truth's Pardon offer not so much a promise but a *practice* of making salvation history immediate through the institutional texts of medieval life. They also offer a means of reshaping the penitential self by participating in the institutional processes by which documents are fashioned into legitimating narratives. These key texts, simultaneously exegetical and documentary, attest both to a past history and present identity. They constitute the procedure by which narratives of selves and communities are made and foundational texts are discovered, glossed, and retained.

Here Deguileville's pilgrimage trilogy once more provides an instructive parallel to *Piers Plowman*. In the *Pilgrimage of the Lyfe of the Manhode*, Tribulation introduces herself to the pilgrim-narrator as heaven's smithy, who specializes in tanning human skin into leather aprons. The narrator is understandably reluctant to accept her office without a commission, and he is surprised to find that she carries two, one from God and one from Satan.[38] God's commission, dated to the Fall, commands Tribulation to reforge the armor of those knights who were commanded to guard the paradisal treasures of the worldly kingdom but were caught off guard by prosperity. The devil's commission, dated to the Crucifixion, commands Tribulation to frustrate pilgrims and lead them into despair. The narrator studies both documents closely ("When þese commissiouns I hadde diligentliche red, seyn and herd, I foolded hem and took hem ayen..." [6573–4]), and he protests to Tribulation that they can't both be applicable because they "strecchen nouht to oon ende" (6577). She replies that, from her perspective, both documents authorize her office, but from the perspective of the reader, the authority of each commission is determined by his spiritual attitude, whether he chooses to thank God or curse the devil. Tribulation's two contracts, I would argue, reflect the *Visio*'s cartulary mode of penitential history in the choices that it offers between Mede's charter and Truth's Pardon, as well as between the two versions of the Pardon. Mede's charter and Truth's Pardon together comprise a linear history of salvation from the Fall to

---

[37] Later in Deguileville's narrative, the pilgrim is offered a chance to atone in purgatory.
[38] Henry, ed., *Pilgrimage of the Lyfe of the Manhode*, ll. 6441–6504 (hereafter cited in the main text by line number).

the Atonement. Yet they correspond to an eschatological ideal – the desired course of self and world – only when the reader considers which document he should transcribe and keep on his person, and what relation that document might bear to other documents issued on his behalf.

Together, Mede's charter and Truth's Pardon comprise a historical writing in which the incursion of the divine into the human condition, the mapping of the soteriological onto the penitential, is understood as a series of legal documents. They also demonstrate how the individual penitent or the community-at-large might be written into salvation history, first, by selecting and ordering the right key texts, and second, by keeping those texts on his/its person by calling them by their institutional names. This is the clerkly procedure of turning legal instruments into cartulary-chronicles, of examining two foundational texts and laying them out as evidentiary scripts for larger narratives. The second sequence of documents in Passus 17–18 – Moses's maundement and Peace's patent – corroborates the earlier one by enfolding documentary procedure into the romance of pilgrimage. If the first sequence invites the slow work of the chronicler, the aligning and glossing of legal texts in order to create a legible history, the second sequence resembles more the documentary tendencies of the romance, the moment of discovery and the rush of the event. Much like Walsingham's story of the seal, this section of the poem illustrates a diplomatic rather than historiographic procedure, and it depicts the encounter with documents rather than the documents themselves.[39]

Moses's maundement and Peace's patent originate in a particularly English tradition of patents that bears a striking similarity to a passage from the *Ancrene Wisse*, the early thirteenth-century spiritual guide for anchoresses. In the seventh book on Love, Christ the king sends the patriarchs and prophets to woo his beloved soul with "leattres isealet" (letters close, i.e. sealed) and then arrives himself with the gospels as

---

[39] Denise Baker and Jill Averil Keen have each briefly considered the relationship among Langland's documents but have arrived at very different conclusions from mine. According to Baker, Truth's "false" pardon is later superseded by an orthodox pardon made efficacious by Christ's death ("The Pardons of *Piers Plowman*"). According to Keen, documentary culture was so corrupt that Langland, in order to depict a divine document, had to simplify the form of his documents from Mede's charter to Piers's pardon (in Passus 19) ("Documenting Salvation: Charters and Pardons in 'Thou Wommon Boute Vere,' the *Charters of Christ* and *Piers Plowman*").

"leattres iopenet" (letters patent) written in his own blood: "On ende he com him seoluen & brohte þe godspel as leattres iopenet & wrat wiþ his ahne blood saluz to his leomon, luue gretunge forte wohin hire wiþ & hire luue wealden."[40] This progression of documents closely follows a common late twelfth-century practice in which English and French kings negotiated peace treaties and marriages by dispatching envoys with oral messages and letters close. These letters protected the envoys and attested to their reliability. The two kings subsequently met at a common frontier and concluded the treaty by exchanging letters patent in duplicate (solemn documents sealed open for general notification or continual application).[41] Like the royal patent, then, the gospels in this passage represent the climax of God's negotiations with humanity, and they attest to the proximity of Christ himself. The open form of the patent in this passage also suggests that the patriarchs and prophets bore temporary letters or letters close to the exclusive audience of the Jews, but Christ demonstrated true charity by offering humanity the universal and perpetual New Testament.[42]

Elizabeth Salter has observed that book 7 of the *Ancrene Wisse* evokes the "many voiced allegory" of *Piers Plowman*, and it is true that the allegory just described amazingly recalls the overall scheme of Langland's gospel narrative: in Passus 17 Moses bears the Ten Commandments as an unsealed patent, and in Passus 18 Love sends Lady Peace the New Testament as (sealed) letters patent ("Lo, here þe patente!" [18.186]).[43] The *Ancrene Wisse* describes the letter born by Christ and his messengers as a love letter or marriage proposal to the soul. Langland likewise

---

[40] *Ancrene Wisse, Parts Six and Seven*, ed. Shepard, 21, ll. 5–7. The French and Latin translations of this passage confirm the meanings of these terms: the French version translates "leattres isealet" as "lettres enseleez closes," and the Latin version translates "leattres iopenet" as "litteras patentes." See *The French Text of the Ancrene Riwle*, 283, ll. 16–24; and *The Latin Text of Ancrene Riwle*, ed. D'Evelyn, 152, ll. 130–4.

[41] Chaplais, "English Diplomatic Documents to the End of Edward III's Reign," in *Essays in Medieval Diplomacy and Administration*, 24–9; and *English Royal Documents*, 18.

[42] Savage and Watson offer a similar interpretation of Christ's patent: "Here they refer to the New Testament which openly declares what was darkly foreshadowed in the Old Testament, here referred to as 'sealed letters'" (*Anchoritic Spirituality: Ancrene Wisse and Associated Works*, 398, n. 11).

[43] Salter, *Piers Plowman: An Introduction*, 78–9. For other parallels between the Christ-Knight topos in *Ancrene Wisse* and *Piers Plowman*, see Waldron, "Langland's Originality: the Christ-Knight and the Harrowing of Hell."

plays up the love letter motif in Peace's patent: "Loue haþ coueited hire longe – leue I noon ooþer/But [loue] sente hire som letter/What þis light bymeneþ" (18.168–70). Langland also retains the image of the patriarchs as a diplomatic (or military) vanguard – here Abraham is a herald and Moses is a scout (a "spie" [17.1]). Although the marriage or "wooing" allegory can be found in any number of late medieval texts, to my knowledge only the *Ancrene Wisse* and *Piers Plowman* develop the diplomatic version. The *Ancrene Wisse* was widely circulated in the fourteenth century, and Langland could very well have known it: it survives in seventeen manuscripts copied between the early thirteenth to the late fifteenth century (five manuscripts in the fourteenth, at least one of which contains *Piers Plowman*) and was quickly translated into French and Latin as well.

Langland's version of the wooing allegory differs from the one in the *Ancrene Wisse*, however, by invoking late medieval documentary procedures; in doing so, it integrates this later sequence of documents into the earlier one represented by Mede's charter and Truth's Pardon. For example, the "wooing" letters carried by the patriarchs and Christ in the *Ancrene Wisse* are re-imagined in *Piers Plowman* as letters of "mainprise" or temporary pardons on bail. Abraham predicts that "out of þe poukes pondfold no maynprise may vs fecche" until Christ offers his life as the security that will "deliuere vs som day out of þe deueles power" (16. 264, 66). Moses then presents the release form, which, when properly sealed by Christ, will ensure that "Luciferis lordshipe laste shal no lenger" (17. 8). In Passus 17 the dreamer asks Moses if his document is sealed, and Moses explains that he is presently searching for the seal:

> [I] seke hym þat haþ þe seel to kepe,
> And þat is cros and cristendom and crist þeron to honge;
> And whan it is enseled [þerwiþ] I woot wel þe soþe
> That Luciferis lordshipe laste shal no lenger. (17. 5–8)

Moses seems to be saying in this passage that the seal that will authenticate his document is Christ's body suspended from the cross. When the writ is sealed with the dangling body of the crucified Christ, Lucifer's dominion will end. The dreamer's description of the writ as a patent ("[He plukkede] forþ a patente" [17. 11]) further substantiates this reading of the seal. Letters patent were always sealed open for public proclamation or recurrent application and were marked by impressive seals that hung (*pendant*) from parchment tags looped through the border of the document. At B 17.16 the image of Christ hanging from the cross like a seal from a patent is further punned on in the line from Matthew that forms the "gloss" of Moses's text: "*In hijs duobus mandatis tota lex pendet et prophet[e]*" (On these two commandments *depend* [lit. *hang*] the whole law and the prophets) (emphasis mine). The verb *pendere* (to hang) in this context suggests that the continued applicability of the Old Law depends ("pendet") on both the dictates of the New Law and the security of Christ's body hanging from the cross like a seal on a patent.[44]

The point here is that Langland is rewriting salvation history, and especially the Pardon, into the exploits of the romance through contemporary documentary practice: the manufacture and transmission of the letter patent of pardon. In this way, Langland's documents make salvation history available as a penitential practice, but they do so by justifying different forms of historical writing, the chronicle and the romance, at the same time that they justify different forms of documentary procedure (pardon, patent, mainprise). After Christ's "battle" on the cross, Peace receives a letter saying that Christ has released on bail "Adam and Eve and oþere mo in helle" (18. 178) from the devil's prison, and that she and Mercy should stand surety for all humanity:[45]

> Loue, þat is my lemman swiche lettres me sente
> That mercy, my suster, and I mankynde sholde saue,
> And þat god haþ forgyuen and graunted me, pees, & mercy
> To be mannes meynpernour for eueremoore after.
>
> (18. 182–5)

---

[44] For a more in-depth discussion of this passage see chapter 4 of this book.

[45] Alford, *Piers Plowman: A Glossary of Legal Diction*, 94. See also Baldwin's helpful article, "The Debt Narrative in *Piers Plowman*," 37–50. Baldwin argues that by the late fourteenth century, vicarious ownership of debt had been replaced by personal debt, or a written bond. As she explains, "the written bond was itself proof of the debt; the seal represented the actual body of the debtor over which the creditor had power until his debt was repaid" (38). She argues further that vicarious debt (Christ stands surety for man's debt) is replaced in the poem by personal debt represented by Christ's patent (we now owe Christ and our neighbors a debt of charity). This last point is not entirely substantiated by the poem. Christ's patent, touted by Moses and Peace, is not a new debt of obligation but a pardon for debt which also insists upon certain conditions ("love God and thy neighbor").

We can see, then, how Langland has made two significant changes to the allegory of the *Ancrene Wisse*: first, he has overlaid the diplomatic procession with a routine chancery procedure, the issuing of a letter patent of pardon, and second, he has brought the concept of a divine patent in line with the soteriological narrative that characterizes the other documents in the poem: Mede's charter, Truth's Pardon, and Hawkyn's patent. Langland calls Truth's document a pardon, but, as in the contextual literature, this pardon is surely Christ's original pardon drawn up on the cross and, as such, offers final pardon only to those sinners who adhere to its prescriptions; in that sense, it is only conditional or temporary. Hawkyn's patent is likewise a quittance or pardon for debt issued at Christ's Passion, but it is effective only for those who follow Christ's example. Similarly, the patent anticipated by Abraham and Moses and publicized by Peace offers only a temporary pardon on bail – a mainprise – from the devil's prison by forgiving original sin. Like Truth's Pardon and Hawkyn's patent, however, the patent carried by Moses and Peace will continue to protect repentant Christians from their own consciences or from the machinations of the devil. Moses explains that this "charm" will save many a soul from the devil who fulfills its dictates ("*Dilige deum & proximum tuum*" (Love God and thy neighbor) [17. 13a]): "Whoso wercheþ after þis writ, I wol vndertaken,/Shal neuere deuel hym dere ne deeþ in soule greue" (17. 18–19). And Peace further reminds us that the terms of this document are continually underwritten and strengthened by Christ's death on the cross: "'Lo! here þe patente!,' quod Pees, '*In pace in idipsum* (in peace in the selfsame),/And þat þis dede shal dure, *dormiam & requiescam* (I will sleep and I will rest)'" (18. 186–7). In effect, then, Moses and Peace are describing the same document as Truth's Pardon and Hawkyn's patent, only re-historicized in its scriptural context and redefined as the product of Christ's merciful sacrifice.

This second movement of documents should consequently be understood as a penitential reflection upon and clarification of Truth's Pardon. The Pardon may seem ambiguous in Passus 7, but Moses and Peace redefine it as Christ's loving contribution to human salvation and clarify its legal status as a mainprise, or temporary release on bail, which remains effective for those who adhere to the conditions of the New Law. It is temporary insofar as it offers absolute pardon in respect to the

Atonement but only conditional pardon in respect to the Last Judgment. Likewise, if the first progression of documents insists upon humanity's contractual role in its full salvation and pardon, the second progression records the divine charity that made that contract possible in the first place. Many readers of *Piers Plowman* would like to see a linear progression from the Old Law and strict justice of Truth's Pardon to the New Law revealed in Peace's patent, but in fact *Piers Plowman* contains two complementary narratives of salvation, one in the *Visio* and the other at the end of the *Vita*, both articulated by overlapping documentary discourses, ranging from the exegetical to the diplomatic, and from the cartulary to the romance. Truth's original pardon thus assumes different guises depending upon the context in the poem. It appears stern in the Pardon episode as it offers an alternative to Mede's charter by shaking its readers out of their spiritual sloth. It appears merciful when offered by Moses and Peace as a saving patent and a love letter to humanity.

More important, finally, than the rehabilitation of the Pardon as a key text of penitential practice and salvation history, is the clerkly method by which that rehabilitation is accomplished. The poem shows that the archive of salvation might be simultaneously conservative and institutive, to use Derrida's terms.[46] It insists, on the one hand, on the recursive self-inscription into a damning past. It asks us to relive the contract of original sin in Mede's marriage charter, and it asks us to turn documents into chronicles, mapping the penitential life onto a chronology of exegetical documents. At the same time, on the other hand, the poem offers the hope of discovery, of coming across a newly redemptive document – Hawkyn's quittance, Moses's patent, Peace's letter – materially produced within the "unstable amalgam of unexhausted past and unaccomplished future," or what we might call the expectations of romance.[47] Significantly, too, the life and death of Derrida's figural archive is rendered in *Piers Plowman* as discreet encounters with literal archives and the narratives that they engender: the substantiation of history through the acquisition of legal documents and the making of history into romance through the events of documentary practice. In the end, it is the literal archive that makes the past comprehensible, just as it converts the work of the penitent into the work of the clerk.

[46] Derrida, *Archive Fever*, trans. Prenowitz.
[47] Strohm, "Chaucer's *Troilus* as Temporal Archive," in *Theory and the Premodern Text*, 80.

TEARING THE PARDON – CONFRONTING HISTORY

To say that the legal documents in *Piers Plowman* constitute a redemptive process is not to deny that they are sites of squabbling and debate, nor is it to reject the consensus of recent criticism that "often what might seem to be definitive determinations in the poem, turn out to be partial, provisional, or mistaken."[48] Rather, as I have already argued, such contention must be read within and against late medieval discourses about documents, discourses rooted in exegetical and penitential traditions and shaped by medieval documentary practice. The poem does seem to disorient its readers deliberately by shifting the names and terms of each document: pardon, quittance, writ, maundement, patent, and mainprise. It then proceeds to redefine these documents through debate and detraction (two versions of the Pardon are presented, the priest questions its authenticity) but more significantly through "historicizing." It requites Mede's charter with Truth's Pardon and reconciles the contradictory versions of the Pardon by rehearsing its creation in the biblical past: Moses carried it, Christ sealed it on the cross, Peace offered it to all humanity. This procedural retrospection shows that the same document in which the priest "kan no pardon fynde" is at once stricter and more generous than any contemporary indulgence. It also suggests that the penitential writing of salvation history is, at its heart, a clerical practice.

In the second half of this chapter I argue that Augustinian exegesis of Colossians 2:14–15 offers new insights into the contentiousness of the Pardon scene – the tearing of the Pardon – and particularly into the ways in which that scene translates Atonement theology into documentary practice. Specifically, I argue that the Pardon scene embodies the documentary historicizing of the poem as a whole, but it also makes that historicizing project the very *condition* of its contentiousness. Several critics have concluded that Piers's tearing of the Pardon is a rejection of its impossible terms: its insistence on justifying works or its promulgation of an Old Testament justice.[49] These readings have been extremely

---

[48] Aers, "*Vox populi* and the Literature of 1381," 439.
[49] Woolf, "Tearing the Pardon"; Baker, "The Pardons of *Piers Plowman*"; Hughes, "The Feffment that Fals Hath Ymaked"; and Simpson, *Piers Plowman: An Introduction to the B-Text*, 82–5. According to Simpson, Piers consequently tears the Pardon because he is

influential, but as I hope I have already demonstrated, a divine pardon *a poena & a culpa* refers to the pardon for original sin, drawn up on the cross, which released humanity from the devil's bond and gave it the chance to regain heaven permanently at the day of judgment.[50] Still, if the Pardon is the text that haunts the poem's dreams, the ruptures and discontinuities of the Pardon episode force us to reckon with the impossibility of that moment. After all, the structural incoherence and dramatic excitement of this passus have divided the poem's critics more than any theological inconsistency.

What becomes clear, however, when reading the Pardon scene against Augustine's commentary on Psalm 144 (his treatise on the *chirographum dei*), is that the contentiousness of the Pardon scene – the tearing of the Pardon, but also the two versions of the Pardon, the stand-off between Piers and the priest, and the dreamer's critique of indulgences – has everything to do with the peculiar nature of its soteriological project. Truth's Pardon embodies not only the historiographical ambitions of the poem as a whole, but also the shock experienced whenever the penitential reader comes up against the transhistorical movement of the divine. To put it another way, the shock of the Pardon is both the realization that history exceeds the everyday moment in which it can be experienced and the sudden knowledge that one is participating in a soteriological contract through the very act of reading a document. Further, if the controversies of the Pardon scene culminate in the tearing of the Pardon, I propose that the tearing of the Pardon is the shock of history materialized within the rituals of everyday life. It is crucial, in this view, that the Pardon is a legal document, because, following Bracton, it is documentary performance that makes the past immediate; conversely, it is history – the perpetual absence of the donor – that elevates the status of written record from probative to (almost) dispositive, and from history to contract.[51] It was Augustine in his *Enarrationes in Psalmos* who first theorized this relationship between documents, redemption, and the shock of history.

---

anxious about the strict and frightening justice of Truth contained in the two lines from the Creed: he cannot see "confidently beyond the 'eye for an eye, tooth for a tooth' world of Truth's 'pardon'."

[50] See Adams, "Langland's Theology," 97.

[51] For Bracton's theory of the absence of the donor, see chapter 1.

Few medieval writers translated or paraphrased the Psalms without the aid of commentaries, and Augustine's *Enarrationes in Psalmos* was one of the most well-used and widely-circulated psalmic commentaries in the fourteenth and fifteenth centuries. In a letter to Boccaccio, Petrarch recommends the *Enarrationes* as an essential guide to the Psalms, and it was one of the major sources for the Middle English glosses on the Wycliffite Psalter, as well as for Richard Rolle's Psalter commentary and the sermon handbook, the *Fasciculus morum*.[52] According to Ker, in the century after the Norman Conquest, thirty-four English cathedral libraries owned at least one volume of the commentary.[53] Lydgate draws on it in his psalmic imitations, and the library of his monastery, Bury St. Edmund's, owned at least two-thirds of it (it usually circulated in thirds: psalm numbers 1–50, 50–100, 100–150).

Langland quotes from the Psalms, by one count, one hundred and seven times; according to the "autobiographical" passage in C. 5, he may even have recited Psalms for a living.[54] While composing *Piers Plowman*, he probably relied on a commentary of some sort (as John Alford and Judson Boyce Allen have demonstrated, "the quotations do not come into the poem naked but as liveried servants").[55] Unfortunately, however, Langland left few clues to his reading habits, whether he had direct access to a copy of the *Enarrationes* or whether he came across passages from the *Enarrationes* in another commentary or sermon, such as the Psalter commentaries of Peter Lombard or Hugh of St. Cher.[56] What becomes clear, however, when placing the Pardon scene next to Augustine's commentary on Psalm 144 is that the latter outlines

---

[52] Kuczynski, *Prophetic Song: The Psalms as Moral Discourse in Late Medieval Literature*, 21–22.

[53] Ker, *English Manuscripts in the Century after the Norman*, 4–5.

[54] Kuczynski, *Prophetic Song*, 189.

[55] Alford, *Piers Plowman: A Guide to the Quotations*, 16. For more examples of Alford's approach, see "Langland's Exegetical Drama: the Sources of the Banquet Scene in *Piers Plowman*."

[56] For a helpful explanation of Peter Lombard's commentary on the psalms and its contributions to Scholasticism, see Colish, "*Psalterium Scholasticorum*: Peter Lombard and the Emergence of Scholastic Psalms Exegesis." Judson Boyce Allen has shown that Langland composed part of the Pardon episode using materials from Hugh of St. Cher's thirteenth-century commentary on the Psalms (on detractors), in "Langland's Reading and Writing: Detractor and the Pardon Passus."

the argument of the former and suggests structures of association that elucidate the tearing as well.[57] Like Langland, Augustine discusses the opposition between absolute and conditional pardon, identifies a divine bond (chirograph) with the Athanasian Creed, stresses the penitential imperative of reading that bond, and includes in the reading of that bond the eschatological separation of good and evil. This Augustinian "solution" does not refuse the dramatic conflict of the Pardon scene. Rather it helps us to describe what we already see, that the transhistorical experience of the divine – the history of generation after generation – is always about conflict on the level of individual reading, whether that conflict has to do with penitential angst, theological conflict, or social reform. Augustine's commentary also helps us to see why the conflict between individual reading and transhistorical experience is necessarily a documentary one: it is the document that allows the penitential reader to bridge the gap between soteriology and contemporary life while at the same inserting himself into a contract of salvation.

Psalm 144 is an unabashedly joyful song of praise, but Augustine characteristically turns it into a thunderous sermon on Matthew 25:46: "and they (the sinful) shall go into eternal punishment [*supplicium aeturnum*] but the just into eternal life [*vitam aeternam*]."[58] This same verse would become the penultimate verse of the Athanasian Creed within a century of Augustine's lifetime, and, nearly a thousand years later, the two bare lines of Truth's Pardon: "*Et qui bona egerunt ibunt in vitam eternam;/Qui vero mala, in ignem eternum*" (And those who do well will go into eternal life, but those who do evil into eternal fire) (7. 110a). Augustine's purpose in this commentary seems to be twofold: first, he wants to remind his readers that God's bountiful mercies, the psalm's ostensible subject, do not include the unrepentant sinner, nor should they lull him into a false sense of pardon; and second, he wants to prove that the lines from Matthew are the very essence of God's contract with humanity and therefore the only true source of pardon. He begins by warning in verses 5–6 ("They shall record your wondrous deeds, and the excellence of your fearful works they shall speak of") that those who truly praise God must take into account his fearful works as well as his wondrous ones: "for they shall not praise your eternal kingdom and be

---

[57] Allen, "Langland's Reading and Writing," 343.
[58] "Et ibunt hi in supplicium aeternum, iusti autem in vitam aeternam."

silent about your eternal fire" (8. 20–1).[59] Similarly at verse 9 ("Sweet is the Lord to all, and his compassion is over his works"), Augustine again cites Matthew 25:46 in order to caution the reader that God's compassion extends only to divine works, not to the works of the sinner: "And when he says, 'Go into eternal fire prepared for the devil and his angels,' this is not his compassion but his severity" (12. 11–13).[60] At verse 8 ("Merciful and pitiful is the Lord") he concedes that God offered forgiveness for original sin ("venia peccatori") so that man might perform good works and thus receive eternal life and fellowship with the angels (11. 7–10). He warns, however, that God promises pardon in the future – and here he chooses the word "indulgentia" rather than "venia" – only to those who turn from their sins right away, not to those who delay (11. 52–4).[61] Again, at the very end of his commentary ("The Lord preserves those who love him and destroys all sinners"), he repeats the same idea expressed in Deguileville's *Pèlerinage de l'âme*, namely that God excludes from his pardon those who persevere in sin, who dispute with him daily, who despair of pardon, or who falsely promise themselves pardon (24. 5–10). Augustine concludes the *enarratio* at verse 20 by quoting once again a credic formulation of Matthew 25:46, that the just will attain the eternal kingdom, and sinners will go to eternal fire (24. 11–14).[62] Medieval fictive documents, as we have already seen, use this same strategy to shake the sinner out of complacency and to comfort him in his despair. In *enarratio* 144, Augustine frequently reflects upon this pastoral tactic. God, he says, doesn't promise without threatening as well, for if he held out no promises, there would be no encouragement, and if he held out no threats, there would be no correction (8. 15–17).[63]

It is clear that the Pardon episode in *Piers Plowman* dramatizes the argument outlined in Augustine's commentary. Truth surely deserves Davidian praise for issuing a pardon *a poena & a culpa* so that people

---

[59] "Non enim praedicabunt regnum tuum aeternum, et tacebunt ignem aeternum."

[60] "Et cum dicit: Ite in ignem aeternum, qui paratus est diabolo et angelis eius, hic non miseratio eius, sed seueritas eius."

[61] "Verum quidem dicis, quia Deus conuersioni tuae indulgentiam promisit; sed dilationi tuae diem crastinum non promisit."

[62] "Veniet tempus ut separentur isti omnes, et fiant illae duae partes, una ad dexteram, altera ad sinistram; accipiant iusti regnum aeternum, eant illi in ignem aeternum: et omens peccatores disperdet."

[63] "Non enim blanditur et non minatur. Si non blandiretur, nulla esset exhortatio; si non minaretur, nella esset correptio."

may enter heaven if they fulfill their spiritual duties – indeed, the expanded Pardon sets forth this system in some detail, and the whole community rejoices and thanks Piers, who secured the document ("and preiseden Piers þe Plowman þat purchased þis bulle" [7. 39]). Confusion and disappointment, however, await someone like Langland's priest, who takes this pardon for granted or who disputes with God – in other words, who fails to count among God's deeds the second half of the verse from the Creed (*"qui vero mala in ignem eternum"*). "Peter," exclaims the priest, "I kan no pardon fynde" (7. 115). Augustine's point in *enarratio* 144, much like Patience's point in his sermon to Hawkyn, is that divine pardon is absolute in respect to the Atonement ("venia") but conditional in respect to the day of judgment ("indulgentia"), and therefore to praise only God's compassion is to take future pardon for granted and be complacent toward sin. This is exactly the priest's crucial mis-recognition and fatal mistake: he assumes in his hubris or complacency that a pardon issued *a poena & a culpa* is absolute in respect to future judgment.

If the priest's confusion between *venia* and *indulgentia* is a problem of spiritual attitude, it is also, at the same time, a historiographical problem – he is confusing the pardon already issued in the past with that which will be granted in the future. By doing so, he fails to establish a relationship between repentance and history. After all, if repentance means to distinguish between *venia* and *indulgentia*, between what one has received and what one deserves, it is also the fulfillment of future promise through the historicizing of the past. Divine justice may be obvious to all those who live and suffer in the world, but divine mercy may be perceived only by true faith and a deep historical understanding.

Like Augustine, too, Langland makes this point about *venia* and *indulgentia* by starkly contrasting God's merciful pardon in the long version with the harsher lines from the Creed in the short version. As Ralph Hanna III puts it, however, Langland never merely "ventriloquize[s] a preexisting discursive totality but remains capable precisely of discursive intervention," and his intervention manifests itself here in his startling substitution of material textuality for exegesis.[64] Whereas Augustine opposes absolute and conditional pardon by ruthlessly glossing the

---

[64] Hanna, "Will's Work," 25.

laudatory Psalm with Matthew 25:46, Langland does it dramatically, by juxtaposing two different versions of the same material text. His is an anti-glossing of sorts, a refusal to distinguish between text and context: the description of a perfectly acceptable pardon opens up into a material text containing nothing resembling an institutional pardon at all, whether royal, papal, or ecclesiastical. Indeed, the formal gap between the two Pardons mirrors that between psalm and commentary, between the absolute pardon of the Atonement (divine mercy) and the conditional one of the Last Judgment (divine justice). As will become clearer below, the successful issuing and receiving of pardon in *Piers Plowman* is an act of discernment that falls between the two texts; hermeneutics here, like history, is an administrative as well as a scholarly practice. It is true that Langland's Pardon, by invoking competing documentary forms, also addresses specific social and theological issues relevant to medieval England. Namely, it deliberately blurs the concept of pardon (*venia*) in order to criticize the abuse of papal pardons (*indulgentia*): the priest is understandably confused by the vagueness of the English term "pardon." Yet even this criticism of indulgences may have been suggested, in part, by Augustine's *enarratio*, which uses two synonyms – *venia* and *indulgentia* – to differentiate between God's absolute and conditional pardon.

Augustine's distinctions between absolute and conditional pardon, and between God's justice and mercy, are typical of medieval religious thought in general, and as far as *Piers Plowman* is concerned, they prove only that the poem makes these distinctions in similar ways, and that the short Pardon is an authentic pardon precisely because it is the promise of the Creed and of Matthew 25:46. What is really fascinating, though, is that Langland, like Augustine, chose to articulate these distinctions as seemingly conflicting legal documents. For at the climax of *enarratio* 144, at verse 13, "Faithful is the Lord in all his words and holy in all his works," Augustine launches into a passionate exposition of the *chirographum dei*, the written bond of God, a figure that represents the contractual nature of divine pardon as stated in the Creed. As mentioned earlier in this chapter, Augustine frequently refers in the *Enarrationes* and elsewhere to the *chirographum decreti* of Colossians 2:14–15, usually in the context of the Atonement. His most extensive and moving discussion of the chirograph, however, occurs in his exposition of Psalm 144:13 in which

he conceives of a new *chirographum dei*, a reverse bond that nullifies
the debt of sin and attests to God's promise of redemption; here the
chirograph represents God's treatise with humanity (*reddire*) rather than
humanity's debt to the devil. The concept of a divine written bond
rarely appears in medieval exegesis between Augustine and the *Fasciculus
morum*. Langland, of course, may have been familiar with the concept of
a divine chirograph from any number of different exegetical and literary
sources – Ambrose's commentary, for example, was widely available
in medieval England, and Hugh of St. Cher and Peter Lombard, citing
Augustine, refer to it as well.[65] To my knowledge, however, the only full-
scale treatment of the *chirographum dei* in medieval exegesis appears in
Augustine's commentary on Psalm 144:13. It is the only place, moreover,
in which the chirograph contains the promise of the last few lines of
the Athanasian Creed, and, in doing so, authorizes a reading practice
intimately related to contract.

To return, then, to *enarratio* 144, verse 13, "Faithful is the Lord in
all his words and holy in all his works," Augustine explains that this
chirograph should be the basis for human faith ("fides") precisely because
it records God's reciprocal faith. In this chirograph, for example, God
has promised to pardon original sin with the blood of his only-begotten
son, resurrect the dead, and send the faithful to eternal life (17. 13–23).
These promises are the very same ones that comprise the last few articles
of the Athanasian Creed:

> [Christ] suffered for our salvation, descended into Hell, rose again
> the third day from the dead. He ascended into Heaven, he sits on the
> right hand of the Father, God Almighty, from whence he shall come
> to judge the quick and the dead. At whose coming men shall rise
> again with their bodies, and shall give account for their own works.
> And they that have done good shall go into life everlasting, and they
> that have done evil into everlasting fire.[66]

For Augustine, this chirograph is the text of the Creed in the form
of a divine bond, some of which, he explains, God already paid to

---

[65] Hugh of St. Cher, *Postilla super Psalterium*, fol. cccxxx; Peter Lombard, *Commentarius
in Psalmos Davidicos* [PL 191:1266C]. Both Hugh of St. Cher and Peter Lombard argue,
following Augustine, that the chirograph accounts both for the gifts already given by
God and for the rest of God's gifts awarded in the future.

[66] See the *Catholic Encyclopedia*, s. v. "Athanasian Creed."

our ancestors through the Atonement, some of which he will pay in our time, and the rest of which will be meted out at Judgment Day. This document covers all of God's promises to humankind, both the pardon of the debt of original sin and the guarantee of a system of works so that those who do well may go to heaven. Augustine explains that God chose not to reveal his bond orally but to write a divine scripture, which anyone throughout time might read and believe (17. 6–7).[67] This written document has been made available to every generation and to all pilgrims: "You don't believe me?!" exclaims Augustine (impersonating God), "Behold, I write to you: for indeed generations come and go, each age of man yielding to the next. In this way there ought to be a writing of God and a kind of chirograph of God that all passersby might read and hold to be the promised way" (17. 9–13).[68] To benefit from the bond is to read the chirograph: God's promise is the reciprocal relation between reading and writing, and therefore he writes so that the history of salvation might be extended into present and future. Assuming the voice of God again, Augustine repeatedly orders his ungrateful audience to read the chirograph and compute the debt owed by God to humanity: "You have my chirograph, there in the chirograph is my whole law that I have promised . . . read the chirograph . . . compute the payment . . . Ingrate, you read the bond, you see the payment and you don't believe the promise!? Read it in my chirograph!" (17. 17–26, 37–9).[69]

What Augustine shows in this impassioned speech is that true penitence is the contractual work of reading. Reading is the passerby's conversion, just as writing is the sacrificial promise of God. Augustine's fury in this passage is directed as much at those who don't read the chirograph correctly as at those who don't stop to read it in the first place. By reading like a clerk, by comparing the claims of the bond with the deeds already performed, each generation will surely recognize the *magnitude*

---

[67] "Possemus illi credere tantum modo dicenti: noluit sibi credi dicenti, sed voluit teneri scripturam suam."

[68] "Non mihi credis, ecce scribo tibi. Etenim quia generatio uadit, et generatio uenit et sic transcurrunt ista saecula cedentibus succedentibusque mortalibus; scriptura Dei manere debuit, et quoddam chirographum Dei, quod omnes transeuntes legerent, et uiam promissionis eius tenerent."

[69] "Chirographum meum tenes . . . Ibi in chirographo meo lege omnia quae promisi . . . Lege chirographum . . . computa redditum . . . Ingrata, legis debitum, cernis redditum, non credis promissum! Lege aliud in chirographo meo."

of God's promise and consequently pledge its faith in that promise. (We are reminded here of the *Long Charter* lyric in which Christ exhorts passersby from the cross, urging them to read his bloody charter: "*O uos omnes qui transitis per uiam,*/Stondeþ and hereþ þis chartre red,/whi I am woundet and al for-bled/*Sciant presentes & futuri,* etc." [ll. 97–8].) Conversely, faith in God's promise will help each generation to recognize the *nature* of the written bond, not only to compute God's deeds correctly, but also, in doing so, to make the necessary differentiation between absolute and conditional pardon, between what one has been given already and what one deserves in the future. By recognizing the magnitude of God's promise and the nature of the written bond, every passerby will benefit from the New Law's contract of salvation by cultivating the right attitude toward divine works.

Finally, and most importantly, by reckoning with this document, Augustine's myopic readers discover their proper place in Christian history, a history that gestures in both directions, past and future, beyond the moment of reading. To read the chirograph, in other words, is to participate in a *contemporary* act of reading: it is to become aware in *one's own moment* of what had been done in the past and what will be done in the future. This history is shocking because it is experienced as a written text – the traveler passes by the billboard and is struck by what he or she reads. According to Augustine, God chose to reveal his chirograph as written rather than oral text, as history rather than revelation, and as absence rather than presence. He did this so that all generations passing by the way would be able to read their own moment into a soteriological framework. As a result, the text itself, the *chirographum dei,* is the site at which the absence of the donor becomes the enactment of his promise, or when history becomes contract through the contemporary act of reading. Salvation history is shocking, then, not just because it is written, but also because it is contractual. At the very moment that we come to terms with a history of divine intercession, at the very moment that we compute God's past and future deeds, we suddenly write ourselves into the contract of the redemption.

The image of a divine bond is one of the most striking images in *Piers Plowman,* and Truth's Pardon is obviously its most puzzling incarnation. Yet, read alongside Augustine's *enarratio* on Psalm 144, the short Pardon can now be understood, I believe, as the *chirographum dei* – the

Athanasian Creed in the form of a divine bond – and the long Pardon as an expansion of the first line of the short Pardon – the institution of a system of works so that the good may attain heaven. As in Augustine's commentary, moreover, the imperative to read the bond is the culmination of the dramatic action of the Pardon: Piers and the priest read it and quarrel over its meaning (" 'Piers,' quod a preest þoo, 'þi pardon moste I rede' " [7. 107]), while Will reads surreptitiously over their shoulders ("And I bihynde hem boþe biheld al þe bulle" [7. 110]). As Augustine reminds us, reading and recognizing the nature of God's pardon is a penitential imperative: the true penitent must read contractually and compare the bond with acts already performed. "Peter," exclaims the priest, "I kan no pardon fynde" (7. 115). The struggle between the priest and Piers is, from one perspective, about the difficulty of conveying truth within the fiction of a fallen world, a difficulty represented by medieval legal practice. From a different perspective, however, that struggle is part and parcel of reading documents: identifying texts and accepting or rejecting their terms by "listening carefully for those key texts" (see the epigraph to this chapter). Like Augustine's commentary, moreover, reading in the Pardon scene is deeply bound up in contract. Truth makes a truce with medieval society, not through the revelation or presence of the divine but through a scripture, a chirograph of God that generation after generation might read and hold to be the promised way: "Treuþe herde telle herof…And purchased [Piers] a pardoun *a pena & a culpa*/For hym and for hise heires eueremoore after" (7. 1–4). Truth, like Augustine's God, is conspicuously absent in order that soteriology be made manifest through text: he sends a written document so that salvation history may be continually known but also so that it may be continually rendered contractual through the very act of reading ("For [Piers] and for hise heires eueremoore after"). It is no wonder, then, that Langland's account of the Atonement is so curiously lacking in affectivity. His christological mode is not affectivity, but history.

As in the case of Augustine's chirograph, moreover, faith in the terms of the short Pardon is portrayed as the first step towards meeting those terms. Just after he tears the Pardon, Piers promptly avows his faith by reciting the well-known statement of faith from Psalm 23: "*Si ambulauero in medio umbre mortis/Non timebo mala, quoniam tu mecum es*" (Though I walk in the middle of the shadow of death/I will fear no evil, for you are with me" [7.120–1]). The last two lines of the Athanasian Creed, which follow the lines quoted in Truth's Pardon, make explicit the relationship between faith and contract: "the catholic faith, which except a man shall have believed faithfully and firmly he cannot be in a state of salvation." Piers's statement of faith in God's protection suggests that he acknowledges the contractual nature and good faith of the charter of the Creed, even if the priest does not. A passage from the *Fasciculus morum* (illustrating John 11:25, "He who believes in me, even if he were dead, will live") similarly illustrates the relationship between faith and contract by linking a redemptive charter of faith to the Creed:[70]

> Faith is a charter for Christians to have and to hold the kingdom of heaven freely and in peace. If anyone holds in good faith a charter given to him rightfully by his lord, over some piece of land or fief, as long as he serves his lord faithfully, the lord is held to keep and protect [*salvare et warantizare*] him from all others. In the same way, as long as we keep our faith that is contained in the charter of the Creed... our Lord Christ will protect us against all the attacks of our enemies and will for our service grant us the kingdom of heaven. (586–7, ll. 204–13)[71]

In this passage, the charter of the Creed represents both the lord's promise to protect the vassal and the vassal's faith in the lord's protection. Like Augustine's *chirographum dei*, or Truth's Pardon, this charter of the Creed is both an indication of mutual faith and written proof that Christ will protect the faithful from their enemies and send them to eternal life, invoking here Psalm 22. Indeed in the Middle Ages the Creed itself was considered to be another one of the psalms.[72]

By reading Truth's Pardon as Augustine's *chirographum dei*, I am not ignoring the fact that it provokes a serious critique of papal indulgences and their abuses (says the dreamer, "A pokeful of pardon þere, ne

---

[70] Here either the Athanasian or Apostolic Creed. See "symbolum" in Du Cange, *Glossarium mediae et infimae Latinitatis*, 686.

[71] "Verum, ipsa est carta Christianorum habendi et tenendi libere et quiete regnum celorum, quia sicut qui fideliter habet cartam alicuius domini sibi iuste concessam super aliqua terra vel tenemento, quamdiu ille fideliter faciat servicium suum domino, debite tenetur eum dominus salvare et warantizare pro quibuscumque aliis. Ita quamdiu fideliter tenemus fidem nostram in carta simboli contentam . . . contra omnes inimicorum insultus Christus Dominus noster warantizabit nos et pro servicio nostro regnum celorum prestabit."

[72] Kuczynski, *Prophetic Song*, 212–13.

prouincials letters, /Thei3 [þow] be founde in þe fraternite [among] þe foure orders/And haue Indulgences doublefold, but dowel [þee] helpe/I sette youre patentes and youre pardon at one pies hele" [7. 197–200]). I am suggesting instead that exegetical traditions wreak havoc with the social practices of ecclesiastical legislation, while at the same time capitalizing on those same practices to make basic distinctions within the theology of the Atonement. On one hand, the papal or ecclesiastical indulgence makes the requirements of salvation legible through specific documentary practices: Truth (or in A, the pope) sends it; Piers requests it (or in A, Will copies it down); the priest, Will, and Piers witness its contents. Similarly, the indulgence shows how credic injunction is relevant to human action (do good and you will go to heaven, do bad and you will go to hell). In its long version, for example, the Pardon lists examples of goods and services, such as alms to the poor, visits to the sick, and free legal counsel.

Yet indulgences also have the effect of fixing the relationship between human and divine, locating that relationship temporally and materially, but also limiting the effects of human agency in its own salvation. This kind of fixing inevitably calls attention to the contested nature of reading that subtends Augustine's reproach in the *Enarrationes* – "You have my chirograph, and still you don't believe?!", and which certainly occupied medieval reformers as well. We have no choice but to read divine scripture in our own generation: to experience salvation history penitentially is to experience it historically, hence Augustine's insistence on the *chirographum dei*. But confined as we are to a historical moment or social practice, can we ever hope to recognize the difference between *venia* and *indulgentia*, a difference founded upon a longer historical view than that which can be experienced individually in one's own moment? Thus, at the same time that *Piers Plowman* names the indulgence as a divine contract, it inevitably undermines it as a social practice. By making the Creed a fourteenth-century indulgence, Langland dramatizes the penitential confrontation with history stipulated by Augustine, while at the same time showing what happens when we fail to confront history correctly, when we fail, that is, to make our own generation legible in the face of the transhistorical movement of the divine.

A similar dynamic between patristic exegesis and contemporary practice occurs in a story from the *Fasciculus morum* about Bishop Odo and the rich man, a story that plays with the documentary language of Colossians 2:14–15 in order to conceptualize a divine contract. Bishop Odo promises those who give alms that they will receive a hundredfold reward. A wealthy man takes Odo at his word and trades a large donation for a promissory note ("cirographum pro promissis"). After the man's death, his widow brings the note (now called a "cirograph[um] debiti") back to Odo who, surprised by her literalism, opens up the grave. He unearths the man's corpse, which is found clutching a beautiful charter ("cartam pulcherrimam") sealed with a golden seal. At first Odo has trouble dislodging the charter from the dead man's grasp, but he prays to God and then easily draws it forth. The charter records the man's happy fate:

> Let all present and future know that for the money I, so-and-so [*talis*], gave to Bishop Odo to be distributed for the use of the poor, I have received a hundredfold return before my death in this world, namely the full remission of my sins, and in the future, as he had promised, eternal life. (554–5, ll. 6–19)[73]

Much like the long version of Truth's Pardon, Odo's charter condones the *quid pro quo* charity of papal indulgences by suggesting that alms-giving incurs a divine debt (*cirograph[um] debiti*) subsequently paid off in the afterlife. The Pardon, too, offers plenary indulgence, the free passage through purgatory, for those who repent for their sins and make amends by giving alms and other charitable activities typically stipulated by ecclesiastical indulgences. Like Truth's Pardon, however, this charter communicates between human and divine because documents express a fundamental relationship between God and humanity, a relationship which originates not in ecclesiastical authority (think of Langland's priest) but in patristic exegesis. That relationship is embodied by the golden charter and the supernatural grasp of the corpse, but it is implicitly gestured to as well by the two references to the *chirographum debiti* from Colossians 2:14–15, here almost ironically misapplied to the promissory note. These references to indulgences have the effect

---

[73] "Sciant presentes et futuri quod ego talis pro pecunia quam pro disposicione episcopi Odonis in usus pauperum distribui centuplum ante mortem meam accepi in hoc seculo, scilicet in plena remissione peccatorum meorum, et secundum eius promissum vitam eternam in futuro."

simultaneously of making salvation history legible through the justification of contemporary material texts, while at the same time proving the discrepancy between *venia* and *indulgentia* to be a social as well as a spiritual problem.

I have argued so far that Augustine's commentary captures the general argument of the Pardon episode: the textual encounter with salvation history, the shock, both historical and contractual, that accompanies that encounter, and the role that legal documents play in dramatizing salvation theology (*venia* and *indulgentia*, the past deeds, and future promise). Augustine's commentary also has fascinating implications for the tearing of the Pardon.[74] Evidence from the *Enarrationes*, in conjunction with late medieval documentary practice, suggests that Piers's tearing of the Pardon makes sense as an affirmative act because it *performs* the contract of the *chirographum dei*. It bridges the historical gap between soteriology and contemporary life while, at the same time, it enacts the promise contained within the Creed itself. In this sense, the tearing of the Pardon is the logical extension of the shock of history – the imperative to read the bond and the startling realization that salvation history stretches backwards (*venia*) and forward (*indulgentia*) beyond the moment of reading. As we will see, the tearing of the Pardon is the dramatization of that shock, but it is also what finally converts history into contract and penitence into act. And it is once again medieval documentary practice – the chirograph again! – that allows the shock of history to be registered as material text.

We have already seen that the tone of *enarratio* 144:13 is impassioned, even furious. Augustine sternly reproves those who recognize neither the contractual nature of God's pardon nor his severity toward the presumptuous, and who consequently feel entitled to mercy. If only they would read the divine bond as contained in the Creed, they would understand the terms of the Atonement, God's faithful promise, and the true nature of his pardon. At the apotheosis of his commentary on verse 13, he fervidly exclaims to such ingrates and skeptics, "Thus God says to you, 'You have my chirograph: I have promised justice, the separation of good and evil, and an eternal kingdom for the faithful,' and still you won't

---

[74] Those critics who defend the integrity of the Pardon tend either to blame the priest for provoking Piers into such a violent act or to ascribe figural significance to the act of tearing. See, for example, Ames, "The Pardon Impugned by the Priest," 62–3.

believe?!" (17.17–19, paraphrasing Romans 8:32).[75] According to Augustine, God deserves the faith and cooperation of humanity because he has issued a contract of salvation in which the good will be separated from the evil and rewarded in heaven. This separation should be understood as the very indication of God's mercy – he has instituted a system of works, as he promised – but also, of course, of his justice – those who don't do well will go to hell. At the end of the *enarratio* (at verses 20–1), Augustine reiterates that the day will come when the good will be separated ("separentur") from the bad, the just sent to the right side and to eternal life ("vitam aeternum") and the wicked to the left and to eternal fire ("ignum aeternum") (24. 10–14). Here Augustine is again citing Matthew 25, which discusses the final separation of good and evil: "and [God] will separate [the good] from the wicked just as a shepherd segregates the sheep from the goats and places the sheep on the right side and the goats on the left" (25: 32–3).[76] The separation of good and evil, in other words, is the basis of the contract of the Creed, and, by extension, of the pardon promised by that contract. If divine pardon entails the forgiveness of original sin and a concomitant system of works, the separation of good and evil is the final implementation of that pardon.

I am arguing, then, that Langland has incorporated this idea from the *Enarrationes* (and perhaps ultimately from Matthew 25:46 or the Athanasian Creed) into the tearing of the Pardon: "And Piers for pure tene pulled it [asonder]" (7.119). By tearing the Pardon apart ("asonder"), or in two ("in twaine") in some *Piers Plowman* manuscripts,[77] Piers simultaneously enacts a psalm and redirects the scene into psalmic

---

[75] "Chirographym meum tenes; iudicium promisi, diremtionem bonorum et malorum, regnum sempiternum fidelibus, et non uis credere?"

[76] "Et separabit eos [gentes] ab invicem sicut pastor segregat oves ab haedis et statuet oves quidem a dextris suis haedos autem a sinistris."

[77] Langland's use of "asunder" – "And Piers for pure tene pulled it [asonder]" – further supports the argument that the violence of the tearing is affirmative rather than purely destructive. Although the alternate scribal reading "in twaine" states more precisely the number of parts in which the Pardon is divided, the word "asunder" refers to the intention behind the action; it means not just to divide mathematically but to divide two things purposely so as to separate one from the other (*MED*, s. v. "asunder." For the scribal history of this line, see Kane and Donaldson, *Piers Plowman*, 377, n. 119). As a verb, it can mean "to fragment" or "to shatter," but as an adverb it nearly always means to be separated irrevocably into two parts, often with intimations of violence, as in the separation of the star-crossed lovers.

contemplation and exegesis.[78] The Pardon episode abounds in references to the Psalms, some of which are boldly quoted, others of which are neatly incorporated into vernacular speeches and actions. After tearing the Pardon, for example, Piers promises to exchange plowing for prayers and penance in what could be called a fictional literalization of a verse from Psalm 41.4: "*Fuerent michi lacrime mee panes die ac nocte*" (my tears will be my bread day and night)" (7. 128a). This same kind of literalization, I propose, occurs in the actual tearing of the Pardon, only this time it is suggested by a commentary on scripture rather than by the scriptural text itself. Piers enacts this line from the *Enarrationes* (and from Matthew 25) by dividing the Pardon into the *boni* and *mali*: "*Et qui bona egerunt ibunt in vitam eternam;/Qui vero mala, in ignem eternum.*" By doing so, he confirms his faith in God's promise, allies himself with the *boni*, and refashions his spiritual self by imitating the eschatological action that Augustine ascribes to God: "diremptionem bonorum et malorum" (the separation of the good from the evil).

Thus the tearing itself should be understood as an affirmative act and an act of faith because it is enacted in imitation of Augustine's commentary and ultimately in *imitatione dei*. By calling attention to the discrepancy between *venia* and *indulgentia*, and *bona* and *mala*, the tearing also makes history into contract. From a divine perspective, Piers's tearing of the Pardon prophesies the contract to come, the eschatological fulfillment of the Creed at the day of judgment. From the perspective of the penitent, Piers's tearing of the Pardon illustrates the discrepancy between two historical modes, *venia* and *indulgentia*, at the same time that it makes salvation history available as a contemporary practice. Mary Carruthers has influentially argued that the Pardon represents the Old Law and Piers's tearing recalls Moses's (hasty) breaking of the Ten Commandments when he witnessed the idolatry of the Israelites.[79] I would argue that this forceful action is neither a refusal

---

[78] David Lawton defends the tearing by assigning it a literal value, arguing that Piers, by tearing the pardon "asonder" (apart), or in some manuscripts "in twaine" (in two), actually divides the two verses of the Pardon – "Et qui bona egerunt ibunt in vitam eternam;/Qui vero mala, in ignem eternum" (110a). In doing so, Piers allies himself with those *boni* who deserve heaven and separates himself from the *mali*. Lawton provides little evidence for this ingenious argument – ultimately, he claims, the tearing of Pardon is unimportant to the scene. See Lawton, "*Piers Plowman*: On Tearing – or Not Tearing – the Pardon."

[79] Carruthers, *The Search for St. Truth*, 70–1.

of the Pardon nor an accident of passion, but a physical enactment of the contract contained in the Creed: the awarding to each one his portion through the eschatological separation of good and evil. In the same way, I would argue, Piers's disturbing "tene" is not the cause of the tearing, but follows from his desire to turn *venia* into *indulgentia* precisely by enacting the difference between the two. Piers's anger is certainly Mosaic in tone, but righteous anger does not belong solely to the Old Testament, and Piers's is reminiscent of Augustine's prophetic anger, a combination of incredulity and anguish.[80] Piers's tearing of the Pardon is in some sense more liturgical than it is typological. In the Sacrifice of the Mass the priest commits an act both affirmative and destructive. He simultaneously re-enacts Christ's breaking of the bread at the Last Supper and his immolation in the Passion, and it is the simultaneity of that action that makes it contractual. The Mass's most influential medieval exegete, Bishop Durandus of Mende (c. 1230–96), explains that the initial fracture of the Host into two parts also signifies the partition of spiritual communities: the half held in the priest's right hand signifies those who are predestined to go straight to eternal glory, whereas the left half signifies those who are still living in temporal misery (that left half is further subdivided into those on earth and those in purgatory).[81]

The translation of legal document into eschatological exclusion is further anticipated in Passus 6 of *Piers Plowman* in which Piers describes the kind of ne'er-do-wells whose company he would rather not keep: robbers, dice-players, wastrels, and jugglers. Truth has warned Piers that these people will be erased from the book of life (Psalm 68:29), and Piers glosses this metaphor literally to mean that his personal salvation

---

[80] Robert W. Frank, Jr. argues that by tearing the Pardon, Piers distinguishes the original pardon sent by Truth from the false pardon offered by some indulgences, thereby exchanging spiritual for material values (Frank, *Piers Plowman and the Scheme of Salvation*, 25–9). I'm not saying the tearing doesn't also serve as a critique of ecclesiastical practices; in fact, as I suggested several times above, it is the very rendering of salvation history into fourteenth-century practices that dramatizes the soteriological imperative of the Pardon at the same time that it inevitably exposes the limitations of those same practices.

[81] The Host is initially partitioned into left and right because (and here Durandus quotes Augustine): "God has two hands, the right with which he pities and the left with which he punishes." Durandus, *Rationale divinorum officiorum*, 529–30 (CCCM 140, 140A–B). Augustine probably meant the left hand to signify those punished in hell but, in the context of the Mass, Durandus made this punishment temporary rather than eternal.

depends upon him actively separating himself from their company: "*deleantur de libro viuencium* [let them be deleted from the book of the living] – I sholde noȝt dele wiþ hem,/For holy chirche is [holde] of hem no tiþe to [aske],/*Quia cum iustis non scribantur* [And let them not be written with the just]" (6. 75–6). In other words, Piers has again translated the idea of God's documentary writing into the sacerdotal separation of evil-doers – here, defined as bad workers – both from himself and from the established church. Interestingly enough, Piers's gloss on Psalm 68:29 is evocative of Augustine's gloss of that same verse, in that it represents the physical separation of the saved and damned at the day of reckoning (again citing Matthew 25:32–3): "that is, many will stumble, and of that number will be those who will hope to be seated with you, and of that number there will be those who will hope to be standing at your right, separated from the goats on the left" (13, ll. 17–20).[82] Immediately after glossing this verse, moreover, Piers literally writes himself into the book of life by drafting his last will and testament, in which he again confirms his faith in the Athanasian Creed: "He shal haue my soule that best hath deserued,/And [defende it from the fend], for so I bileue/Til I come to hise acountes as my [crede] me [techeth] – To haue relees and remission, on that rental I leue" (8. 87–90). Once again, then, the Creed is conceived to be a contract between God and humanity (it anticipates a payment to be rendered), and once again, a legal document becomes the site at which the Creed is translated into penitential and eschatological action.

No literary episode, however indebted to biblical exegesis, may entirely deny the logic of practice. In the end, it is the logic of practice that registers the shock of history. We have seen that Langland, following the lead of Augustinian exegesis, conceptualizes salvation history as the issuing and receiving of a *chirographum dei*, and converts that history into penitential action through medieval documentary practice. In this way, his translation of the *Enarrationes in Psalmos* into the dramatic action of *Piers Plowman* may be described as scriptural modeling.[83] This modeling is formally and aesthetically selective – Piers's tearing triggers a cacophony of dissenting voices that perpetuates the poem's general

---

[82] "Id est, multi scandalizabuntur, et ex eo numero qui se sperabant sessuros tecum, et ex eo numero qui se sperabant staturos ad dexteram tuam separati ab haedis sinistris."

[83] See Alford, "The Scriptural Self," 3; and Allen, "Langland's Reading and Writing," 353.

pattern of confrontation and disputation.[84] But this scriptural modeling is selective in a cultural sense as well: the translation of biblical commentary into legal action evokes the ritual tearing or cutting of a particular legal document – the medieval chirograph. Importantly, then, it is the material, and not just the symbolic experience of legal texts that renders Augustine's commentary into the life of the poem, just as it is the material experience of legal texts in the poem that turns salvation history into a contract of faith.

We saw that Augustine repeatedly invokes the chirograph to describe the written bond drawn up perpetually between God and humanity. It is fair to say that Langland had Augustine's chirograph in mind when writing the Pardon scene, both in the theological and eschatological distinctions that it represents, as well as in its implications for documentary writing generally. But whereas for Augustine "chirograph" probably meant a generic document, a handwritten debt or bond, for later medieval writers, a chirograph referred to a specific physical format and legal function of the written record. In a ceremony analogous to the Mass, the scribe would draw up in duplicate or triplicate a deed called a chirograph or indenture. As in the case of the consecrated wafer, the notary or scribe would ceremoniously rip or, more commonly, cut the indenture in half and distribute the parts to the legal actors. As Bracton explains, "It is clear that there are three kinds of private instruments, for sometimes one makes a writing in his own interest, to which no credit will be given; sometimes against his own interest, to which credit will be given; sometimes in another's favor as well as his own, against his own interest as well as for it. [The latter instrument] is common... a writing of that kind is called a chirographic charter which is cut through the middle, one portion remaining with one party, the other with the other."[85] The term "indenture" referred to the custom either of ripping

[84] As Middleton has shown, this *combative animus* actually facilitates the episodic development of the poem, which relies upon "breaks and discontinuities"("Narration and the Invention of Experience: Episodic Form in *Piers Plowman*," 100).

[85] Bracton, *De legibus et consuetudinibus angliae*, trans. Thorne, 109. "Et sciendum quod privatorum instrumentorum tres sunt species, unde facit aliquando quis scripturam sibi ipsi, et tali scripturae non erit fides adhibenda, aliquando facit contra se, et tali scripturae fides adhibetur, aliquando tamen facit quis scripturam sibi et alii, et contra se et pro se, quae communis est et de superius dicitur... Et talis scriptura dicitur carta cirograffata, quae scinditur per medium, et unde una pars remanet parti uni et altera alteri." For

the document in two, or cutting a wavy line [literally, "bitten"] through the two parts, and indeed some chirographs may have been cut in a wavy line to simulate a manual tearing of the parchment or paper. According to legal formularies and rhetorical handbooks, this form provided more security to a transaction by decreasing the chances of forgery; the tearing of the document determined, rather than questioned, its authenticity. This form, often used in the fourteenth century for letters of retaining, also guaranteed that each actor would have a personal share in the transaction, because each one was making a writing both for and against his own interest.[86] The chirograph entitled each person to his portion, in the sense that it stipulated the forfeit or gain of specific goods or services, and in the sense that it assigned to each person the responsibility to maintain the physical condition of the contract. In order to reconfirm the transaction, the actors had to reproduce the two parts and reassemble the document (a third part was often stored in a municipal archive).

The ritualistic "tearing" of the document, in sum, had at least three important effects: it enacted the conditions of the deed, it attested to the security and validity of the transaction, and it implicated the actors in the preservation of the contract. If Piers's tearing of Truth's Pardon typologically recalls Moses on Mount Sinai, and anagogically the separation of the good from the evil at Doomsday, it recalls more literally the contractual rending of an indenture. By tearing his chirograph, Piers simultaneously declares his faith in its terms and awards to each his or her portion. Like the breaking of the Host in the Mass, or the cutting of an indenture, the tearing of the Pardon at once implements a contract and awards to each his own portion. This portion is one's own deserts, what one writes for and against oneself, but it is also the responsibility to make the *chirographum dei* literally relevant in one's own moment and one's own generation. Indeed, this is the final conceit of the *Charters of Christ*, that the eschatological and the liturgical might be materially linked through the rituals of documentary practice. At the end of the

more information the appearance and use of indentures, see *De legibus et consuetudinibus angliae*, 7, 3, 96–7. See also *The Parisiana Poetria of John of Garland*, ed. and trans. Lawler, 148–51.

[86] Clanchy, *From Memory to Written Record*, 65. For examples of indentures of retaining, see Jones and Walker, eds., "Private Indentures for Life Service in Peace and War, 1278–1476," 10–19.

Long Charter, Christ announces that he has left his body in the priest's hands as an indenture, with which the priest might communicate to each the security of his portion: "On endenture I lafte wiþ þe,/þat euer þou schuldest siker be:/In preostes hondes my flesch and blode,/þat for þe dyede on the Rode" (205–8).

By thinking of Truth's Pardon as a medieval chirograph, moreover, we start to see how the tearing of the Pardon ritually embodies the shock of history: it shows what happens when history (the *chirographum dei*) becomes immediate through documentary performance (the medieval chirograph), and when legal documents become (almost) foundational through historical absence. This documentary shock – the physical rending of the chirograph – is at the heart of the Pardon episode, and of Langland's documents more generally. As such, it forces us to see that redemption has a past and future made available through the material experience, as well as through the collecting and transcribing, of legal texts. This material experience is burdened with all the problems of fourteenth-century society, but it is ultimately a penitential imperative: it is this documentary materiality that translates soteriology into contemporary life, and history into allegory. *Piers Plowman* portrays spiritual pilgrimage as the work of the chronicler or legal clerk as well as the contemplative reader, and as the careful copying, justification, and reinterpretation of a series of legal instruments. The reader of the poem develops spiritually by reconstructing a set of documents that add up to a larger and more coherent narrative than may first appear. But, as the Pardon scene suggests, Langland's documents advertise not only a penitential historiography but also a "puncturing through to history." And as a result, God's document becomes both the poem's historical subject and its transhistorical road.

4

Writing public: Documents in the
Piers Plowman tradition

In the last chapter we saw that *Piers Plowman* displays the making of salvation history as the reading, ordering, and glossing of a number of legal documents: for Langland, to read like a penitent is to read like a clerk. If the poem enfolds, then, as a series of fictive documents, and if it advocates a penitential reading which is also the making of history, it also tells us something about the character of public writing in late medieval England. In this chapter I argue that between the 1370s and the 1420s documentary writing became a paradigm for thinking about vernacular letters in terms of public discourse. More surprisingly, perhaps, it is Langland who invents public poetry from the matter of documentary culture. In making this argument, I am not suggesting that the legal document made "publics" in the sense that it was a precursor to a post-medieval national community or public domain, or that it constituted an open forum of discussion, or even that it was perceived to act for the public good.[1] I am suggesting instead that texts as different as *Piers Plowman*, *Mum and the Sothsegger*, and the 1381 rebel letters used legal documents to define what it means to be a writer who speaks as if at large (as a clerical or lay speaker, as an individual or community speaking), and who writes as if for the profit of the society or realm. As we shall see, moreover, all three texts construct ideals of public writing from documentary culture, and particularly from those strange intersections between documentary practice and literary form. In doing so, as I said, they take their cue directly from *Piers Plowman*.

It is counterintuitive to make this kind of argument about *Piers Plowman*, because the many legal documents in the poem are supposed

[1] For an interesting discussion of the idea of the medieval English public see Ferster, *Fictions of Advice: The Literature and Politics of Counsel in Late Medieval England*.

to be inimical to its author's notion of public writing. Several modern readers have argued, for example, that Langland is deeply critical of what I call "obtrusive" writing, of those "literate practices" that drive social relations, protrude from monuments, constitute the materials of ritual, or are distributed, collected, and hoarded. According to such arguments, obtrusive writing, of which legal documents are the most frequently cited example, is counter to poetry on the one hand, and to learning, on the other, both of which address audiences but are nevertheless only obliquely related to social practice. If obtrusive writing can be said to be public, it is only in the sense of the official pronouncement or the meticulously executed charter, texts that attest to a policy, action or negotiation. These texts are official but not open. They are exclusive or secret, in part because they often give material evidence of privilege or possession, and in part because they are non-discursive (they refuse dialogue or debate). This critical distinction between *obtrusive* documentary practices and *intrusive* poetic expression suggests, in turn, a reading of *Piers Plowman* in which literate practices (i.e., what the poem portrays) are continually undone by literary ones (i.e., what the poem does). In this reading, the literary parodies the literate, it directs it to other purposes, or it transcends it by eschewing its materiality or institutional affiliations. Thus, the poem is public in the sense that it addresses the corruption of contemporary society, as visualized through the institutional writings that help to produce such corruption in the first place. In this reading, the poem is the incisive critic; its documentary practices are its distended subject.

The poem has also been defined as public writing in a slightly different sense, that it concerns, in Middleton's much-quoted phrase, "the constant relation of speaker to audience within an ideally conceived worldly community."[2] In this relation, the poet addresses the community as a whole as opposed to a patron or coterie, and to this purpose, he represents himself in all sorts of guises: cleric, layman, pilgrim, or vagrant. The problem with this definition is not Middleton's formulation but rather the way it has been taken up to make distinctions between the poem itself and the documentary culture that it represents. The poem's address to the community, and its concomitant interest in constructing

---

[2] Middleton, "The Idea of Public Poetry," 95.

authorial identities, are generally presumed to be contrary to the documentary modes that it critiques. If we refrain, however, from taking these distinctions for granted, we start to see that *Piers Plowman* portrays documentary literacy not only as a commendable, even spiritual practice, but also as an ideal of writing which mediates between the intrusive and the obtrusive, between address and disclosure, and between the literary and the literate. In fact, it is the very obtrusiveness of Langland's documents, by which I mean both their *trenchant materiality*, and the way that they *project* or *disclose* themselves into the society of the poem, that reveals what is at stake in public writing, both for Langland and for those who followed him. In short, if documentary writing helps to define a *Piers Plowman* tradition (*Mum and the Sothsegger*, John Ball's letters), it does so not in its inherent difference to that tradition but as the very heart of public writing itself.

OBTRUSIVE DOCUMENTS: DOCUMENTARY LITERACY IN *PIERS PLOWMAN*

In a recent article, Wendy Scase asks the critical question, "What theory of literacy is implicit in the text of *Piers*?" She identifies a "spiritual literacy" in which written forms are used in figurative expressions of religious truths but usually with "some negative or pejorative implication with regard to literate practices."[3] It is true that *Piers Plowman* offers many examples of dysfunctional literacy, several of them in the episode of Lady Mede, the personification of financial reward.[4] Mede distributes her favors recklessly, agreeing, for example, to finance stained glass windows as long as she receives credit by having her name engraved on them. The dreamer fumes at such egotistical display: "Ac god alle good folk swich grauynge defendeþ,/To writen in wyndowes of hir wel dedes,/An auenture pride be peynted þere and pomp of þe world" (3. 64–6). In another example of literacy gone wrong, the dreamer rebukes ignorant priests who deceive the laity by making mistakes in the liturgy: "So is it a goky, by god! þat in his gospel failleþ,/Or in masse or in matyns makeþ any defaute" (11. 307–8). In several places, too, the poem

---

[3] Scase, "Writing and the Plowman," 126–7.
[4] All citations to the B-text of *Piers Plowman* are to *'Piers Plowman': The B Version*, ed. Kane and Donaldson.

implicitly questions the necessity of clerical learning for salvation. In the scene of Conscience's dinner, for example, one of the guests, a pompous friar, lectures impressively but chooses fried eggs over "soul" food (13. 40–1, 61–3).

All three examples associate literacy, or its perversion, with moral deficiency, especially with pride or greed. They do not imply, however, that *Piers Plowman* condemns literacy itself; rather, they present different registers of medieval literacy – pragmatic, liturgical, and scholarly – among which Langland himself surely discriminated.[5] It makes sense, at least, to start with the assumption that a poet acutely aware of corrupt literate practices would be ideologically invested in literacy generally. Not only did Langland make his vocation an extremely learned poem, but he probably also worked as a professional literate of some kind: a scrivener, a legal clerk, or a prayer-bidder for patrons, if he resembled any manifestation of his literary persona. Despite providing examples of corrupted literacy, moreover, *Piers Plowman* challenges its readers to think about spiritual literacy *in terms* of pragmatic or bureaucratic literacy, the literacy of the written record, the legal transaction, and the scribe. It suggests, for example, that documentary literacy may actually describe a spiritually efficacious writing. It further suggests that the efficacy of documentary writing is bound up in the very thing that seems to indict it – its obtrusiveness, the way that it is materially disseminated, circulated, and received. The obtrusiveness – or publicness – of documentary writing has two interrelated aspects: performance and disclosure. The first has to do with the relation of text to act; the second with the relation of text to audience, the way that it makes its subject available for public consumption and public participation.

To take the first point, the spiritual efficacy of documentary writing, let us return to the example of ignorant priests mentioned above. Towards the beginning of B. 11, the Emperor Trajan breaks into the narrative with a contemptuous "baw for bokes!" (140), declaring that love exceeds logic or law, and loyal labor saves sooner than Latin learning. As a saved pagan, Trajan has a vested interest in the primacy of faith and good works and a natural antipathy to Christian academics

---

[5] For more formal divisions of late medieval literacy, see Parkes, "The Literacy of the Laity"; and Coleman's recent update to these divisions in *Public Reading and the Reading Public*, 88.

and sacraments: he declares, for example, "that al þe clergie vnder crist ne my3te me cracche fro helle,/But oonliche loue and leautee and my laweful domes...And I saued, as ye [may] see, wiþouten syngynge of masses" (144–5, 151). Yet his interruption also introduces a larger anti-intellectual and anti-literate sentiment to the passus, which is taken up by an unidentified speaker, possibly Trajan again but more likely the dreamer himself (a speech ascribed to Rechelessnesse in C).[6] The speaker uses Trajan's experience to stress the importance of charity over canon law and to disparage the learning of the clergy. He even accuses the clergy of exalting their Latin learning over the common people:

> Forþi lakke no lif ooþer, thou3 he moore latyn knowe,
> Ne vndernyme no3t foule, for is noon wiþoute defaute.
> For whateuere clerkes carpe of cristendom or ellis,
> Crist to a commune womman sede in [comen] at a feste,
> That *Fides sua* sholde sauen hire and saluen hire of synnes.
>
> (ii. 213–18)

The speaker then turns to the related issue of priests who can barely pronounce the liturgy, comparing them to sloppy scribes who copy their charters incorrectly:

> A chartre is chalangeable bifore a chief Iustice;
> If fals latyn be in þat lettre, þe lawe it impugneþ,
> Or peynted parentrelynarie, parcelles overskipped.
> The gome that gloseþ so chartres for a goky is holden.
> So it is a goky, by god! þat in his gospel failleþ
> Or in masse or in matyns makeþ any defaute. (ii. 304–8)

The scribe (the "goky" or fool) who errs in his Latin or omits words, only to insert them later above the line or in the margins ("peynted parentrelynarie"), has invalidated ("impugneþ") his charter and consequently prevented the beneficiary from claiming the rights or freedoms contained therein. If the analogy holds true, the priest who stumbles through the liturgy deprives his listeners not only of the correct words but, by implication, of the spiritual benefits that those words effect. It is true that this analogy starts to resemble the heterodox position that

---

[6] For discussions of Trajan as speaker and pagan, see Gradon, "*Trajanus Redivivus*"; Simpson, *'Piers Plowman': An Introduction to the B-Text*, 126–7; Grady, "*Piers Plowman, St. Erkenwald*, and the Rule of Exceptional Salvation"; and Wenzel, "Langland's Troianus."

sacramental efficacy depends on the moral state of the priest – a reckless position indeed. However, the interest of this analogy is clearly educational rather than moral reform, and its effect in the passus is to shift Trajan's emphasis on the dispensability of Latin learning to an emphasis on the indispensability of liturgical skills.[7]

If the charter-liturgy analogy undermines the anti-clerical tone of the passus by implying that sacramental efficacy does depend upon the clergy's command of Latin, it also posits a scribal or, really, a documentary conception of the written word, which refocuses the earlier attacks against clerical literacy. Trajan, we remember, has previously conflated liturgy and learning by saying that he was saved without Christian works or knowledge: "and I saued, as ye [may] see, wiþouten syngynge of masses" (II. 51). By comparing the recitation of the liturgy to the drafting of a legal record, the analogy also highlights important similarities between legal and spiritual records. Both, for example, are official scripts, which derive their authority from their originators (royal or divine) and from their Latinate origins. The efficacy of each text depends, moreover, upon whether or not the scribe or priest has observed the proprieties of transmission and performance. They both represent, in some sense, the fundamental text properly executed when stripped of its gloss, whether that gloss is conceived of as scribbling or stammering. The performativity of the liturgy, in other words, is imagined through the material practices of documentary literacy. Thus the dreamer disparages Latin learning, but presents a surprisingly literal assessment of the power of writing. According to his analogy, word equals act, and therefore beneficial literacy consists of the accurate and authoritative performance of official texts. In short, his contempt for clergial learning does not extend to Latin literacy *per se*. Rather, it implies that an ideal spiritual literacy exists in which official texts are used not to belittle or exclude the unlearned but to further their salvation. It is a literacy that enacts rather than declaims, and in doing so, it takes its conceptual form from legal documents and the bureaucratic activities that produce them.

Langland revisits this documentary mode of writing in Passus 12 in Imaginatif's eloquent defense of the clergy. Imaginatif soberly refutes the anticlericalism of Passus 11 by warning the dreamer neither to scorn

---

[7] For an interesting reading of this passage, see Holsinger, "Langland's Musical Reader."

clergial learning nor to contradict clerks: "Forþi lakke þow neuere logik, lawe ne hise custumes,/Ne countreplede clerkes, I counseille þee for euere" (12. 97–8). He explains that God communicates doctrine to the clergy in the same way that the master of a well-ordered chancery or scriptorium does to his scribes – he provides a perfect exemplar: "Alþou3 men made bokes, [þe master was god]/And seint Spirit the Samplarie, & seide what men sholde write" (12. 101–2). Thus Will should not formally oppose clerks, because their knowledge is generated by an exemplary, here even trinitarian, chain of scribal transmission. Just as clerks are themselves "mirours to amenden [by] defautes" (12. 95), so their texts accurately reflect the divine Word. Significantly, this scribal metaphor, like the charter analogy in Passus 11, has a distinctly legal flavor. "Countreplede," as it concerns the dreamer's satire, probably refers to the rhetorical argumentation of academic disputation. Yet in the context of Imaginatif's exemplar analogy, it also means to plead against someone in court, a useless activity if the written evidence is incontestable.[8] According to Imaginatif, then, sacred texts and the clerks who write and teach them have the same kind of performative authority as an impeccably written legal document. Granted, Imaginatif's defense of the clergy is as utopian as the earlier charter metaphor is contentious. What is remarkable, however, is that both Imaginatif and the dreamer arrive at similar definitions of ideal literacy, even if they disagree about the value of clerical learning. For both characters spiritual literacy, whether liturgical or scholarly, is justified in terms of documentary culture: the proper dissemination of sacred texts depends upon adherence to technical form, to a notion of writing as material object, and, correspondingly, to a belief in the authority and efficacy of the written word.

We have seen that B. 11 and B. 12 justify the official literacy of the clergy as a kind of bureaucratic competency. The charter-mass analogy in B.11 also supposes that the legal record, like the liturgy, is a sacred and inviolable trust. It follows, then, that the scribe who correctly transcribes that record, or the legal actors who execute it, reveal their moral integrity. In other words, if a charter constitutes a moral act, the process of producing a charter might just reveal an individual's condition, and

---

[8] *Middle English Dictionary*, s. v. "countreplede." See Galloway's insightful comments on counterpleading and Will's complaint against the law in "Making History Legal: *Piers Plowman* and the Rebels of Fourteenth-Century England."

conversely, an exemplary moral act may be described in terms of documentary production. This peculiar correspondence between moral and documentary acts appears repeatedly throughout the poem. In the biblical flashback of Passus 17–18, for example, *Spes*/Moses conveys his hope in salvation by longing for a knight who will provide an authorizing seal for his writ: " 'I am *Spes*, [a spie', quod he], 'and spire after a Knyght/That took me a maundement vpon þe mount of Synay/To rule alle Reames wiþ; I bere þe writ [riȝt] here' " (17. 1–3). It is his very desire to complete the transaction, to turn the adventure of sacred history into a bureaucratic exercise, that guarantees his redemption. And by reading that writ, however incomplete it may be, the dreamer may progress spiritually as well. Likewise Peace confesses her faith in Christ's victory and proves herself a redemptive agent by displaying her patent from Love: " 'Lo! here þe patente" ' (18. 186). Most significantly, Piers communicates with Truth solely through procuring, writing, and performing legal documents. Much to the priest's surprise in the Pardon episode, Piers knows how to interpret scripture for his own life, but his spiritual literacy is specifically documentary: he facilitates documentary disclosures from above at the same time that he initiates other documentary acts himself. The Athanasian Creed *is* a charter of pardon that Piers acquires from Truth, and, as already discussed in chapter 3, Piers avows his faith in Truth by tearing the Pardon in half, an act that imitates the ritualized tearing of an indentured document.[9]

All these examples suggest that to communicate directly with Truth is to participate in documentary culture: to witness, copy, send, or receive legal documents. Langland never claims, of course, that the legal or liturgical performer is inherently perfect. Mede's charter is technically accurate but damns its actors, and we may guess that the friar at Conscience's dinner delivers flawless sermons at St. Paul's Cross, even if he lacks charity. Yet, as we have seen, more creditable characters demonstrate belief in and conformity to spiritual truths by participating in documentary culture.

[9] To be sure, lawyers have the least pardon in the A-text because "lettrid þei ben alle" (8. 45), and they know how to manipulate language at the expense of the poor (Kane, ed., *'Piers Plowman': The A Version*). I am saying not that legal documents are inviolable or inherently charitable, but rather that, in *Piers Plowman*, documents faithfully executed and deployed are used as a privileged means to describe spiritual acts and attitudes.

These examples suggest further that documentary literacy is capable not only of describing moral or spiritual acts but also of producing the right relations between God and humanity; this literacy both creates and attests to the relationship between human and divine. *Piers Plowman* repeatedly portrays God's relationship to humanity as a legal relationship of homage, debt, or pardon; but that relationship is expressed through the written instruments of the law. For example, the dreamer defends the importance of baptism for salvation by arguing that a baptized Christian may no more abjure his Christianity than a bondsman may exercise his will through a charter (i.e., transfer rights to property) without his lord's consent: "For may no cherl chartre make ne his c[h]atel selle/Wiþouten leue of his lord; no lawe wol it graunte" (11. 127–8). Elsewhere, Anima explains to Will that the moral faculty of the soul, Conscience, serves as "goddes clerk and his Notarie" (15. 32) because it indelibly records the soul's decisions like a supernatural report card: "whan I chalange or chalange noȝt, chepe or refuse" (15.31). Other faculties of the soul may appeal to God through prayer (for example, *memoria*), but it is only the bureaucratic industry of Conscience that maintains a truthful exchange between human and divine.

If Conscience's writing potentially damns the soul, as does Mede's marriage charter and Synderesis's testimony in Guillaume de Deguileville's *Pèlerinage de l'âme*, this passage nevertheless links the directing of the will and the disclosure of the self to the drafting of a charter. In other passages, Langland imagines the very movement of the will to be a documentary act. For example, Piers's inaugural act of piety is composing his last testament. Before he can embark on the "pilgrimage" of the half-acre, Piers, "old and hoor" (6. 83), must put his spiritual affairs in order:

> Forþi I wole er I wende do write my biqueste.
> *In dei nomine, amen.* I make it myselue.
> He shal haue my soule þat best haþ deserued,
> And [defende it fro þe fend], for so I belieue,
> Til I come to hise acountes as my [crede] me [techeþ] –
> To haue relees and remission, on þat rental I leue. (6. 85–90)

Piers sometimes appears to be a rural champion of pious illiteracy, as, for example, in his retort to the priest in the Pardon episode, "Abstynence þe Abbesse myn a b c me tauȝte" (7. 138); yet his literacy, expressed almost entirely in his interactions with legal documents, attests to his moral and spiritual condition. His testament, for example, leaves instructions for the burial of his body ("The kirke shal haue my caroyne and kepe my bones" [91]), but it also rehearses his beliefs, serving as a literary self-reckoning. It confesses his faith in his own redemption or "relees" at the day of judgment, as well as his commitment to the basic tenets of Christianity as stated in his "crede." Much like other English testaments of the period, Piers's testament is a religious instrument that disposes of both soul and body. Take, just for example, the 1395 testament of one Lady West, which states first, the beneficiaries of her soul (God and Mary), next her charitable donations, and only then her household items: "*In dei nomine*, Amen . . . I, Alice West, lady of Hynton Marcel, in hool estate of my body, and in good mynde beynge, make my testament in the maner as hit folweth here after. In the begynnyng, I bequethe my soule to god almyghty and to his moder seynt Marie," etc.[10] As Julia Boffey has observed, the testament became a popular literary form in the fifteenth century precisely because it had this connotation of moral introspection and confirmation in addition to its strict legal connotation of bequeathal.[11] Significantly, however, Piers insists on writing his testament himself ("I make it myselue," versus the more conventional, "this will was made"), an act that is at once assertive and bureaucratic. It represents the will to write, but also the will to write oneself into a contractual relation. Not only does Piers lay claim to documentary literacy, as he does in the Pardon episode, but he shows that the act of writing a document, unmediated by clerk or parish priest, describes a higher level of moral responsibility and spiritual enlightenment. If Piers may be taken as a Christ-like model of behavior, we may conclude that in writing a document, a Christian can both conform to and imitate God.

Piers's testament also suggests that the spiritual efficacy of documentary writing, the way that it correlates literacy and redemption, and textuality and moral will, depends not simply on its institutional performativity, the strict relation of word to act, but on its broader publicness, the way that it discloses through documentary performance. The testament is already public in the sense that it inscribes its author *postmortem* into the communal and civic relations of institutional charity.

---

[10] Furnivall, ed., *Earliest English Wills*, 4.
[11] Boffey, "Lydgate, Henryson, and the Literary Testament."

Clive Burgess argues that medieval testaments were essentially private documents dealing with the immediate future of the individual rather than with the relation of the individual to the community (most testators had already made oral pre-obit negotiations in front of witnesses, even in taverns).[12] In late medieval England, however, future arrangements were often profoundly corporate. Not only did testaments stipulate funds for church projects and the poor so that the testator would be communally remembered after death, but they also served as a public confession of spiritual allegiance, often written down or dictated in the presence of several lay witnesses and a parish priest.[13] Piers's testament can be said to be public, then, in several different ways: it literally writes the individual penitent into the redemption of Christian society, it contributes materially to the welfare of the local community, and it is corporately manufactured. But it is by calling attention to the production and performance of his testament that Piers transforms personal confession into a public event dramatically enacted before all would-be pilgrims. And by assigning a testament to Piers in particular, Langland elevates the document from the conventional to the superlative and from a personal bequest to the public production of the moral will – both Piers's will and the collective will of the humanity that he allegorically represents. He publicly affirms his allegiance to Truth with a document that is simultaneously his death-deed and a model for every living Christian: "I wol worshipe þerwiþ truþe by my lyue,/And ben his pilgrym atte plow for pouere mennes sake" (6.101–2).

All of Langland's documents, in fact, are freely broadcast, and it is their very accessibility, their material presence, that makes them appear to benefit *or* incriminate the entire community of the poem. As noted above, obtrusive or documentary writing, insofar as it describes a spiritually efficacious textuality, is intrinsically non-discursive. It posits a performative relation of writing to salvation, it attests to the legal ramifications of self-inscription, but it doesn't invite exchange or debate – it is not a public discourse in the strict sense of the term. Yet, as we started to see with Piers's testament, documentary writing comes into being in the poem as a textual performance which designates *and* implicates a public. It concerns the public welfare because it is materially accessible

---

[12] Burgess, "Late Medieval Wills and Pious Convention."
[13] See Pollack and Maitland, *A History of English Law Before the Time of Edward I*, 337–9.

as text, and it constitutes a public through its very dissemination. In this respect, Langland's documents do not *confer* benefits to the public as much as they *model* the public benefits of documentary writing. Thus the legal actors in Mede's charter are aristocratic personifications, but their document is witnessed by a beadle, reeve, pardoner, and miller, and reconfirmed by every new reader who happens upon the poem. Mede's notaries "stonden forþ boþe" and "vnfoldeþ þe feffement that Fals hath ymaked" (2. 72–3), and they read the charter aloud so that all earthly inhabitants might hear the symptoms and penalty of sin: "[Th]us bigynnen þ[e] gomes [and] greden [wel] hei3:/*Sciant presentes & futuri, &c.*/Witeþ and witnesseþ þat wonieþ vpon erþe" (2. 74–5). The Latin tag *sciant presentes & futuri* (let those present and future know) marks the conventional beginning of a charter, but its English "translation" further emphasizes the charter's aural delivery and inclusiveness. Thus Langland has expanded the conventional *sciant* into the more participatory "witeþ and witnesseþ," and redefined *presentes & futuri* as all those "þat wonieþ vpon erþe," the entire field of folk jostling and crowding the *Visio*. Whoever is notified, who sees and hears this charter, is part manufacturer and part "beneficiary." Ironically, of course, this charter damns all who see and hear it, but it also constitutes the damned as a documentary public formed through the public performance of a material legal text.

Truth's Pardon is in many ways the reverse of Mede's charter – it is society's disclosure of the divine rather than society's self-disclosure to the devil. In the last chapter we saw the important soteriological relationship between the two. Like Mede's charter and Piers's testament, however, the Pardon can be said to be public text because it implicates the whole community through the very conditions of its publication. In this view, Piers represents the aspect of humanity that permits the divine to disclose its purposes, while Will represents the aspect of humanity that receives divine communication, that makes it manifest and relevant through the acts of reading and transcription. It is, moreover, this double process of procuring and receiving the Pardon that brings the community of the poem into being as a legal entity, the benefiting public. This process is also what makes the Pardon both corporate – it inscribes all members of the community into a mutually interdependent contract – and civic – it uses the indulgence rhetoric of civic charity to describe the terms of the contract. For example, Truth sends the merchants in the margin a special letter sealed with Truth's secret seal, instructing them to seek their redemption in repairing bridges, visiting criminals, endowing hospitals and religious orders, and providing dowries for poor girls. These are exactly the kinds of community and church projects prescribed by ordinary ecclesiastical indulgences.[14] But the merchants' letter is importantly no secret at all – "secret" here refers to its exceptional rather than its private character – and it becomes contractually available to the merchants through its public dissemination.[15] In the A-text, Will himself transcribes Truth's letter to the merchants, caught up as he is in the moral action of that scene. The merchants, for their part, gratefully reward him: they "ʒaf Wille for his writyng wollene cloþis;/For he copiede þus here clause, þei [couden] hym gret mede" (A. 8. 43–4). In the B-text it is Piers who is so profusely thanked for soliciting Truth in the first place: "Thanne were Marchauntʒ murie; manye wepten for ioye/And preiseden Piers þe Plowman þat purchaced þis bulle" (7. 38–9). In all versions of the poem, Will is also privy to the disturbingly short version of the Pardon. Piers unfolds it at the priest's request ("And Piers at his preiere þe pardon vnfoldeþ" [7. 109]), Piers and the priest read it together, and Will, peering over their shoulders, triumphantly confirms its contents, "And I bihynde hem boþe biheld al þe bulle./In two lynes it lay and noʒt a [letter] moore,/And it was writen riʒt þus in witnesse of truþe (7. 110–12). Medieval readers knew what to picture. A marginal illustration in Bodleian Library MS Douce 104 depicts a very young priest clutching Truth's Pardon, a partly folded patent with an oversized seal dangling from the bottom (Figure 10).[16]

---

[14] For some examples of these indulgences, see *Richard D'Aungerville of Bury, Fragments of His Register and Other Documents*, ed. Dean of Durham, 17–20. See also Orme's helpful article on ecclesiastical indulgences, "Indulgences in the Diocese of Exeter 1100–1536."

[15] Scholars often assume that the "secret seal" is secret, but in fact the term may refer either to the Privy Seal or to the king's signet with which he marked legislation of personal interest. On this point see Tout, *Chapters in the Administrative History of Medieval England*, vol. 5, 168.

[16] As Kathryn Kerby-Fulton explains, "the artist has 'downgraded' the iconographical authority stereotypical of the cleric holding the document by manipulating his age and gesture and making a sharp juxtaposition of images . . . his boyish face and the company that he keeps on this folio (bringing up the rear after the False Friar and the Sleeping Bishop) don't give him or the church a chance of looking authoritative, and suggest

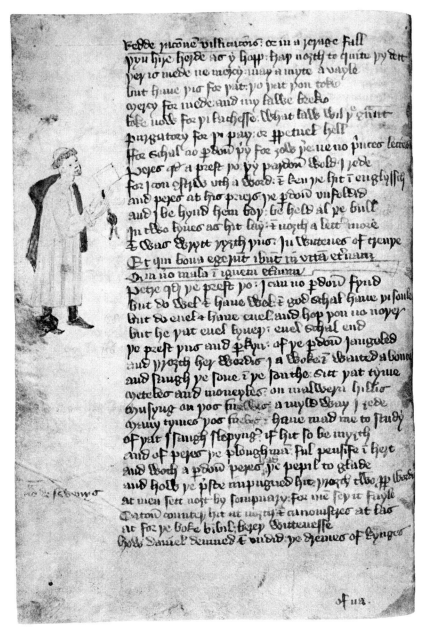

Figure 10 The priest examines the Pardon. From William Langland, *Piers Plowman*. Oxford. Bodleian Library, MS Douce 104, fol. 44v. (1427). (With permission of the Bodleian Library).

In short, *Piers Plowman* contains hundreds of Latin quotations, which may be read, misread, glossed, and debated, but only legal documents promise a physical encounter with an official text. It is precisely this possibility of a physical encounter that transforms documentary texts into public actions: they represent obtrusiveness deliberately writ large. Remarkably, for all his Latinity and legal sophistication, Langland does not confine his view of literacy to textuality; rather, his documents are peculiarly characterized by an "insistent materialism," which translates into several modes of public writing: performance, disclosure, accessibility, and inclusiveness.[17] Once again, this is not to say that real medieval documents, by virtue of their presentation, conferred benefits onto all their hearers (excepting, maybe, blanket pardons issued after a revolt or usurpation). Rather, it is to say their presentation offered a *fiction* of publicness, which was attractive to medieval poets.

Certainly, in terms of public performance, legal documents were perhaps the most familiar texts in medieval England, and as such came to define an idea of publicness indebted to the materialities rather than to the legalities of disclosure. This is especially true for certain forms of royal and ecclesiastical documents, and it is these forms that come to exemplify public writing in later medieval poetry. For example, although few official documents in English were produced before the fifteenth century, royal officials periodically recited proclamations such as the Magna Carta throughout the realm in Latin and both vernaculars, perhaps as many as four times a year. Likewise indulgences, the ostensible purpose of which was to collect funds for public charities, were recited by pardoners and parish priests in town squares and pulpits, and presumably in English as well as in Latin. In both cases, moreover, the visibility of the material document was as important to its performance as the aural delivery of its text. By the end of the thirteenth century, for example, copies of the Magna Carta were being posted in cathedrals and other central places where everyone could inspect as well as hear the document.[18] Indulgences, too, were nailed to church doors, displayed by pardoners like relics, or otherwise exhibited by institutions that wanted

that the illustrator's sympathies in this argument were with Piers" (*Iconography and the Professional Reader*, 23).

[17] See Kirk, "Langland's Narrative Christology," 32.

[18] Clanchy, *From Memory to Written Record*, 265.

to impress or solicit visitors. In this way, certain legal instruments were public events in themselves involving aural and visual performances as well as active community participation. They were designed to be read aloud and required an audience to witness the performance.

These documents were public, not because they claimed to represent the political interests of the community at large (public-spiritedness), nor because they necessarily integrated civic responsibility with the communal operations of the afterlife (public welfare). Rather, they were public because their rhetoric of universal notification and their open presentation established a reciprocal relation between the proclamation and the reception of a text that was nothing less than contractual. The publicness advertised by legal documents was located, in other words, not in the interplay of texts and voices or in benefits conferred but in the relation of disclosure to audience, a relation that is public insofar as it conflates participation with benefit. This idea of publicness is exemplified in literary texts by letters patent, a documentary form already discussed briefly in preceding chapters. The patent gripped the imagination of English writers because it was an institutional writing that captured the public aspirations of vernacular poetry. Patents were documents sealed open and distinguished by large pendant seals suspended from the bottom of the parchment by a tongue of parchment or ribbon. The patent was further characterized by its universal salutation – *Omnibus Christi fidelibus ad quos presentes litere peruenerint* (To all those faithful in Christ to whom these present letters should reach) – and by its special execution clause advertising its open format – *In cuius rei testimonium has litteras nostras fieri fecimus patentes* (In witness of this thing we have had our letters made open). Because the patent was used for public proclamation or recurrent application, its validity depended upon the integrity of its hanging seal and visible text. Letters close, by contrast, were used for singular, in-house directives, and for that reason they were sealed in such a way that the receiver could not read the message without breaking the seal.[19] Patents were used for a wide variety of legal acts, such as indulgences and testaments, and royal patents were

[19] Tout, *Chapters in the Administrative History of England*, vol. 5, 122–6; and Hall, *Select Formulas of English Historical Documents*, 53–78.

often used for matters of personal interest to the king such as pardons, safe-conducts, and confirmations of older charters.[20]

Fourteenth-century authors often invoke letters patent to link spiritual and hermeneutic "openness" with the disclosure of important information to the community. For example, the charter from the sermon-handbook, the *Fasciculus morum*, adopts the patent execution clause in order to emphasize the availability and inclusiveness of Christ's body and Word: "In witness thereof I have written this present charter with my own blood, read it and published it through the whole world, and sealed it with the seal of my divinity... Written, read, confirmed, and given to humankind on Good Friday on Mount Calvary, publicly and openly [*publice et aperte*] to last forever..."[21] Similarly, the *Pilgrimage of the Lyfe of the Manhode* contains a last will and testament of Christ, the patent execution clause of which proclaims its universal applicability and public benefit: "*openliche* I haue signed my testament. To *alle folk* I haue yiven pees and graunted and confermed" (emphases mine) (ll.1408–9).[22] This Middle English version of Deguileuille's *Pèlerinage de la vie humaine* is a very literal translation of the French, and it is significant therefore that "openliche" translates the original French word "publiquement": to publish openly, i.e. visibly, is to make legal information universally accessible and universally relevant. Medieval readers of Deguileville imagined this testament to be sealed letters patent: late fourteenth and early fifteenth-century illustrations of this testament depict Charity showing Moses or Penance an unfurled parchment with two appended seals. In the illustration of this scene in Douce 300, fol. 19v (Figure 11), for example, Penance is literally armed to the teeth with painful instruments of torture, and Charity displays Christ's testament as a letter patent with pendant seals (see also Figures 2 and 3). The *Charters of Christ* manuscripts likewise call attention to the "vnder-honged seale" of the patent in order to compare the openness of Christ's crucified body with the relevance of

[20] Clanchy, *From Memory to Written Record*, 220, 264–5.
[21] Text in Wenzel, ed. and trans., *Fasciculus morum*, 146–7, ll. 92–7 (hereafter cited in the main text by page and line number). "In cuius rei testimonium hanc presentem cartam sanguine proprio conscripsi, legi, et per totum mundum publicavi, sigillumque divinitatis mee apposui... Scripta, lecta, confirmata, et generi humano tradita feria sexta Parasceves supra montem Calvarie, publice et aperta, in eternum duratura."
[22] Guillaume de Deguileville, *Pilgrimage of the Lyfe of the Manhode*, ed. Henry (hereafter cited in the main text by line number).

Figure 11 Charity presents the last will and testament of Jesus Christ; Penance presents her instruments of torture. From Guillaume de Deguileville, *Le pèlerinage de la vie humaine*. Oxford. Bodleian Library MS Douce 300, fol. 19v (ca. 1390–1400). (With permission of the Bodleian Library).

his Word. For example, the scribe of CUL Additional 6686 has transformed the poem into an open document with the large painted seal
that appears to hang from the text (Figure 7), and the illustrator of BL
Additional 37049 has portrayed Christ's body as an oversized patent
pinned to the cross like a broadside or sandwich-board for all to see
(Figure 8).

Piers Plowman contains several examples of patents: Hawkyn's patent,
Moses's maundement, and Peace's patent. In all of these examples,
Langland is deeply interested in the way that the material production
of patents can be used to describe the contract of the Atonement. In
Passus 14 Patience reminds Hawkyn that if the devil punishes him in
his conscience, he should avoid despair by showing the devil his divine
"acquitaunce." This document promises release from sin to those who
successfully conform to Christ's example. This promise can only be accomplished, explains Patience, by making oneself the very parchment
of the quittance, a divine patent: "Ac þe parchemyn of þis patente of
pouerte be moste,/And of pure pacience and parfit bileue" (14. 192–3).
Patience cites the salutation of this quittance to prove his point that
such a document exists and is continually available to Hawkyn: "*Pateat
&c: Per passionem domini*" (Let it be manifest: through the passion of
the lord) (14. 190a). This salutation which, incidentally, only simulates
a patent – to my knowledge, no such salutation really exists in medieval
diplomatics – deliberately puns on the verb *patere*, in order to make
the etymological connection between *pateat* ("Let it be manifest") and
patente (open or exposed). By doing so, it suggests that the document's
very parchment is imagined to be Christ's vulnerable body splayed upon
the cross, which, by virtue of its openness, every reader may simultaneously witness and emulate. To be open is to be at once universally
imitable and publicly accessible.

We see a similar poetics of publicness in Passus 17, where the dreamer
meets *Spes* or Moses bearing the Ten Commandments as an unsealed
letter patent: "I bere þe writ [riȝt] here"(17.3). The dreamer, eager to
read it, inquires, "Is it enseled?...may men see þ[e] letteres?" (17.4).
Moses replies to the first question in the negative and to the second
(apparently) in the affirmative: it is not yet sealed and it is available for
public scrutiny:

'Nay . . . [I] seke hym þat haþ þe seel to kepe,
And þat is cros and cristendom and crist þeron to honge;
And whan it is enseled [þerwiþ] I woot wel þe soþe
That Luciferis lordshipe laste shal no lenger' (5–8).

Encouraged by this explanation, Will insists upon seeing the writ at
once, "Lat se þi lettres . . . we myȝte þe lawe knowe" (17. 9), and carefully inspects it: "This was þe tixte trewely; I took ful good yeme./The
glose was gloriously writen wiþ a gilt penne" (17. 14–15). He reports
that the text of the writ is taken from Matthew 22: 37 and 39, "*Dilige
deum & proximum tuum*" (Love God and thy neighbor), and that
the gloss, taken from the next verse in Matthew, explains the significance of the text: "*In hijs duobus mandatis tota lex pendet et prophet[e]*"
(On these two commandments hang the whole law and the prophets)
(17. 15).

   What is so remarkable about this passage is the way that Langland uses
the material production of patents to construct a relationship between
typology and gloss, a relationship crucial for establishing the relevance
of the Old Testament to the New. Moses/*Spes* describes the Ten Commandments as an unsealed writ, which anyone may read, not because it
is unsealed but because the seal itself will be a patent seal hanging from
the parchment, ensuring that the parchment remains open and the seal
remains intact. The patent seal signifies that the document is a public
notification for recurrent application: everyone should know about it,
and it will continue to be effective for years to come. Moses/*Spes* further
indicates that the seal confirms the text, in part because it is a material
sign of Christ's sovereign will, but in part because the seal hanging from
the document resembles Christ's body hanging from the cross with his
arms outstretched: "And þat is cros and cristendom and crist þeron to
honge" (17.6). Just as the seal symbolically represents the fulfillment of
the Old Law in the New Law, so it literally imitates the crucified body
of Christ, which authorized the Redemption and made it universally
accessible. This image of Christ as a pendant seal also appears in the
prose tract called the "Charter of Heaven" from *Pore Caitif* (ca. 1380s):
"& by þese two lacis hangeþ þe seel of oure chartre . . . þe printe of þe
seel is þe schap of oure lord ihesu crist hanginge for oure synne on
þe cros as we moun se bi þe ymage of þe crucifix . . . he haþ his armes

spred abrood redi to bicliipe hem."[23] The gloss of Moses's writ makes the same point, that the Old Law is confirmed in the New, insofar as it predicts the coming of Christ, and insofar as it can be interpreted by means of the twofold principle of charity: love God and thy neighbor. You might say that, according to Moses's writ, the Old Law is both the gloss that *depends* upon the text of the gospels – it is marginal without it – and the text *elucidated* by the gloss of the gospels; it is the gloss that makes the prophecies manifest and relevant. The Latin verses concretize this relationship between typology and gloss by punning once again on the patent seal. The phrase, "*In hijs duobus mandatis tota lex pendet et prophet[e]*" puns on the verb "pendere," meaning both literally "to hang" and figuratively "to depend," suggesting that the continued relevance of the Old Law *depends* upon its fulfillment in the New Law at the same time that Christ's open body *hanging* from the cross authenticates the dictates of Moses's writ. The patent seal acts, in other words, as the physical incarnation of the gloss, and as such mediates between history and interpretation, showing how history is made continuously relevant through the public act of reading. Just as the Ten Commandment's "pece of a hard roche" (17.11) is first described by Moses as a material text so the material text, in its turn, comes to represent an open hermeneutics, the typological manifestation of the New Law through the hanging body of Christ.

Together Patience's patent and Moses's maundement posit a theory about public writing through the practices and poetics of obtrusive writing, a writing characterized by its projection and reception within the poem. Critics have argued, however, that the documents in these two scenes illustrate Langland's New Testament poetics of paradox in which secular values and legal practices are reversed in Christ. In these readings, Patience offers a saving document to Hawkyn but then reveals it to be no document at all: Langland, according to James Simpson, "explodes its *purely legal, documentary status* by insisting on the *necessary spirit behind the words* of the document."[24] Likewise, according to Jill Keen, the juxtaposition of legal form and biblical gloss in Moses's maundement

---

[23] Text in Spalding, ed., *The Middle English Charters of Christ*, 101–2 (hereafter cited in the main text by page number).

[24] Simpson, *Piers Plowman: An Introduction to the B-text*, 160–1 (italics are in the original).

suggests an erasure of documentary materiality altogether: "In *Piers*," she argues, "strict adherence to earthly legal forms indicates a departure from God's law."[25] I would argue, however, that it is the reverse of Simpson's and Keen's formulations that is significant: the point is not that Langland's documents dissolve into scriptural texts, but rather that scriptural texts or divine revelation are imagined to be documentary in the first place. Granted, there is always some irony in comparing divine and worldly images, especially when the latter is implicated in the dissemination of power and justice. But in these two scenes Langland puns on documentary terms to describe the spiritual immediacy and hermeneutic openness of the Word. Both paradoxes and puns rely on connections between two terms, but where medieval paradox derives its effect from contradiction, puns usually point to surprising similarities between material objects and abstract concepts.

Indeed, the capacity of documentary writing to describe not just spiritual literacy, but the way that that literacy defines public writing, can be seen equally well in reprehensible documentary performances as in exemplary ones. In Chaucer's *Pardoner's Prologue*, for example, the Pardoner proves his authority to distribute indulgences with an amazing collection of ecclesiastical warrants: "Bulles of popes and cardynales,/Of patriarkes and bishopes I shewe, announces the Pardoner." But a few lines earlier he insinuates that his very body is like one of these patents: "First I pronounce whennes that I come,/And thanne my bulles shewe I alle and some./Oure lige lordes seel on my patente,/That shewe I first my body to warente."[26] By associating his body with a presumably forged patent the Pardoner suggests that, like the fraudulent relics in his pouch, his wanton body is on display to the public. It is a public letter open to the perusal of any passerby and ostensibly a source of spiritual benefit to anyone who should receive him. Of course, the Pardoner's comparison of his body with a sealed patent also calls attention to the discrepancy between them: the bishop's patent with its hanging bulls offers an unfortunate contrast to the Pardoner's gelded body, which hides untold secrets – or perhaps nothing at all. In this way too, the Pardoner's forged patents resemble the fake relics in his pouch: both underscore

[25] Keen concludes that Langland had no choice but to simplify his legal instruments in order to make them spiritually viable ("Documenting Salvation," II, 125–56).
[26] *The Pardoner's Prologue*, Benson, ed., *The Riverside Chaucer*, 335–8, 342–3.

his physical deficiency and attest to his dubious authority.[27] In short, what signifies common profit in *Piers Plowman* and other penitential literature becomes in the *Pardoner's Prologue* duplicitous exhibitionism.

LANGLAND'S POETICAL ADDRESS

In *Piers Plowman*, I have argued, legal documents model a public writing constituted between disclosure and reception, and between the text that obtrudes and the reader who unfolds it. There is nonetheless a visible gap between the dreamer, who wishes to address the ills of society, and Piers, who makes possible the incrimination and regeneration of the community. In the second half of this chapter, I consider two texts composed in the wake of *Piers Plowman*: the 1381 rebel letters and the alliterative dream-vision, *Mum and the Sothsegger*. Both works attempt to close the gap between agent and author, and both works attempt to redefine publicness in order to serve overtly political ends. In the process, both texts end up making more forceful claims about the relationship between poetry and documents than *Piers Plowman* can sustain. That they are able to do so, however, has everything to do with the way that they respond to reflexive passages within *Piers Plowman* – the dreamer's conversation with Lewte in Passus 11 and Imaginatif's rebuke of the dreamer in Passus 12. What is at issue in these passages is not writing poetry *per se*, but the problem of using poetry to address, rather than to disclose, the condition of society.

In Passus 11, the dreamer twice takes on the public voice of the satirist and is twice reprimanded.[28] At the beginning of the Passus, he denounces the hypocrisy of friars who place more value on the lucrative sacrament of confession and the rite of burial than on baptism and confirmation. He appeals in his cause to Lewte (equity or justice), asking if he has

---

[27] Carolyn Dinshaw offers a similar reading: "The Pardoner's scraps and chips of saints substitute for his lack of virility . . . his other artifacts, those sealed documents from Rome, are just as closely associated with his own masculine lack . . . As rolled-up parchments with seals dangling from them, the Pardoner's documents and bulls, placed conspicuously in his bulging 'male' present an iconographic substitute for his own lacking masculinity" (*Chaucer's Sexual Poetics*, 164).

[28] See Bowers's discussion of Langland's ambivalence towards language and satire in *The Crisis of Will in 'Piers Plowman,'* 191–201. For an entirely different reading of satire in Passus 11, see Simpson, *Piers Plowman: an Introduction to the B-text*, 129–31.

the right to publish his visions: "'If I dorste,' quod I, 'amonges men this metels avowe'" (II. 86). Lewte confirms that the laity have the right to decry the vices of the clergy publicly: "þyng þat al þe world woot, wherfore sholdestow spare/To reden it in Retorik to arate dedly synne?" (II.101–2). He subsequently qualifies this statement, however, warning that satirists should not be too eager to uncover evil in others, nor should they expose private sins to the public eye:

> Ac be [þow] neueremoore þe firste [þe] defaute to blame;
> Thou3 þow se yuel seye it no3t first; be sory it nere amended.
> [Th]yng þat is pryue, publice þow it neuere;
> Neiþer for loue [looue] it no3t ne lakke it for enuye. (II. 103–6)

While Lewte appears to authorize moral satire, his qualifications reveal the dreamer's critique to be motivated by a private vendetta rather than a genuine desire to counsel and amend. Notably, Lewte does not insist that the lay critic himself be morally perfect ("It is *licitum* for lewed men to [legge] þe soþe" [II. 96]), but he does question the dreamer's ability to address the sins of others without some measure of pride and self-interest. Scripture agrees with Lewte and underlines the need for personal repentance by citing the parable of the wedding feast in which many are called but few are chosen: God "plukked in *Pauci* pryueliche and leet þe remenaunt go rome" (II. 114). Taken together, Lewte's qualification and Scripture's parable imply that satire, by subjecting "pryue" sins to public view, may exclude the dreamer from the few "pryueliche" chosen for salvation. Scripture's sermon shakes the dreamer out of his smug satirical stance and throws him into a moral crisis, a debate with himself, rather than with the friars: "Al for tene of hir text trembled myn herte,/And in a weer gan I wexe, and wiþ myself to dispute/Wheiþer I were chosen or no3t chosen" (II. 115–17). Although the dreamer understands publication to be a public act, in fact, it threatens to exclude the speaker from salvation at the same time that it makes the friars' sins common knowledge. The problem with "lakking" in this passage, in other words, is that it proceeds from the individual speaker, and therefore from a position of pride or self-interest – it inevitably reflects back on the one speaking, on his moral and social status. It speaks both to the moral problem – who am I to cast the first stone? – and to the related social problem – who may legitimately address whom? But "lakking" also refers to competing models of public writing. It speaks, that is, to the critical opposition between address and disclosure, between what one reveals about others and what one confesses about oneself or what one reads in the texts produced by society on its own behalf.[29]

This tension between public writing and personal salvation and between "lakking" and amending reaches a climax in the Imaginatif episode, the most explicitly reflexive episode of *Piers Plowman*. Imaginatif introduces himself as the personification of moral memory, the faculty of the soul that recalls past sins in order to imagine future salvation or damnation ("I haue folwed þee, in feiþ, þise fyue and fourty winter,/And manye tymes haue meued þee to [mynne] on þyn ende" [12. 3–4]).[30] It is through this faculty that the dreamer should be moved to re-evaluate his life and amend his soul before old age keeps him from doing proper penance: "To amende it in þi myddel age, lest myȝt þe faill[e]/In þyn olde elde, þat yuele kan suffre/Pouerte or penaunce, or preyeres bidde" (12.7–9). In this way, Imaginatif serves as the soul's confessor or auto-biographer, allowing the soul to imagine itself and translate itself into text. The dreamer, says Imaginatif, has been wasting time with poetry:

> And þow medlest þee wiþ makynges and myȝtest go seye þi sauter,
> And bidde for hem þat ȝyueþ þee breed, for þer are bokes y[n]owe
> To telle men what dowel is, dobet and dobest boþe,
> And prechours to preuen what it is of many a peire freres (12. 16–19)

According to this passage, one problem with the dreamer's writing is that it fails to help him to amend his own faults or reflect productively upon his life. Another problem is that it claims the authoritative voice of clerical writing, but it is neither a sermon nor any other socially useful text, such as the Psalter, with which the dreamer claims to make a living. How then can the dreamer's writing legitimately represent both society and self? How can writing be a penitential transcript or mirror of the soul, and at the same time transcend the self to serve as a legitimate address to the world?

---

[29] For other relevant passages on "lakking" and penance, see *Piers Plowman* B. 11. 376–405.
[30] Much illuminating scholarship has been devoted to defining Imaginatif as a faculty of the soul. See, for example, Jones, "Imaginatif in *Piers Plowman*"; Minnis, "Langland's Ymaginatif and Late-Medieval Theories of Imagination"; and Kaulbach, *Imaginative Prophecy in the B-text of Piers Plowman*. In this chapter I restrict my analysis to what Imaginatif says about himself.

The dreamer fumbles for an answer and comes up with two contrary excuses, neither of which responds directly to Imaginatif's questions. First, he gives a standard academic apology (from Cato's *Distichs*), excusing writing as a pleasurable respite from other work (12. 20–4). He then changes tactics and protests that his writing *is* a kind of spiritual work. He claims that he has received little guidance from institutional authorities on this subject and that his writing is at least a substitute for action, if not a proper action itself:

> Ac if þer were any wight þat wolde me telle
> What were dowel and dobet and dobest at þe laste,
> Wolde I neuere do werk, but wende to holi chirche
> And þere bidde my bedes but whan ich ete or slepe" (12. 25–8).

Critics have understandably found the dreamer's response to Imaginatif to be inadequate and evasive, and I am not proposing to defend it here.[31] It does, however, introduce a third component to ideal writing. If writing should ideally be a transcript of confession and at the same time a public address (such as a sermon), it should also be an effective action, a verb such as "dowel," or a performative action like prayer. The dreamer's public writing is superfluous, smug, and often inappropriate, but as a mode of knowledge production it has the potential to be a legitimate – even essential – moral action. Thus with the dreamer's answer to Imaginatif, the function of public writing becomes more complex: what authoritative model of writing exists for the poet who wants to address the world and to attend to his own salvation, to write and act at the same time?

If we now return to the earlier discussion of documentary literacy, we see that the documents in *Piers Plowman*, and particularly Mede's charter and Truth's Pardon, offer a forum in which the condition of

---

[31] The latter passage especially has provoked much discussion about Langland's attitude toward poetic making. George Economou, for example, has shown – and most readers have thought – that Will's exchange with Imaginatif reveals Langland's ambivalence toward writing poetry. He concludes that Langland omitted this exchange in the C-text because he had gained more confidence in the value of his poetry ("Self-Consciousness of Poetic Activity in Dante and Langland," 191). By contrast, James Simpson has interpreted the exchange between Will and Imaginatif as a "radical defense" of poetry as a source of moral authority, and as a direct challenge to institutional authority (*Piers Plowman: An Introduction to the B-Text*, 136–9).

society may be judiciously and publicly addressed. They reveal actions both laudatory and reprehensible, but importantly they disclose these actions rather than expose them. They function as textual self-disclosures, and it is in this capacity as a record of a life or event that they maintain their authority and effectiveness. Disclosure might refer to what society projects of itself into the life of a poem, the way that it inscribes itself contractually into social relations and by extension into legal and moral action. Or disclosure might refer to that document sent down to society from above, the making of contract available through the public dissemination of information. The contents of such a document might concern pardon, freedom, or protection, anything that stipulates an action resulting in benefit or punishment. Piers's testament, for example, legally renders his secular and spiritual accounts, and Conscience's record destines the soul to heaven or hell. In a larger capacity, Mede's charter and Truth's Pardon damn or save the societies whose offenses or good deeds they record and, in that sense, they are produced and activated through society's confession of itself. The document is, in other words, the confession that acts: it is how society discloses itself to itself and to its God, but also the means by which it amends its condition, both in the present and the future.

We saw that Imaginatif opposes the dreamer's "making" to prayer and penance, and the dreamer claims that his writing is a kind of spiritual labor that prevents him from spending all his time going to church or saying his beads. The dreamer never really substantiates this claim, but the examples of divine writing in the poem certainly do. In Passus 11, as we have seen, the proper performance of the liturgy is compared to a perfectly executed charter, and likewise Truth changes the spiritual and social status of the poem's inhabitants by turning sacred texts into public broadcasts and redeeming contracts: patents, quittances, writs, and mainprises. Mede's charter damns many of the poem's inhabitants, but Truth's Pardon, by addressing each estate and occupation, reverses the transgressions contained in Mede's charter. We saw that the poem repeatedly blames Latin literates (like the dreamer) who use scripture for egotistical purposes, for disputation or self-aggrandizement. Yet Langland's documents transform the language of scripture into a legal record and effective action such as prayer or a mass. In this way, they offer a model for public writing based on a contractual rather than a confrontational relationship to the world.[32]

In conclusion, Langland's documents offer an alternative to the dreamer's uncharitable satire by depicting a public writing that goes beyond satire, that simultaneously confesses the life of the universal subject and acts on that subject's behalf. This writing is nothing less than the efficacious Word, the redemptive and indisputable embodiment of the divine, yet its public incarnation is the medieval legal document in all its multiplicity of forms. But just as love-stricken Will searches constantly for Piers but never fully apprehends him, so poetic making only estimates or approximates the divine documents that pervade *Piers Plowman*. The dreamer and his creator continually seek a writing that may benefit both author and audience and a public writing that may amend without "lakking." A disjunction always remains, however, between Will's work and the poem itself, as if it had been produced somewhere else and at another time. As Middleton observes, "paradoxically, it seems to be a condition of the integrity of [Will's] 'work,' or the defensibility of the project, that it never be fully identifiable or coexistent with any form of its (merely) textual incarnation."[33] This disjunction proceeds in part from the poem's queries about writing and the writing matter that it actually contains. It may also have something to do with the largely vernacular project of the poem and the Latin institutional culture from which the poem's documents are ultimately derived. Yet the labor of documentary writing may nevertheless clarify the poem's understanding of poetic making, regardless of whether that making is in Latin or the vernacular. Lewte and Imaginatif blame Will for addressing the public without proper authority, and Langland's strategy in both episodes is to excuse his speaker by making him a layman, with indubitably confusing results. In a persuasive analysis of the poem, Wendy Scase argues that Langland is concerned to differentiate a "new" anticlerical voice from a traditional one precisely by exploiting the "lewed"-"lered"

---

[32] Steven Justice argues about the *Visio* that it constitutes a search for a genre that will "accommodate an authority neither abusive nor idiosyncratic," but ultimately Langland's "discontinuous choices" of genre allows the poem to approach religious authority as it "progressively abandon(s) claims to poetic authority" ("The Genres of *Piers Plowman*," 291–306). I'm suggesting that Langland's documents offer a generic ideal which accommodates religious and poetic authority alike.

[33] Middleton, "Acts of Vagrancy," 292.

impasse. In this way, she argues, he substitutes the language of the vaguely clerical outsider for the "irremediably clerical" insider.[34] The poem suggests, however, that legal documents are, professionally speaking, neither clerical nor lay texts, but texts produced by a newly ambiguous subset of the clergy (legal clerks, scribes, and notaries), as well as by all kinds of lay actors and witnesses. Consequently, Langland's documents have the strange effect of both uniting and dividing the far-flung reaches of what medieval writers called "clergie," and of transcending institutional authority while at the same time drawing liberally from it. It is by means of these documents that Langland begins to outline vernacular public writing and validate his own.

GENRES OF SOCIAL ACTION: THE LETTERS OF JOHN BALL

Two fourteenth-century chroniclers, Henry Knighton and Thomas Walsingham, copied into their Latin histories a total of six English letters. They attributed these letters to the itinerant priest John Ball, as well as to other supposed leaders of the 1381 uprising with pseudonyms such as Jackke Trewman, Jakke Mylner, and Jackke Carter. According to Walsingham, a letter was found in the pocket or sleeve (*manica*) of a man about to be hanged, and when John Ball confessed to writing one such letter, he too was hanged.[35] The letters have long intrigued modern readers, first, because they are written in English and therefore reveal something about lay literacy in the fourteenth century, as well as about the relationship between literacy and violence; and second, because they borrow conspicuously from *Piers Plowman* and therefore attest to the wider reception of the poem beyond its original, presumably more erudite or specialized, audience. The letters, for example, refer to allegorical figures in Langland's poem such as "peres þe plowman" and "hobbe robbyoure," and several of them exhort their readers, "doþ welle and ay bettur and bettur."[36] The letters also borrow the official salutations of legal documents, ranging from the simpler notifications

---

[34] Scase, *Piers Plowman and the New Anticlericalism*, 165–8.
[35] Justice, *Writing and Rebellion*, 26.
[36] Richard Firth Green also locates sources for the rebel letters in vernacular religious lyrics and sermons, for example, the preaching poetry of Friar John of Grimstone. See "John Ball's Letters: Literary History and Historical Literature."

of broadsides or pamphlets such as "Jakke Trewman doþ ʒow to understande" (Trewman, 1) and "Jakke Carter preyes ʒowe al þat ʒe..."
(Carter, 1) to John Ball's more elaborate imitation of an official patent:
"Johon schep som tyme seynte marie prest of ʒork. and now of
colchestre. Greteth wel... etc." (Ball₃, 1–2).³⁷ However strange they may
have seemed to the chroniclers who collected them, these letters were
evidently meant to rally people into action by drawing upon two cultural discourses: legal documents and Langland's popular religious allegory. And if Walsingham may be believed, the combination of the two
produced a political statement sufficient to hang a man.

In *Writing and Rebellion*, Steven Justice memorably calls these documents acts of "assertive literacy."³⁸ They are assertive, he explains, because
they demonstrate how the rural laity appropriated official instruments to
serve an alarming, if deeply reactionary, program, one that called for the
eradication of middlemen, and the restoration of justice as a principle of
royal – as opposed to local – dispensation. Justice supports his argument
with the findings of Rosamund Faith and Michael Clanchy, who show
that urban craftsmen and small rural landowners alike had increasing
contact with documentary culture in the later Middle Ages, and used
it to acquire or regain privileges, including freedom from services and
access to the royal courts. The phrase "assertive literacy" suggests, in
other words, that the rural laity wrote these vernacular letters because
they recognized the performative work of documentary writing, and
were willing and able to use it against those who would withhold their
privileges.

This idea is certainly compelling as it stands, but it is less so when
it is applied to the relationship between the letters and *Piers Plowman*.
Justice argues that the letters reshaped the inchoate social matter of
the poem into a performative document. More specifically, he argues
that Ball appropriated material from Wit's speech in B. 9 and, in doing
so, radically reinterpreted Langland's vocabulary of labor and of the
natural order to support a rural-based movement for social equality.³⁹
In short, whereas Ball took from documentary culture a model for a
performative writing that "enacts something, gets something done," he

---

³⁷ Texts in Justice, *Writing and Rebellion: England in 1381*, 13–15 (hereafter cited in the main
text by name of the "author" and line number).
³⁸ Justice, *Writing and Rebellion*, 13–66.   ³⁹ Ibid., 111.

had to transform Langland's "curious and insistently literary" poem into a "social document" in order to articulate a concrete plan of social or redemptive action. In this way, Will's response to Imaginatif in B. 12, why he meddles with "makyngs," reflects the poem's true *modus operandi*; in *Piers Plowman*, poetry is merely a form of "delay and compensation" until the seeker discovers the true course of action. By contrast, writes Justice, "Ball's conception of the written word owes more to this bureaucratic culture of instrumental writing than to the culture of theological commentary or the literary form that Langland derived from it."[40]

Justice's comparison of *Piers Plowman* and the rebel letters has changed the way we read the poem and its political interventions. Nevertheless, I would like to present a very different way of reading these two works together, namely that the rebel letters are, to quote Victor Turner, "genres of social action."[41] Rather than transforming or adapting *Piers Plowman* to fit a bureaucratic model of writing, the purveyors of the 1381 letters were converting poetry into social action *on the poem's own terms*. They were, in effect, closing the gap between the dreamer and Piers, between the singularity of satire and the redemptive possibilities of disclosure. It is true, as Justice points out, that the culture of theological commentary bequeathed to Langland a model of glossing and disputation, and in that sense a parallel does exist between Imaginatif's accusations of Will in B. 12 and the dilatory structure of the poem as a whole. But if Langland uses that commentary model to explore competing genres and opinions, he finally challenges its inability to act and its tendency to exclude. And as suggested earlier, the poem responds to Imaginatif's accusations by showcasing an obtrusive model of public writing, official written documents, which simultaneously disclose and enact spiritual legislation.

I am saying, in other words, that the rebel letters put into circulation the very text that Langland advertises as a model of public writing but never acknowledges as his own: *not* the historical legal document but the fictive legal document, the legal document *as* poetic form. This is not to say that the rebel letters aren't real in the sense that they didn't have serious effects; rather, it is to say that they capitalize on the documentary process by which vernacular allegorical poetry becomes a mode of public

---

[40] Ibid., 117.   [41] Turner, *The Anthropology of Performance*, 23–7.

address. It is as if these letters are the ones that Piers might carry on his person, if he were really as sympathetic to labor as his name suggests. Like Langland's documents, for example, the rebel letters disclose crucial information, ("jakke trewman doþ ʒow to understande þat falsnes and gyle haviþ regned to longe" [Trewman, 1–2]), and, in doing so, they implicate those whom they address in contracts both spiritual and social ("jakke carter preyes ʒowe alle.þat ʒe make a gode ende. of þat ʒe haue begunnen. and doþ wele and ay bettur and bettur. for at þe euen men hery[e]þ þe day" [Carter, 1–3]).

Like the documents in *Piers Plowman*, moreover, the rebel letters disclose and include in large part because they have unlocatable subjects. They draw upon the *talis* or generic "so-and-so" of documentary personhood – they can be filled in with anyone's name – and it is this *talis* that makes them public texts: they may be kept in anyone's pocket or sleeve (*manica*) because they may be sent by, directed to, or received by anyone. It is, moreover, the generic or personified character of these letters that suggests that they are produced by society on its own behalf, just as Truth's Pardon is procured by Piers and transcribed and read by Will; Mede's charter is issued at the request of False and witnessed by a miller, reeve, beadle, and pardoner; and Piers writes his testament as an exemplary Christian in front of all pilgrims. Similarly, in the rebel letters Jack Trewman and Jack Carter implicate all people, Piers the plowman evokes all honest laborers ("lat peres þe plowman my brothur. duelle at home and dyʒt vs corne" [Carter, 3–4]), while Hobbe the Robber represents, as he does in *Piers Plowman*, those objected to in the present and excluded in the final assessment ("chastise wel hobbe þe robbere. and takeþ wiþ ʒow johan trewman and alle hijs felawes and no mo" [Ball₃, 5–6]).

Notably, too, the *talis* of documentary writing, the "anyone" or "everyone" that makes up society's transcription of itself, is represented both in *Piers Plowman* and the rebel letters by urban and rural laborers. Despite Langland's deeply ambivalent position on rural labor and the natural order, he imagines the documentary *talis* to be exemplified by Piers the plowman, as if "everyone" and "anyone" were social as well as rhetorical constructs. In both texts, too, it is the juxtaposition of the generic laborer with moral personifications – "jakke mylner" and "jakke trewman," Wrong and the reeve, Truth and the plowman– that makes documentary writing not simply a public act, but one with profound eschatological meaning. Walsingham, an expert in all sorts of legal documents, complained that the letters were "full of enigmas," by which he was probably referring to their riddlic character, that they don't refer to identifiable persons or actions. The *talis* of these letters is neither a template for history ("N grants to M") nor is it a historical person. Walsingham may have also been commenting on the fact that the letters' cryptic injunctions are more prophetic than heraldric. They prophesy the final end of social contract ("Nowe regneþ pride in pris. and couetys is hold wys...Enuye regniþ wiþ tresone. and slouthe is take in grete sesone. god do bote. for nowe is tyme amen" [Ball$_2$ 4–7]), at the same time that they alert us to immediate actions. Several letters prophesy, for example, that "johan the mullere hath ygrounde smal smal smal þe kynges sone of heuene schal paye for al" (Ball$_3$, 7–9). Thus the rebel letters, by positing the generic laborer as an eschatological figure, have not appropriated *real* documents, which depend on historically specific situations and actors. Rather, they have borrowed the *vernacularized legal fictions* of documentary culture, in which the whole of society is implicated by the documentary *talis*. In this respect, they are following the lead of *Piers Plowman*: it is precisely Langland's fictionalizing of documentary culture that provides a viable model for public writing, one that is indebted to – but ultimately goes beyond – real documents.

John Gower, in his vision of the 1381 revolt, offers a useful counterexample to the rebel letters. In the *Vox clamantis* he continually subordinates the eschatological to the heraldric in order to portray the revolt as an exceptional and punishable act, and its actors as identifiable criminals, even though he gives them the names of generic laborers. "There appeared a Jackdaw," he writes, "well instructed in the art of speaking, which no cage could keep at home" and later he writes, "Wat calls, Tom comes to him, and Sim does not loiter behind Bet...Jack tears down houses and kills men with his sword...The prophet Ball teaches them."[42] By contrast, the rebel letters use the commonness of documentary person

---

[42] Translation printed in *The Major Latin Works of John Gower*, ed. and trans. Stockton, 65, 67. The contrast I am illustrating is more apparent in Gower's original Latin: "Watte vocat, cui Thomme venit, neque Symme retardat Bette...Iakke domos que viros vellit et ense necat...Balle propheta docet" (Macauley, ed., *The Complete Works of John Gower*, ll. 783–4, 790, 793).

("Jack Trewman") to direct the generic toward the eschatological. No doubt the authors of the letters were probably using laborers' names to project an undifferentiated consciousness or identity distinct from those accused of manipulating justice. Yet arguably it is the way that both Langland and the rebels deploy personification allegory that makes public writing documentary in the first place.

Another example of how the rebel letters borrow from Langland's documents is the way that they capitalize on the universalizing salutation of patents and charters in order to designate an inclusive subject. For example, the two letters attributed to John Ball mimic official patent addresses, but where a conventional patent might greet all officials and loyal servants ("Omnibus ballivis et fidelibus suis...salutem"), or at least the universal Christian subject ("Omnibus Christi fidelibus ad quos presentes litere peruenerint" [To all those faithful in Christ to whom these present letters should reach]), these letters greet that diverse subject, at once anonymous and common, which looms so large in *Piers Plowman* and which its fictive documents address: "John balle seynte marye prist grete3 wele *alle maner men*" (Ball₂, 1–2; emphasis mine, cf. the salutation to Mede's charter, "*Sciant presentes & futuri, &c.*/Witeþ and witnesseþ þat wonieþ vpon erþe" [B. 2. 74–5]). And where Ball names himself specifically (e.g., "John balle seynte marye prist"), the way that he addresses his audience suggests that in certain contexts historical specificity itself is as much a legal fiction as the template. In his second letter, for example, he writes, "Johon schep...greteth wel *johan nameles*, and johan the mullere and johon carter" (Ball₂, 1–2; emphasis mine), a salutation that conflates the personified laborer with Everyman. In this way, the rebel letters draw on a poetics of publicness indebted to the patent, which was already available in *Piers Plowman* itself.[43]

It is true, as Justice points out, that the documents in *Piers Plowman*, even if they are instrumental to salvation, lack the explicit imperatives of the letters, such as "nowe is tyme" and "make a good end." Nonetheless,

---

[43] Justice argues about the letters that they transform the exclusions of contemporary practice into documentary inclusion. Because the reading of letters patent was only an ephemeral "act of information" that caused the audience to be "left out of, or behind in, the action, belated witnesses to the language of record," the rebel letters "aimed instead to make the language of record and official action identical with the language of information and everyday exchange, a language by definition open of access to those native-born" (*Writing and Rebellion*, 71).

the point remains the same, that the rebel poets, by citing documentary formulas and ascribing them to allegorical agents, were collapsing the poem's ideal into the linguistic mode of the poem itself. The poem presented itself as a public archive to those whose major platforms were the issuing of charters of freedom and the liberation of ancient charters from monastic archives. Thus we could say that the rebel poets were not simply imitating bureaucratic forms, but rather they were borrowing from *Piers Plowman* what the poem itself advertises as a legitimate public discourse. Rather than transforming *Piers Plowman* by appropriating documentary culture, they were transforming documentary culture by appropriating Langlandian poetics. Justice argues that the rebels "recognized the written document as something powerful but also malleable, something that, once written, could be rewritten," but that very rewriting belonged to what was starting to look suspiciously like a literary tradition.[44] For Justice, documentary literacy is a writtenness that participates in literature only at moments of political crisis and popular insurrection. In his view, it is an institutional production, which is subject to appropriation without reference to those aspects of a culture that make literacy into textuality, and even into poetry. Yet Ball, like Langland, was caught up in a larger movement in which the vernacular literary subject increasingly found its public voice in the legal document, and in which official discourse was appropriated to serve vernacular piety in its incarnation as public poetry. Middleton observes that "to write a work of literature is at once to use and to deform instrumental discourse, to open the way of foolish or dangerous understanding of the culture's almost blunted purposes as the way to their full subjective repossession and communal renewal."[45] Would it be so strange if what the rebels stashed in their pockets was not an act of "assertive literacy," but another one of Langland's documents – not the imitation but the double?

BAGGING COUNSEL IN *MUM AND THE SOTHSEGGER*

Like the rebel letters, the alliterative dream-vision *Mum and the Sothsegger* (ca. 1400), a member of what Helen Barr calls the "*Piers Plowman*

[44] Ibid., 48.
[45] Anne Middleton, "The Audience and Public of *Piers Plowman*," 121.

tradition," closes the gap between Piers and the dreamer.[46] It does so, however, not by emulating Piers and writing the material of the poem into the texts of legal documents, but rather by making legal documents the desired end to narrative action. As we shall see, *Mum* turns the Langlandian predicament of satire into the post-Langlandian predicament of counsel by appealing to a literature of disclosure rather than address, and specifically by appealing to material legal documents. Whereas in *Piers Plowman* the legitimacy of public writing is bound up in debates about whether the laity has the right to critique the clergy, and whether the clergy have the right to publicize internal disputes, public writing in *Mum and the Sothsegger* is bound up in debates about the effectiveness of the parliamentary Commons, whether or not they inform the king of the grievances of the realm. Consequently, whereas *Piers Plowman* is concerned with the relation of morality to social status, *Mum and the Sothsegger* is concerned to find a balance between tyranny and sedition. Like Langland, however, the *Mum*-poet's strategy for inventing public poetry, and justifying his own agency within it, is to turn his subject – the condition of the realm – into material archives available to public perusal and royal correction.

The *Mum*-poet was preoccupied with the status and function of public writing, and seems to have deliberately misread *Piers Plowman* as the search for a legitimate mode of truth-telling. Langland portrays Truth as a multivalent concept, usually representing God, but also justice, integrity, and honesty. These shifting meanings are reflected in the rebel letters as well, one of which urges its readers to "stonde manylche togedyr in trewþe. and helpeȝ trewþe. and trewþe schal helpe ȝowe" (Ball₂, 3–4). By contrast, the *Mum*-poet has sifted through Langland's allegorical mix for a more literal definition of Truth to fit his secular project.[47] As a result, his narrator is preoccupied with finding a political

---

[46] For the *Mum*-poet's debts to and transformations of *Piers Plowman*, see Barr, *Signes and Sothe*, ch. 5. Two important earlier essays on the relationship between *Mum* and *Piers* are Blamires, "*Mum & the Sothsegger* and Langlandian Idiom"; and Simpson, "The Constraints of Satire in *Piers Plowman* and *Mum and the Sothsegger*."

[47] Simpson makes the same observation, that the Lewte passage appears to advocate satire but then reveals it to be a judgmental posture to the world that produces a limited form of Truth, a literal rather than theological truth. The author of *Mum and the Sothsegger*, on the other hand, is only concerned with how one may legitimately reveal the vices of society without getting into trouble ("The Constraints of Satire," 23).

"truth-teller" rather than pursuing a larger spiritual truth.[48] This narrator is continually discouraged in his efforts to tell the truth by the omnipresent Mum who, as his name suggests, extols the benefits of silence, and indeed, the poem's larger critique of the court, university, and fraternal orders develops from this tension between knowing the truth and preserving diplomatic silence.

About one third of the way into the poem, however, the narrator begins to be convinced of his own truth-telling role, and he invokes the legal document as the justification for and very structure of his literary enterprise. He complains, echoing Langland's dreamer, that he is weary of wandering about, never knowing whether to rest or to go forward, always wondering whether Mum or the sothsegger should have the "maistrie" in the end.[49] Mum, decked out like a bishop "with his myter," menaces the narrator continually, counseling him to submit and save his own skin: "And leste I soughte sorowe, cesse by tyme" (581). At that moment, the narrator suddenly receives a divine document that permits him as God's proxy to waive legal responsibility for his writing.

> And boode til a baron, blessid be he euer,
> (His name is y-nempnyd among the ix. ordres)
> Sent a saufconduyt so that I wolde
> Maynteyne no matiere to amende myself,
> Ne caicche no colour [that] came of my wittes,
> But showe for a souurayn to shewe it forth after.
> This boldid me to bisynes to bringe hit to ende
> Thorough grace of þis good lord þat gouuerneth al thing. (584–90).

A safe-conduct might be issued for any number of reasons, but it primarily served to protect an ambassador, civil servant, or messenger on a mission, requisitioning arms and provisions for the bearer of the

---

[48] Barr has already noted that "the pervasiveness of legal vocabulary in the [*Piers Plowman*] tradition reflects, in part, the textual force of *Piers Plowman*" and further, that in the *Piers Plowman* tradition, legal diction helps to define "the ethics of a truth-telling practice" (*Signes and Sothe*, 133). She proceeds to argue that the *Piers Plowman* tradition departs from *Piers Plowman* in deploying legal diction and motifs which are "distinctly social and political in temper" (134), rather than spiritual.

[49] Text in Barr, ed., *The Piers Plowman Tradition*, ll. 570–5 (hereafter cited in the main text by line number).

document, or soliciting the overlord for protection.[50] It was also issued to protect a traveling layman, who would otherwise be accused of vagrancy or sedition under the various incarnations of the Statute of Laborers. This statute sought to eradicate competition by forcing laborers to stay on their lords' estates, and sought to alleviate labor shortage by forcing all able-bodied people to work.[51] After 1400, an archbishop or bishop might also issue a safe-conduct to authorize and protect an unaffiliated religious, as in the case of Margery Kempe, thereby mapping labor regulations onto anti-heresy provisions.[52] The safe-conduct in *Mum and the Sothsegger* seems to draw upon all three situations. It is sent by a divine "baron," famous among the nine celestial orders, suggesting that the narrator is a civil servant of sorts, perhaps a member of the delinquent court responsible for counseling the king. The document also accounts, however, for the narrator's errancy, both his wandering and the implications of wandering for sedition or heresy, as alluded to by Mum's bishop costume. The safe-conduct thus prevents the narrator from being harassed in strange lands or having to defend himself in court should he be interrogated by bishop Mum or accused of sedition. Like those addressed by the rebel letters, he may "bringe hit to ende" without having to account for himself ("mayntene no matiere") or to make up fictitious excuses ("caicche no colour").

It is difficult not to read this passage as a response to the self-interrogations of *Piers Plowman* B. 12 and C. 5. Importantly, too, it is a response conditioned by Langland's documentary modes. In B. 12, as discussed above, Imaginatif berates the dreamer for wasting his time (12. 16–18), and the dreamer protests that poetry is a necessary "werk" until someone else can tell him the meaning of doing well (12. 25–8). Satirical poetry, he argues, is a substitute for adequate spiritual instruction, and as such it gives the vernacular writer license to address society without claiming a particular social identity. It is a labor that replaces both the work of prayer and the speaker's social identity only because the clergy are such negligent teachers. The dreamer's argument is also a

---

[50] For examples of royal safe-conducts, see #162 in Chaplais, *English Medieval Diplomatic Practice, Part I*, 308, or "Letter for Protection of T. Gray" in *Richard D'Angerville of Bury, Fragments of His Register and Other Documents*, ed. Dean of Durham, 58.

[51] On safe-conducts and vagrancy generally, see Middleton, "Acts of Vagrancy."

[52] For more discussion of Margery Kempe's documents, see the epilogue to this book.

means of fashioning a poem by justifying delay: the poem both anticipates and proceeds from Imaginatif's interrogation, just as Imaginatif
himself is both the memory and projection of the dreamer's moral life.
In C. 5, by contrast, Reason and Conscience take the dreamer to task
for *not* working, for idling about when he should be applying himself
to fieldwork or crafts. The dreamer defends himself first by citing his
clerical status, and second by apologizing for the fact that his unlicensed
praying for others has not always profited his own soul.[53]

The safe-conduct episode in *Mum and the Sothsegger* effectively responds to B. 12 and C. 5 at once. In response to B. 12, the *Mum*-narrator
justifies his poetic work as compensation for those who should exemplify truth but fail to do so (for Langland, the clergy; for the *Mum*-poet,
the knights of the shire); and like the dreamer in B.12, the *Mum*-narrator
imagines himself to be at once a member of that group and its marginal
critic. In response to C. 5, however, the narrator justifies public writing
and exonerates himself by invoking the safe-conduct that Langland's
dreamer so visibly lacks. This document, in effect, allows the narrator
to dodge the vagrancy statutes evoked in C. 5, while at the same time
explicitly constituting himself as public writer by collapsing vagrancy,
sedition, and civil service. Like the dreamer in C. 5, moreover, the *Mum*-
narrator wants to defend his writing against accusations of vagrancy and
sedition, but he does so not by referring to a work "already 'out there' in
the world" (Middleton's phrase) but by recuperating the public work of
Langland's documents. More specifically, he recuperates Truth's Pardon,
with all of its implications for divine protection and maintenance, for
his new and deeply secular enterprise. Thus, whereas C. 5 refers to a
poem previously circulated by Langland, but ungraspable as a written
text, the *Mum*-poet's safe-conduct simultaneously cites an earlier poem –
Piers Plowman – and forecasts a new form of public poetry about to be
written.

I mentioned that the self-interrogations in *Piers Plowman* B. 12 and
C. 5 are part of Langland's poetics of delay, a point that Justice and
Middleton make as well: in B. 12 the poem bodies forth from the

---

[53] As Middleton has persuasively argued, the dreamer realizes himself as a public writer in
this scene through his interrogation for vagrancy, as "a worker without papers" whose
"authorizing document is none other than that which he has already made (of) himself –
the work that is already 'out there' in the world" (Middleton, "Acts of Vagrancy," 292–3).

imperative to bide one's time – even though the poem is complete, it doesn't end – and in C. 5 the poem is already written but circulated in a different place at a different time. In both episodes, the publicness of the poem – its consciousness of itself as an address to the world – is, from the perspective of the dreamer, infinitely deferred, even if it is realized as text within the poem itself. In *Mum and the Sothsegger*, however, the narrator eventually resolves the work of public writing by subordinating address to disclosure and spoken counsel to the documentary modes advertised in *Piers Plowman*. He does this first by invoking the divine safe-conduct. Then, in the last several hundred lines of the poem, he musters up his courage and tells the king the truth by emptying a sack of "bokes vnbredid in balade-wise made/Of vice and of vertue fulle to þe margyn" (1345–6), that is, the unbound leaves of ballads or broadsides, crammed to the margins with revealing information about the realm. The dreamer tells us that his sack contains secret poetry ("pryue poyse" [1344]), but the poetry in question turns out to be a literal archive of vices and virtues, satirical documents that the dreamer publicizes in the name of counsel. These documents effectively disguise satire under the cover of documentary disclosure: each document is a bullet point on the narrator's list of grievances, and each one listed is followed by increasingly longer commentary, virtually indistinct from Langlandian satire. The dozen or so documents in the bag range from the institutional to the fantastical. They include, for example, an official record of goods bequeathed to the cathedral church, a "quayer of quitances of quethyn goodes" (1348), a "rolle of religion" recording the incomes from monastic estates (1364 ff.), a last will and testament revealing the crimes of their executors (1697 ff.), and a report of rumors circulating among the common people, "a copie for comunes of culmes foure and twenty" (1388).

Just as the divine safe-conduct justifies the work of public poetry by offering the narrator a warrant of protection, so the narrator's bag represents the means by which society confesses to or witnesses its own corruption. This motley collection of documents asks, in other words, how public poetry might eschew the agency of the self-interested speaker, not just by receiving protection from above – the divine safe-conduct – but also by allowing society as a whole to disclose itself to public view, and, in doing so, to translate disclosure into incrimination and reparation.

Some of these documents, for example, are themselves evidence of nefarious practices but end up reporting those practices, such as the "writte of high wil y-write al newe/Y-knytte in a cornier of the bagge-ende" (1498–9) that tells how neighboring landowners try to dominate each other by initiating criminal action suits, and consequently "annoyen thaire neighborowes nyne myle aboute" (1509). Other documents report the bad practices directly, such as the "paire of pamphilettz of prelatz" (1370) stuck in the bottom of the bag, which reports that prelates enjoy their pluralities and imitate the lives of lay lords: "Thus leden thay thaire lyves in lustes and in sportes" (1378). Still other documents are supposed to be used to assess institutions for corrupt practices, but they may or may not be used effectively. An example is the volume of visitation, which records every time a beneficed priest goes uncorrected for abandoning his parish.

In sum, the narrator's bag explores what it means to disclose in poetry: it contains reports of what people are doing wrong, but these reports are issued by the people themselves. Together these documents constitute a public discourse, which is at once the *statement* of the community to itself, and a response to documents issued from above, a discursive realm that opens up between the safe-conduct and the bag of books, the content of which is vernacular alliterative poetry. From this perspective, it comes as no surprise that among the leaflets in the sack is the allegorical "copie of couetise" – a document written both by and about Greed, describing how rich men buy mansions and only leave money posthumously to the poor. Likewise the bag contains a devil's patent, a "raggeman rolle that Ragenelle hymself/Hath made" (1565–6) (punning on "raggeman," meaning both the Devil and a document with a tattered fringe of pendant seals), which proclaims the abuses of maintenance and the oppression of the common people.[54] These allegorical and supernatural documents look back to Mede's charter in *Piers Plowman*, or the devil's record in Deguileville's *Pèlerinage de l'âme:* they disclose the deeds of their makers and expose those deeds to public scrutiny and divine or royal correction. Nor is it surprising that the very last document in the list, sporting a red silk tassel, is a "cedule soutelly

[54] For more information on ragmen, see Alford, *Piers Plowman: A Glossary of Legal Diction*, 125. See also *Pierce the Ploughman's Crede*, in Barr, ed. *The 'Piers Plowman' Tradition*, line 180.

indited" (1734), filled not with the excesses of contemporary society but with prophecies of wonders which have now come to pass since the first and second estates fell out of step: "wordes of woundres that han falle,/And fele-foldes ferlees wythynne thees fewe yeris,/By cause that the clergie and knighthoode to-gedre/Been not knytte in conscience as Crist dide thaym stable" (1736–9). Frank Grady rightly argues that the poetry written at the beginning of the Lancastrian regime – of which *Mum* is one example – was defined by the substitution of the document for the dream-vision as a means of truth-telling.[55] Importantly, however, *Mum and the Sothsegger* does not just substitute documentary culture for the dream-vision which it "remembers" yet chooses to put aside; rather it extracts from Langland's dream-vision the operative mode of public writing.

It might be argued that the jumble of copies, quires, schedules, and pamphlets in *Mum* resembles more those broadsides anonymously posted on doors and churches in the fifteenth century than it does official legal documents. As such, the documents in the narrator's bag could be said to parody and subvert official channels of communication, which admit no debate and which are irremediably corrupt. Yet if the bag of books evokes the practice of bill-casting, the fiction of bill-casting was not the creation of a public domain distinct from the official written record. Rather, it was the same fiction that informs medieval documentary practice, namely that a community of public action is constituted within the reciprocal relation between disclosure and reception, and between official proclamations and the documents produced by society as whole. This reciprocal relation tends to be hierarchical, rather than lateral. For example, in her essay on fifteenth-century bill-casting, Wendy Scase describes a bill circulated by John Cade's supporters in 1450, urging the king to issue a proclamation by means of royal letters patent ("openly to be redde and cried"). This royal proclamation should state that the king wants the people to help him bring traitors to justice.[56] What is so interesting about Cade's bill is not just that it pretends to articulate a "hidden transcript" (Judith Ferster's phrase), that it replaces the parliamentary petition with an anonymous one, but that it imagines communal disclosure in relation to official proclamation. The

[55] See Grady, "The Generation of 1399."
[56] Scase, " 'Strange and Wonderful Bills,' " 238.

Mum-poet is very careful, in fact, to distinguish documentary poetry from the unsubstantiated complaint of the commons. It is as if he is worried that broadsides and documents, because they both disclose the condition of the realm, might *seem* to be issued by the commons at large. For example, one of the documents in the bag, the "copie for comunes of culmes foure and twenty," does not report the general complaint of the realm, as we might expect. Instead it reports the error of those common people in the shire who fabricate stories about the events in the center, even about private conversations among the peers. Says the narrator,

> I mervail but thay mette so how hit might be
> That thay finde fables and been so ferre fro thens
> That though thou ride rennyng, and reste but a lite,
> Fro London forth the long waye to the land-is ende,
> And comes right from the king-is courte and his cunseil bothe,
> Fro prelatz vnto peris in pryuete or elles,
> Yit shal tidingz bee y-tolde tenne dayes ere thou come,
> That neuer was of worde spoke ne wroughte, as thou shal hire.
>
> (1394–401)

In the midst of this diatribe against the commons, the *Mum*-poet launches into a story about Genghis Khan, who, to drive home a point about loyalty, forced the kings of conquered nations to murder their first-born sons. The *Mum*-poet concludes this story by saying that he disapproves of the rumor-mongering of the commons, but by commons he is referring not to the "knightz that cometh for the shires," the delegates in parliament, but to the laborers in the localities (1460–2).

We have seen that the *Mum*-poet draws upon the obtrusiveness of documentary writing, a writing that discloses and performs, in order to describe his own counsel poetry. It is significant in this regard that he chooses to locate public poetry within the materialities of documentary practice. Earlier in this chapter, I suggested that Langland equated legal inclusiveness with the open format of letters patent, and, in doing so, made universal notification a form of public legal action. In this way, *Piers Plowman* projects an ideal writing through the material document: the unfolded proclamation, its hanging seal, and its attendant puns. In *Mum and the Sothsegger*, however, thingness itself becomes a figure for counsel poetry, and obtrusiveness an indicator of disclosure achieved.

Indeed, the very materiality of the documents in *Mum* leads us back to the question of the status of material form within the literate practices of the law. We might suppose, for example, that the specificity of the sizable "volume of visitacion of viftene leves" (1353) the "writte of high wil y-write al newe/Y-knytte in a cornier of the bagge-ende" (1498–9), and the fancy "cedule soutelly indited/With tuly silke intachid right atte rolle-is ende" (1734–5) reflect the desire of the poet to transcend the obtrusive literacy of contemporary society, those things that corrupt by the very fact that they are crafted, flourished, and stored away. After all, the "title of a testament" reports that executors secretly hide wills and the records of their fees, casting them in a coffer "leste thay copied were" (1697–701). Likewise, the bishop is so thrilled with the "quire of quitances of quethyn goodes" that he begs that it be bound "al newe" (1348–9). Yet these examples show only that those people who deal in material documents want to appropriate their benefits for themselves. Their executors understand the *relationship* between copying and exposure: the bishop, for example, treasures the records of bequeathals just as he loathes the account of poor men's suffering bound in its frayed cover (1586). In fact, society suffers only when its material documents, its capacity to reveal or usher in the truth, are concealed or buried away, when, as Jack Trewman's letter puts it, "trewþe. hat bene sette under a lokke" (Trewman, 2).

From a different perspective, the materiality of the documents in *Mum* once again recalls fifteenth-century bill-casting, the physical dislocation of which would seem to challenge the writtenness of institutional documents. Wendy Scase argues, for example, that broadsides conform to an oral model (and thus ostensibly serve public interest) because they feature ballad verses, and are therefore easily communicated and remembered; because they are ephemeral (except, of course, for those who happened to collect them); and because they are intrinsically opposed to the self-serving writtenness of official channels of counsel (such as the failure of the Commons to petition on behalf of the community as a whole).[57] Richard Firth Green takes a different position

[57] According to Scase, bill-casting "signified the absence of the official or legitimate mode of publication even as it 'took its place,'" and it "textualized the political aspirations (purportedly) of a silent populace denied access to public platforms." Sheila Lindenbaum makes a similar argument about documentary writing among London poets of the late

from Scase on the materiality of the institutional word, and especially in relation to *Mum and the Sothsegger*. He argues that the "physical solidity" of the *Mum*-poet's bag of books implicitly contrasts the duplicity of the law's "literate technology" with the "solid materiality of the wed [the physical token]" and the "good faith of the human messenger."[58] For both critics, however, the virtuous making of publicness is at odds with the written record. In Scase's view, materiality represents the privatizing, corruptive nature of documentary literacy and is opposed to the public domain; in Green's view, materiality is opposed to documentary literacy and represents communal negotiation.

I propose a very different reading of this passage than those offered by Green and Scase. In *Mum and the Sothsegger*, it is the obtrusiveness of the written word, the codified and collectible record, that comes to stand for the public disclosure of the "hidden transcript." First of all, from the very beginning of the poem as we have it, the narrator depicts counsel as a spoken enterprise. Whereas the unspoken problems of the realm are imagined to be a written text (the realm needs a truthteller "forto telle [the king] the texte, and touche not the glose/How the worde walketh with oon and with other"[141–2]), that text is one that bad counselors now "parle priuyly to thaire owen peeris" (155), and which any "burne" used to be able to "bable" when Henry took the throne. Now it can only be heard in the inaudible cry of the "comune clamour." When the narrator is finally emboldened to speak, however, he chooses to do so by dumping a bag of material texts "of vice and of vertue fulle to the margyn" (1346). Indeed, it is this striking exchange of the dislocated oral for the physical solidity of the written that enables the *Mum*-poet to

---

1370s and 1380s, namely that they recognized that "official forms of writing had been abused by privileged interests," and, as a result, they tried to revalidate documentary forms by presenting their own work as common plea petitions, documents less obviously connected with instruments of power and more connected with the concerns of the common profit ("London Texts and Literate Practice").

[58] Green, *A Crisis of Truth*, 279–81; and see also his comments in "Medieval Literature and Law," 419. For Green, the very writtenness of documentary practice makes it inherently unliterary. In his view, whereas documentary practice is opposed to traditional values, non-negotiable, and morally suspect, literary texts, like physical tokens, are on the whole nostalgic, socially adaptable, and morally responsible. These distinctions become especially problematic at moments such as the one when Green sympathizes with one medieval claimant who forced his female opponent to eat her charter and seals, which, Green speculates, "she may well have just obtained from the nearby Rolls House" (*A Crisis of Truth*, 144).

differentiate his own counsel poetry from that which has previously been left unsaid. In doing so, moreover, he exchanges the speaking up/keeping mum opposition, which defines "secret" as something unspoken, for the open/closed opposition, which defines "secret" as something physically hidden. Right before he unknits his bag of documents, the narrator mentions that the sothsegger tried for many years to find the salve to heal society, but Mum and his company had stolen the "bagges and many a boxe eeke" (1342). A few lines earlier the narrator converses with a wise beekeeper who urges him to get busy writing, to "make vp thy matiere," and who warns him, let "no feynt herte/abate thy blessid bisynes of thy boke-making...Care thou not though knyghtz copie hit echone" (1280–1, 1286). But when the moment finally arrives at which the narrator is ready to identify his own literary making with the counseling of the king, he describes it as the unpacking of a literal archive, the bags and boxes that refer not to the hasty equipment of thieves but to the real containers in which documents were stored and transported. As we have already seen, this archive is abstracted from the narrator himself – they are not his original compositions; rather, the act of writing has been transmuted into the activity of restoring and unpacking the archives of the realm, what society presents to itself about itself. The "pryue poyse...preyntid withynne" (1344) is made public, not through the poem itself but through the transformation of poem into material archive.

It is the very solidity of these documents, moreover, that recommends a model of counsel poetry indebted as much to chivalric knighthood as to the failures of the parliamentary Commons. In the episode directly preceding the bag of books, the narrator consults with the sothsegger who says that knights of the shire elected to parliament need to "shewe the sores of the royaulme" and "berste out alle the boicches and blaynes of the heart" (1120, 1122). Rather than doing that, though, they allow "sores" to remain "saluelees in many sundry places" (1130), and they end up bringing home to the shires "a bagge ful of boicches vn-y-curid" (1139), that is, a bag of swelling or running sores. It is clear that this language is not simply medical but also chivalric, the idea being that parliamentary counsel becomes a noble endeavor when it links the manifestation of an illness to its miraculous healing. When they keep their counsel to themselves, the knights of the shire become nothing more than messengers who return to their shires with a bag of sores, sores unaddressed and un-dressed because they have been allowed to remain hidden. The narrator later adapts this metaphor to justify his own writing. At lines 1278–9 the beekeeper promises the narrator that his writing may "amende many men of thaire misdeedes," and a few lines later the narrator begins to reflect upon his own writing, how he will begin to redress the sores of society in the very act of diagnosing them: "Thenne softe I the soores to serche thaym withynne/And seurely to salue thaym and with a newe salue" (1338–9). He thus likens his own writing both to the process of "searching" sores, of revealing those things which protrude from the sick body, and to the process of salving those sores in the very act of bringing them to light. He observes, as we just saw above, that the sothsegger has been searching for the salve for years, but Mum and his cohorts have stolen away the bags and boxes (1342). The narrator thereupon counters Mum by opening his bag, which turns out to contain neither a medicinal salve nor the sores themselves but physically tangible documents "in balade-wise made" (1345). Clearly the sothsegger's earlier "bagge ful of boiches" is a metaphor for grievances and for counsel unspoken, but it also anticipates the narrator's bag of books, the portable bags and boxes of poetry with which he will finally counsel the king. In this way, counsel poetry, by announcing itself as obtrusive writing – sores and legal documents – aspires to a chivalric model on the one hand (as if Launcelot were a knight of the shire instead of the Round Table), and to a very materialist notion of social reform on the other. For the *Mum*-poet literary making becomes public healing when encased in legal documents.

We have seen that the *Mum*-poet offers more assertive readings of *Piers Plowman* than Langland could have ever anticipated. In *Piers Plowman* divine documents enable the Truth to be told, but this Truth is derived from revelation rather than counsel, and is not explicitly linked to Langland's written work. Langland portrays the legal document as a spiritually exemplary but secularly inimitable form of writing; in *Mum*, public writing has become a sack of documents hand-delivered by the poet. In the rebel letters and *Mum and the Sothsegger*, the document becomes a vernacular "genre of social action," one continually advertised in *Piers Plowman* but never entirely identified with the dreamer's "retorik," "poyse," or "makyngs." All three poets differ significantly, however, from a writer such as Thomas Hoccleve, who plays with documentary forms (such as in his *Letter of Cupid*), but nonetheless contrasts his poetry to his job at the Privy Seal where he and his fellow clerks "stowpe and stare upon the sheepes skyn" and must keep their "song and wordes in."[59] Langland, Ball, and the *Mum*-poet seem deliberately to elide this distinction between writing as occupation and writing as literature; for these poets bureaucratic and specifically documentary activity became a means of conceptualizing and justifying poetic work.

[59] Text in *Regement of Princes*, ed. Charles Blyth, ll. 1014–15.

PART III
Identity, heterodoxy, and documents

5

Lollard community and the *Charters of Christ*

Sometime in the mid-fourteenth century a strange literary form appeared on the English scene: the fictive legal document, a lyric or prose tract in the form of a charter of feoffment, or last will and testament, often "issued" by a supernatural agent. This literary phenomenon is not entirely surprising, emerging as it did during a period in which justice was increasingly centered on the written record (such as conveyances of property and bonds of debt) and in which the royal bureaucracy and some personal bonds (such as wills and letters of retaining) were verging on vernacularization.[1] But fictive documents can be understood not simply as a prescient moment in the history of the English language, but also as the point of intersection between what Nicholas Watson calls "vernacular theology," and what Bruce Holsinger calls "vernacular legality." They represent the point at which the stuff of documentary culture (charters, seals, coffers) and its agents (grantors, notaries, witnesses) were being translated into the rhetoric and ideologies of popular piety.[2] On the face of it, legal documents don't seem like especially promising candidates for vernacular pious literature, and indeed, medievalists have long regarded documents as sites of Latinate bureaucratic corruption and as instruments of repression and insurrection. Studies by Susan Crane, Steven Justice, and Richard Firth Green, for example, have delineated the contentious political and juridical space that documents occupied in late medieval England, especially in regard to the Peasants' Revolt of

---

[1] For a brief history of the proliferation of documents in medieval England, see the introduction to this book.

[2] Watson, "Censorship and Cultural Change in Late Medieval England: Vernacular Theology, the Oxford Translation Debate, and Arundel's Constitutions of 1409"; Holsinger, "Vernacular Legality: The English Jurisdictions of *The Owl and the Nightingale*."

1381.[3] With these studies in mind, the fictive document might be taken to be an inherently conservative genre, one that reproduces a dominant ideology by means of an opaque textual apparatus or an official language. But, as the *Charters of Christ* literature suggests, documentary culture, when translated into the vernacular, provided an intergeneric framework that might be stretched to accommodate an astonishing variety of spiritual, political, and literary agendas. To this end, fictive documents reveal some important features of Lollard polemic as well. As we will see, late medieval preachers and polemicists used documentary culture both to challenge orthodox notions of textual authority and to construct an oppositional rhetoric. Patently heterodox sermon-writers borrowed the image of Christ's charter to contest the legitimacy of indulgences and letters of fraternity, and to describe what would come to be identified as a Lollard ideal of spiritual community. In short, legal documents came to represent for all sorts of medieval readers and writers the critical relationship between authoritative texts and textual community, what Brian Stock defines as "a group that arises somewhere in the interstices between the imposition of the written word and the articulation of a social organization."[4]

CLAIMING THE CHARTER OF CHRIST

If one poem alone could stand for the traditional pieties of late medieval English literature, it would be the *Long Charter of Christ*, a well-attested and intriguingly versatile Passion lyric appearing around 1350. As we already saw in chapter 2, the *Charters of Christ* lyrics constitute a daring experiment in poetic form, but they have equally fascinating implications for the development of vernacular piety, and it is worth describing them one more time. The *Long Charter* is essentially an apocryphal retelling of Christ's life, as might be found in any number of late medieval cycle plays or didactic poems: Christ as speaker recounts his life (the Incarnation, Temptation, and Last Supper) and concludes with a brief description of post-Crucifixion events (the Resurrection,

---

[3] Crane, "The Writing Lesson of 1381"; Justice, *Writing and Rebellion: England in 1381*; Green, *A Crisis of Truth*.

[4] Stock, *Listening for the Text: On the Uses of the Past*, 150.

the Harrowing of Hell, and the Celebration of the Mass). The poem allegorizes these events as the production of a land-grant: the Incarnation
is the initial "sesyng" or formal occupation of heaven, the Crucifixion
is the bloody inscription of the charter on Christ's body, the Harrowing
of Hell is the renegotiation of the contract, and the Eucharist is the
indentured copy of the charter issued for security and remembrance.
The charter itself, the centerpiece of the poem, grants heavenly bliss
to all readers and listeners in exchange for a "rent" of perfect penance.
The poem survives in at least twenty manuscripts and was continuously
copied until the end of the fifteenth century, usually in lyric collections
and pastoral miscellanies. Its popular appeal was such that, by the end
of the fourteenth century, it had already generated an abridged version
of itself, which modern editors call the *Short Charter* (surviving in at
least twenty-five manuscripts), as well as a prose tract called the "Charter of Heaven" which circulated with a compilation of vernacular pious texts called *Pore Caitif*. Antiquarians labeled the *Charters of Christ*
"curiosities," a term that only underscores what would seem to be their
unforgivable ordinariness.

Sometime after 1400, however, the *Long Charter* was twice revised
and expanded. The two revisers together contributed over four hundred lines to the original, most conspicuously a new introduction. This
chapter takes these revisions as its focus, arguing that they gesture in one
way to the peculiar censorship strategies of the early fifteenth century,
but in a much more striking way to the fierce competition in that period
for the language of vernacular piety. Despite the fact that the *Charters*
originate in mainstream preaching texts and espouse strictly orthodox
doctrine, the image of Christ as a legal document posited a relationship
between author and audience that, by the 1410s and 1420s, served orthodox and heterodox agendas alike. Sermon-writers and polemicists seized
upon the image of Christ's charter to promote radical theories about official texts (indulgences, letters of fraternity, royal charters, the gospels)
and the political and spiritual communities that those texts claim to
represent. As I argue, such controversial appropriations of Christ's charter caused the *Long Charter's* fifteenth-century revisers to re-affiliate
the poem with an unambiguously orthodox polemic. In the process,
they reshaped the textual community that a divine document might
represent.

The fifteenth-century anti-Lollard initiative, spearheaded by the Archbishop of Canterbury Thomas Arundel at the turn of that century, tracked down Lollards primarily by their books and book learning, with the result that most of vernacular literary production was affected in some way by anti-Lollard legislation.[5] Fifteenth-century censorship accordingly took on a number of shapes and guises. The most conspicuous form, external censorship, ranged from the confiscation and burning of heretical books, to the expurgation of offensive material (as in the case of a Lollard sermon cycle discussed by Anne Hudson), to the excision of particular words (as in Huntington Library MS 143, a *Piers Plowman* manuscript in which a scribe systematically erased nearly every occurrence of "Piers" and "Plowman," suggesting, perhaps, some kind of "police-action").[6] External censorship supposes, of course, that forces outside a given text – legislation, critics, errant readers, or unorthodox texts – may call attention to the presence of heterodox material within that text, and, consequently, may identify both the text and its transmitters as disciplinary sites. By contrast, internal or self-censorship supposes a deliberate authorial act to fashion a text that will successfully escape correction, discourage errant readings, or counter heterodoxy. For example, new authors or translators such as Nicholas Love might offer up their work to official scrutiny, or, like Thomas Hoccleve, actively collaborate with the Lancastrian "counter-offensive."[7] But late medieval internal censorship also involved more cunning strategies. A careful writer might conceal seditious material in ambiguous or codified language (such as the author of *Mum and the Sothsegger*), or, like the author of *Jack Upland*, transfer theological conflict to fictionalized interlocutors, unreliable or naïve characters who debate with institutional authorities.

---

[5] See Hudson, "'Laicus Litteratus'"; and McNiven, *Heresy and Politics in the Reign of Henry IV*.

[6] See Hudson, "The Expurgation of a Lollard Sermon-Cycle"; and Bowers, "*Piers Plowman* and the Police." Bowers argues that this excision constitutes a "police-action," although Russell and Kane suggest the possibility that the erasures were done to prepare for the rubricator to replace these words in red ink. See Russell and Kane, *'Piers Plowman': The C-Version*, 15.

[7] In the *Regement of Princes*, for example, Hoccleve goes so far as to define his whole writerly enterprise against the Lollard threat, arguing that good counsel counters heresy and deserves remuneration (Blyth, ed., ll. 281–385).

Naturally, external and internal censorship are artificial categories insofar as they act together to shape a given text – a writer will often modify his work to meet the expertise or taste of a particular readership or the temper of a political climate. As the *Long Charter* makes clear, however, revision might embody a peculiar relation of text to readership, and of what I have been calling internal to external censorship. Namely, the reviser, who serves as both internal and external censor, recognizes the original text to be at once doctrinally ideal and hermeneutically fraught. That is not simply to say that the reviser fears the text will be misread by errant readers, but rather that he or she perceives that the language with which that text is supposed to convey doctrine – and in this case Christ's charter – has become common property. As such, the text elides distinctions not only between orthodox and heterodox doctrine, but, more insidiously, between orthodox and heterodox reading practices. The first four lines of the revised *Long Charter*, for example, pretend to respond to a heterodox threat emanating from outside the text.[8] The original text begins quite conventionally with Christ's voice urging readers and listeners to take note of his suffering:

> Jhesu, kyng of heuene and helle,
> Mon and wommon, I wol þe telle
> What loue I haue i-don to þe;
> Loke what þou hast don to me! (A. 1–4)

The revised texts, by contrast, are introduced by a new speaker, who warns his audience that a certain school will not save them from the devil, and who proposes the *Long Charter* as a preventive to its teachings:

> Wo-so wil ouer-rede this boke
> And with gostly eyen ther-on loke,
> To other scole dare he not wende,
> To saue his soule fro þe fende. (B. 1–4)

If we take its "self-declarations" (Paul Strohm's phrase) at face value, this new introduction suggests that the threat of heresy lies comfortably outside the text; the reviser is merely noting the doctrinal fitness of this

---

[8] The three versions of the *Long Charter* are printed in *The Minor Poems of the Vernon Manuscript*, vol. 2, ed. Furnivall and Horstmann, 637–57 (hereafter cited in the main text by line number).

vernacular religious poem.[9] After all, "scole" might just refer to any unwholesome doctrine or deviant course of study.[10] But if the original *Long Charter* was really such a model of orthodoxy, why did it need this strange new introduction? In their capacity as external censors, the revisers of the *Long Charter* found little material to excise. Their labors consist of several noteworthy deletions but mostly of seemingly unmotivated insertions, which bloat the slender original into a nearly unrecognizable form. They include, for example, a garrulous clerical narrator (a fastidiously orthodox version of the fictionalized interlocutor) and long asides on the sacraments. Nor are these additions gratuitous exercises in *amplificatio*; they seem, rather, to be a coherent program to point readers in the right interpretive direction and divert their attention from heretical misreadings. Why did the poem require such extensive revision throughout, and what obstacles did the original text present?

The subversive implications of the *Long Charter* are hardly obvious. The original *Long Charter* (ca. 1350) contains no overtly suspicious material or evidence of Lollard tampering. It proffers no criticism of possessioners, friars, pardoners, or popes. It acknowledges, if briefly, the necessity of auricular confession ("soþfast schrifte"), and it supports the orthodox position on transubstantiation in the image of the Host as an indentured copy of Christ's charter-body: "On endenture I lafte wiþ þe,/þat euer þou schuldest siker be:/In preostes hondes my flesh and blode,/þat for þe dyede on the Rode" (A. 205–8). Further, the image of Christ's body as a bleeding charter nailed to the cross belongs to an

---

[9] Strohm, "Chaucer's Lollard Joke: History and the Textual Unconscious," 23.

[10] It is by no means certain whether the *Long Charter* reviser is referring here to a doctrine or a school, or whether the doctrine or school is supposed to be Lollard or merely an oppositional group or behavior (e.g., "the devil's school"). That this "scole" might refer to a coherent set of heterodox beliefs or educational program becomes more apparent after working through the revisions. Official statutes and confessions of prosecuted heretics indicate that Lollards did form underground schools in which the vernacular Bible and other texts were discussed in intimate groups. The statute *De heretico comburendo* asserts, for example, that the Lollards "make unlawful coventicles and confederacies, they hold and exercise schools (*scholas*)," and in 1430 Thomas Moon confessed to having "kept, holde, and continued scoles of heresie yn prive chambres and places of myne, yn the which scoles Y have herd, conceyved, lerned and reported the errours and heresies wiche be writen contened in these indentures" (Tanner, ed., *Heresy Trials in the Diocese of Norwich, 1428–31*, 179). See also Anne Hudson's comments on Lollard schools in *The Premature Reformation*, 176–80. For a lucid account of Lollard schools (and pedagogy), see Copeland's introduction to *Pedagogy, Intellectuals, and Dissent in the Later Middle Ages*, 8–19.

iconographic tradition antithetical to Lollard sensibilities. Early Lollards were ambivalent about religious images, regarding them as necessary if faulty teaching aids, but later Lollards were notorious iconoclasts who denounced crucifixes as vain and distracting images.[11] The "Charter of Heaven" from *Pore Caitif* tries to make Christ's charter more vivid to its readers by reminding them of familiar images of the crucifix: "þe printe of þis seel: is þe shap of oure lord ihesu crist hanginge for oure synne on þe cros. as we moun se bi þe ymage of þe crucifix."[12] Notably, several Lollard manuscripts of *Pore Caitif* omit the last part of that sentence, "as we moun se bi þe ymage of þe crucifix," one scribe replacing it with the phrase, "as the gospel þat is our believe techiþ us."[13] In short, the charter of Christ motif belonged to a literary and artistic tradition that Lollards should and did find in extremely bad taste.

The reception of the *Long* and *Short Charters* also suggests that they appealed to squarely orthodox readers who identified them with practices of the established church. Some readers, for example, associated the *Charters* with indulgences and relic worship, practices especially repugnant to committed Lollards. One fifteenth-century reader doctored his *Short Charter* into a pardon granting an indulgence of 26,030 years and 11 days (an odd addendum since the *Charters of Christ* insist on the strictest terms for salvation: true love of God and neighbor). Another *Short Charter* may have been carved on a gravestone in Kent (c. 1400) (Figure 4), a custom usually reserved for indulgences, which were sometimes carved into the tombs of dignitaries. Passersby who prayed for the souls of the dead earned a specified number of days off purgatory.[14] The image of Christ as a crucified charter also reminded readers of illustrations of the *arma christi* and of Christ as the Man of Sorrows. Both these images were used to decorate indulgences and often served

---

[11] Sawtre, the first Lollard martyr, protested the idea of worshipping a dead image of Christ on the cross when he could very well worship the "quicke ymage of God" among the poor and sick (Hudson, *The Premature Reformation*, 304–5). Likewise the *Twelve Conclusions* (1394) decry the homage paid to images of "tre and of ston," especially during the twice-yearly services of the cross in which "þe rode tre, naylis, and þe spere . . . ben so holiche worschipid" (*Twelve Conclusions*, #8, Hudson, ed., *Selections from English Wycliffite Writings*, 27, ll. 105–7).

[12] Text in Spalding, ed., *The Middle English Charters of Christ*, 102.

[13] In BL Harley 2322. For more information on the manuscript tradition of this text, see Brady, "Lollard Interpolation and Omissions in Manuscripts of the *Pore Caitif*."

[14] Orme, "Indulgences in the Diocese of Exeter 1100–1536," 21.

as substitutes for relic-worship.[15] The fifteenth-century illustrator of British Library MS Additional 37049, for instance, depicts the charter of Christ as a juxtaposition of the Man of Sorrows and the *arma christi* (Figure 8). In this graphic illustration, Christ gazes down sorrowfully at his mid-section, which has been expanded into an unfurled parchment nailed to the cross. On the parchment are written the verses of the *Short Charter*, floating around the cross are the instruments of Christ's torture, and affixed to the stem of the cross is a pierced and bleeding heart which does double duty as the charter's seal.

For many medieval readers, then, Christ's charter resembled a number of ostentatious pardons already in circulation, textual relics which could be displayed and adored. It would surely follow that the multiple connections among the *Charters*, indulgences, and relic-worship would repulse Lollard preachers, who notoriously campaigned against relic-worship and who denounced pardons as the insidious workings of the Roman Antichrist.[16] More to the point, the "mainstream" reception of the *Charters* should suggest that the *Long Charter* revisers attached an anti-Lollard introduction in order to advertise the poem's orthodoxy. In fact, as will become clearer below, both the new introduction and other revisions show that the poem required serious rehabilitation to serve that purpose. One readership may have treated Christ's charter as an exaggerated pardon, but another, clearly heterodox, readership could just as well recruit it *against* indulgences and letters of fraternity. The problem with the *Long Charter*, then, concerned not so much the doctrine it espoused as its potential for interpretative and rhetorical transformations. And as we shall see, the indeterminacy of Christ's charter was produced not so much by the extended metaphor of Christ as charter but by the radical relationship among reader, text, and author that such a metaphor might imply. As a result, Lollard writers ably adapted Christ's charter to heterodox notions of textual authority and spiritual community. By doing so, they challenged institutional beliefs and practices, but they also challenged the literary affiliations of vernacular piety.

---

[15] See Lewis, "Rewarding Devotion: Indulgences and the Promotion of Images"; see also the illustrated York indulgence recorded in Simmons and Nolloth, ed., *The Lay Folks' Catechism*, 159, n. B. 13.

[16] See, for example, the confessions of John Skylly and Robert Cavell in Tanner, ed., *Heresy Trials in the Diocese of Norwich*, 53, 58, 95.

INDULGENCES, CHARTERS, AND THE TEMPER OF
VERNACULAR PIETY

Lollard writers were notoriously hostile to legal documents, particularly to indulgences and letters of fraternity, but also to preaching commissions, certifications, and trial depositions, all of which would bring no end of grief to Lollards on trial. Their hostility stemmed simultaneously from their positions on ecclesiology and their lived experience with the law. Consequently, to understand how Lollards could have transformed Christ's charter into an "anti-pardon" and a symbol of Lollard textual community it is necessary to keep in mind the range of objections to indulgences and to other documents of the institutional church. One of the most common objections to pardons and to letters of fraternity was that they were simoniacal and hence uncharitable: by selling spiritual benefits for material gain, the clergy excluded the poor and meritorious. The Lollard speaker in *Jack Upland*, for example, incensed that Friar Daw withholds letters of fraternity from poor men, facetiously suggests that friars demand the same letters from poor men that rich men demand from the friars: "Frere, whi axe ye not lettris of brithered of other pore mennes preieris, good and Christen levers...as ye desire that other riche men axen you letteris for a certayne summe bi yeer?"[17] Indulgences were also considered uncharitable because they were doled out without respect for the common profit. The pope, who claims to be the "tresorer of holi chirche," is really a "tresourer most banisschid out of charite," both because he exchanges pardon for money and because he does so "at his owne wil."[18] An early Lollard writer likewise explains that "þese pardouns bene not grauntid generally for fulfillyng of Goddis hestis and werkis of mercy to most nedy men, as Crist biddis, but for syngulere cause and syngulere place."[19] According to the *Sixteen Points* of Lollard belief, popes and bishops may issue pardons as long as they do so according to scripture, to release those who have entered into foolish bonds or forgive those who have personally trespassed against them.[20] But pardons that release the sinner from divine punishment in return

---

[17] *Jack Upland, Six Ecclesiastical Satires*, ed. Dean, 125, ll. 151–3.
[18] *Twelve Conclusions*, #9, Hudson, ed., *Selections from English Wycliffite Writings*, 27, line 131.
[19] "*Octo in quibus seducuntur simplices christiani*," Arnold, ed., *Select English Works of John Wyclif* 3: 460.
[20] *Sixteen Points*, Hudson, ed., *Selections from English Wycliffite Writings*, 21–2, ll. 105–18.

for money or service are damning both because they exchange spiritual for material goods – an oft-repeated Lollard objection – and because the grantor assumes an exclusive power belonging to Christ alone.[21] Finally, indulgences and letters of fraternity were criticized as newfangled documents lacking confirmation in scripture and authorized by sinful men who, according to one Lollard preacher, deceive the common people with "here nouelerie of massis... & newe pardons & pilgrimages."[22]

These objections to ecclesiastical documents were derived from two basic tenets of early Wycliffism. The first concerns the predestined community of the faithful, a notion of spiritual brotherhood that necessarily undermines the works of the established church, the prayers of religious associations, and the intercession of the saints. According to this tenet, indulgences and letters of fraternity, which draw from the works of others and are authorized by the clergy, are at best ineffectual and at worst deceptive because they pretend to influence or even override divine judgment.[23] Additionally, these documents, when exchanged for money, create privatized, worldly communities of the rich, as opposed to the "open" and inclusive spiritual community of the meritorious. The second tenet concerns the authority and antiquity of scripture. As one early Wycliffite writer argued, the authority of scripture (meaning the gospels and Pauline Epistles) is based on its antiquity, and therefore other

[21] This last reason points to a more theologically significant objection to spiritual letters, namely, that they are not only uncharitable and singular, but also superfluous and distracting. They purport to draw from the merits of saints or of the fraternal orders, which have no bearing on the salvation of the individual Christian. As one sermon-writer comments about fraternal letters, "ʒif men schewen þanne þese lettres oþur to God or his lawe, þei profiʒte nothing to hem, ne defenden hem aʒen God. And so þese lettres ben superflew, as ben þese ordres þat maken hem" (*English Wycliffite Sermons*, vol. 1, ed. Hudson and Gradon, 329).

[22] Matthew, ed., *The English Works of John Wyclif*, 102.

[23] Technically, of course, indulgences were only intended to reduce purgatorial punishment, but predestinarianism has little room for purgatory, and indulgences were often misunderstood by Lollards and others to release sinners from both *poena* and *culpa*. There were, however, notorious cases of extravagant pardons issued *a poena et a culpa* in the fourteenth century. One Lollard sermon-writer rails against a particular papal pardon that offered release from "peyne and blame" and granted 2000 years off from purgatory – probably the plenary indulgence issued by Boniface VIII at the request of Philip IV (Hudson and Gradon, eds., *English Wycliffite Sermons*, vol. 4, 49). Another sermon-writer complains that "hyt were ydel to traueylon for any pardoun, siþ a man myʒte at home geton hym fowrty thowsande ʒeer by noon!" (Hudson and Gradon, eds., *English Wycliffite Sermons*, vol. 1, 436).

more recent scriptures, commentaries, and man-made documents are inherently false.[24] Consequently, indulgences, charters, and all "new" texts should be upheld only if they are supported by the gospels. According to a debate recorded in the *Fasciculi zizaniorum* by one of Wyclif's opponents, Wyclif argued that even if the Magna Carta itself promises to maintain the temporalities of the Church, this ordinance can be interpreted properly only in light of the gospels, which advocate clerical poverty.[25] Together, the two Wycliffite tenets, the predestined community and the primacy of scripture, posit an inclusive spiritual community constituted by Christ at the originary moment on the cross and authorized by scripture alone.

Contempt for ecclesiastical documents generated a wealth of anti-materialist rhetoric ridiculing their worthlessness and frailty. One Lollard writer, infuriated by the sale of pardons, objected that they are made up of a "litel leed not weiynge a pound, hengid with an hempryn thrid at a litil gobet of a calfskyn, peyntid with a fewe blake draugtis of enke."[26] Yet if some Lollards vilified the written record in order to discredit indulgences and emphasize the authority of scripture, others seized on Christ's charter to point up the weaknesses of indulgences and to describe heterodox ideas of spiritual and political community. Christ's charter appealed to orthodox and heterodox readers alike because it had come to signify a public and open letter available to all Christians, and a foundational grant coequal with Christ's crucified body and with scripture. I argued in chapters 2 and 4 that charters and patents were used to represent the Word because they were perceived to be inherently public texts directly addressed to a universal audience of readers and listeners. As I suggested in chapter 2, in my discussion of the lyric, fourteenth-century writers also imagined certain kinds of legal documents to be transhistorical and performative: they seemed to transmit the voice of their authors to future generations and continually put into effect his or her wishes. We can see this desire for documentary accessibility and

---

[24] Matthew, ed., *The English Works of John Wyclif*, 287.

[25] This is John Kenningham reporting Wyclif in his own determination. See *Fasciculi zizaniorum*, 4–5, 18–19.

[26] Quoted in Hudson, *The Premature Reformation*, 300. This kind of anti-materialist rhetoric is rarely about literacy for its own sake, but rather about anti-authority sentiment in the guise of anti-literacy. See Clanchy on the dispute between St. Anselm of Canterbury and Henry I (*From Memory to Written Record*, 261–2).

agency in conventional Latin formulas, as in the typical land-grant salutation: *Sciant presentes et futuri quod ego, Johannes... dedi et concessi et hac presenti carta mea confirmaui* (Let all those present and future know that I, John... have given and granted and with this present charter confirmed), but even more so in their devotional transformations, as in the salutation to the *Charter of the Abbey of the Holy Ghost*: "*Sciant presentes & futuri &c.* Wetiþ ye þat ben now here, & þei þat schulen comen after you, þat almighti god in trinite, fader & sone & holy gost, haþ gouen & graunted & wiþ his owne word confermed... etc."[27] Within the context of vernacular piety, then, legal documents came to signify the original, continuous, and public proclamation of crucial spiritual legislation (i.e., the contract of the Redemption). But whereas for mid fourteenth-century lyricists and exegetes Christ's charter was largely a penitential strategy of making Christ's Word and Passion immediate and relevant, for later writers with Lollard sympathies, it came to represent a relationship between text and community diametrically opposed to that represented by ecclesiastical letters. If ecclesiastical letters constituted private and privileged communities organized by the pope and ecclesiastical orders, Christ's charter might serve as the foundational text for a spiritual brotherhood inclusive of all (saved) Christians, unmediated by institutional authorities and texts, and authorized by the crucifixion and the gospels.

We see this kind of drastic re-contextualization of Christ's charter, for example, in an interpolation of *The Lay Folks' Catechism*, in which Christ's heavenly grant is opposed to indulgences and equated with the gospels.[28] What we take to be a copy of the original vernacular text, written down in Archbishop Thoresby's register in 1357 and attributed to the archbishop's reforming efforts, was intended for the sacerdotal instruction of the laity and includes a lengthy exposition on the Ten

---

[27] Text in Horstmann, ed., *Yorkshire Writers: Richard Rolle of Hampole and His Followers*, 338–40.

[28] In Lambeth Palace Library MS 408 and Bodleian Library Douce 274. For a discussion of the manuscript tradition of *The Lay Folks' Catechism* and its interpolations, see Hudson, "A New Look at *The Lay Folks' Catechism*." As Hudson shows, the Lollard-sympathetic views of the Lambeth interpolator are often riddled with contradictions (for example, he does not omit Thoresby's injunction that any lay person who learns their catechism will enjoy an indulgence of forty days), and, moreover, no interpolated manuscript of the wildly variant *Lay Folks' Catechism* corpus is the same.

Commandments. But whereas Thoresby's copy merely extols the virtues of the Ten Commandments, the Lollard-sympathetic interpolator finds an occasion to denounce pardons, temporalities, and liturgical works. If you break the Ten Commandments and do not amend, he says, you will be "dampnyd in helle in body and sowle withouten ende," despite your impressive collection of a "þowsand bullys of pardoun lettris of fraternite and Chauntres."[29] Conversely, if you obey the Ten Commandments, you will enjoy perpetual bliss in heaven, whether or not you have ever purchased a pardon. In short, concludes the interpolator, pardons and fraternal letters have no legal bearing on salvation. Heaven is a grant issued in the gospels and authorized by Christ's crucified body: "þe erytage of heuyn ys þyn be graunt of cristys gospel. aselyd with his precious blod þat may neuer be fals: for no creature in erthe ne in heuyn."[30]

It is certainly not necessary to insist on the Lollard affiliations of this interpolator to see that his statements about ecclesiastical documents might be controversial. Granted, his diatribe against indulgences is not so different from that of the dreamer in *Piers Plowman* who, after seeing Piers tear the Pardon, complains that, despite his own grudging belief in the power of indulgences, he is amazed that rich men use them as an excuse to break the Ten Commandments ("but dowel [þee] helpe/I sette youre patentes and youre pardon at one pies hele!" [7.199–200]).[31] Significantly, however, the *Lay Folks' Catechism* interpolator has creatively re-imagined documentary culture to express clearly heterodox positions, and has borrowed from the *Charters of Christ* literature in order to do so. Like the *Lay Folks' Catechism*, the *Carta Dei* also imagines Christ's charter to be sealed with his own blood: "To this charte trewe and good/I have set my seal, myn herthe blood."[32] And where the *Lay Folks' Catechism* insists that Christ's charter is legally incontestable and physically indestructible because it is sealed with his own blood (it "may neuer be fals: for no creature in erthe ne in heuyn"), so the "Charter of Heaven" confirms that Christ's charter is imperishable because it is inscribed upon Christ's body: "þis chartre may not fiyr brenne ne watir

---

[29] Simmons and Nolloth, ed., *The Lay Folks' Catechism*, 57, ll. 879–83.
[30] Ibid., 57, ll. 888–91.
[31] *'Piers Plowman': The B-Version*, ed. Kane and Donaldson (hereafter cited in the main text by line number).
[32] Spalding, ed., *Middle English Charters*, 98, ll. 27–8.

drenche: neiþir þeef robbe neiþir ony creature distroie ... þis scripture is
oure lord Ihesu crist: chartre & bulle of oure eritage of heuene," and a few
lines later, "alle þe creatures in heuene neiþir in erþe neiþir in helle moun
not robbe it neiþir bireue it fro þe."[33] As in the *Charters of Christ*, then,
the *Lay Folks' Catechism* interpolator argues for the primacy of scripture
by identifying a divine charter with Christ's crucified body, but notably
by doing so he has also adapted the materialist rhetoric of Christ's charter
to articulate what would become distinctly Lollard concerns.

A second, more explicitly Lollard sermon also evokes Christ's charter
to discredit other spiritual letters and to posit a predestined community
of believers. In this sermon for Quinquagesima Sunday, compiled in
an early fifteenth-century manuscript with the "Charter of Heaven"
(Bodleian Library, Rawlinson MS C. 751), the sermon-writer has
provocatively sandwiched a description of Christ's charter between con-
demnations of letters of fraternity and indulgences.[34] He admonishes
those who think that, by becoming lay brothers of a fraternal order "bi
lettre and bi seel," they will partake of the good deeds performed by
the brothers. Rather, they should believe that those who will be saved
are free partners of all good deeds performed from prelapsarian Eden
to the day of judgment through the mercy of God and according to
their deserts. They should steadfastly believe, moreover, in a universal
brotherhood of the predestined constituted by Christ's charter, rather
than in the elitist brotherhoods founded by profane letters:

> Alle we beþ breþeren of oo Fadir in heuene, and breþeren to oure Lord
> Jesus Crist, and into his broþerhede we beþ receyued bi þe worshipeful
> chartre of þe hooli Trinyte: Fadir, and Sone, and Hooli Goost. The
> chartre of þis breþerhede is þe blessid bodi þat hynge on a cros; writen
> wiþ þe worþi blood þat ran doun fro his herte, seelid wiþ þe precyous
> sacramente of þe auter in perpetuel mynde þerof. And þis blesside
> bretherhede schal abiden foreuere in blisse (whanne alle false faitouris
> schullen fare) wiþ hire Fadir.[35]

The sermon-writer proceeds in the same vein to denounce another deceptive document, the "bulle purchasid of a fals pardener," which further

[33] Ibid., 102.
[34] For a description of this manuscript, see Jeremy Griffith's introduction to Cigman, ed.,
Lollard Sermons, xxiv–xxv.
[35] Ibid., 113, ll. 266–84.

distracts the sinner from the true righteousness and severity of God. As in the case of the interpolated *Lay Folks' Catechism*, this passage links Christ's body on the cross to a divine charter and, by doing so, quite deliberately evokes the *Charters of Christ* tradition. As in the passage from the *Lay Folks' Catechism*, moreover, this one borrows Christ's charter to formulate a spiritual fellowship authorized by scripture and by the liberating terms of the Passion. Conversely, it uses Christ's charter to prove that the documents of the institutional church – pardons and letters of fraternity – represent new practices and exclusive communities lacking proper authorization. Finally, this passage reveals once again how heterodox concerns may sharpen even specific literary borrowings into pointed polemic. As in the *Charters of Christ* literature, here Christ's charter is written with his own blood, but uniquely its seal is the Eucharist ("seelid wiþ þe precyous sacramente of þe auter"), which is described as a reminder ("in perpetual mynde therof"), rather than an extension or re-enactment of Christ's body on the cross. By contrast, the author of the *Long Charter* describes the Eucharist as an indentured copy – a duplicate and binding copy of Christ's charter-body – continually issued to priests at their altars: "On endenture I lafte wiþ þe,/þat euer þou schuldest siker be:/In preostes hondes my flesh and blode,/þat for þe dyede on the Rode" (A. 205–8).

In short, both the *Lay Folks' Catechism* and the sermon for Quinquagesima Sunday suggest that heterodox writers were critical readers of the *Charter of Christ* literature and deliberately adapted it to polemical ends. We may speculate, too, that the "Charter of Heaven" served as a kind of "bridge" text, relaying the rhetoric of Christ's charter to heterodox readers. This tract was the most frequently copied of the fourteen texts in *Pore Caitif*: it survives in forty-seven out of fifty-six manuscripts containing the full text or extracts from *Pore Caitif*, and it was circulated independently of the rest of its compilation in five manuscripts, all of which, interestingly enough, contain the "variant" version of the text. Also, several non-interpolated versions of the "Charter of Heaven" were published in fourteenth and fifteenth-century manuscripts with a fervent "Lollard-style" treatise, further attesting to a heterodox readership.[36] At least one medieval reader, moreover, directly identified this text with a

---

[36] For example, Bodleian Library Rawlinson C. 209, and Bodleian Library Douce 13. Some Lollard concerns of this treatise include the integrity of the "felawschip of perfite men,"

Lollard program. The "Charter of Heaven" warns that Christ's charter is too precious to be locked in a chest; rather it should be inscribed on the hearts of those who hope to receive their heavenly inheritance: "þis scripture is oure lord Ihesu crist: chartre & bulle of oure eritage of heuene! locke not þis chartre in þi coffre: but sette it eiþir write it in þin herte."[37] In the margin of one non-interpolated "Charter of Heaven" a fifteenth-century reader wrote the words "letters of fraternite" next to the line, "locke not þis chartre in þi coffre," implying that the kind of charters that *are* locked away in chests are the fraternal letters decried in the sermons just discussed.[38]

This marginal gloss in the "Charter of Heaven" manuscript further shows how Christ's charter might link a Lollard anti-ecclesiological program to a radical and even insurrectionary politics. Wycliffite arguments for the antiquity of scripture were deeply implicated in the question of clerical endowments, and they tended therefore to lump together royal charters and ecclesiastical donations (for example, the Donation of Constantine), both of which were considered to be recent texts with insufficient authority to administrate divine affairs. Concerning the related question of civil dominion, however, royal charters trumped ecclesiastical instruments because they, like scripture, possessed a plenitude of power within their *proper sphere*: the dissemination of secular authority over goods and persons.[39] So whereas Wycliffite writers might technically have been interested in separating "sacred origin from

the imitation of the first church, the ability of each man to determine the moral character of his own works, the necessity of "trewe compuncioun of herte," and the conspicuous absence of the clergy or of oral confession (Douce 13, fols. 7v–14r).

[37] Spalding, ed., *Middle English Charters*, 101.

[38] In CUL Ff. 6.34, fol. 74r. The same reader may have had Lollard sympathies generally. Most of his *notae*, consisting of "be war" and "tak good heede," mark passages on the evils of swearing, a favorite Lollard issue.

[39] According to the account in the *Fasciculus zizanorum*, Wyclif supposedly argued against charters in order to make a case for the antiquity of Scripture, but upon closer examination of the debate, it becomes clear that his opponent was putting words into his mouth. Kenningham would like to have pretended that Wyclif, who was arguing against the authenticity of the Donation of Constantine, was equating written instrument ("genus") with mode of authority: "scripturae recentissimae sunt falsissimae et exemplificavit de cartis donationum et instrumentis notariorum: quantum ad huiusmodi instrumenta relinquens legistis discussionem objeci quod genus cartulorum non est recens, sed valde antiquum" (18). He argues, against Wyclif's supposed position regarding charters, that charters are in fact as old as scripture. He cites God's perpetual feoffment of Abraham, to which Wyclif easily responds that the issue is not charters themselves but the nature

historical beginning" in order to support the idea of *scriptura sola*, the *Charters of Christ* offered a language with which one might be mapped very suggestively onto the other.[40] More specifically, Christ's charter, collapsing as it did the rhetorical opposition between divine scripture and royal charter, showed how inclusiveness and accessibility might be foundational principles. It showed how the exclusionary acquisitiveness of ecclesiastical donations (the Donation of Constantine, but also fraternal letters and indulgences) might be equated with the desire to compromise royal dominion, and to intervene treacherously in the relationship between king and realm.

To return then to the glossed passage from the "Charter of Heaven" ("locke not þis chartre in þi coffre"), we see at first glance that it posits the superiority of open to closed forms of spirituality, and of the spiritual to the material. Christ's charter is no pricey object to be stowed in a chest (as charters were, of course) but is, rather, a message of salvation at once personally relevant and publicly inscribed. Yet, at second glance, we see that its language of archives and locks recalls much more radical political texts such as the 1381 broadsides, one of which famously warns that "Trewþe" is "under a lokke," suggesting a peculiar equation of legitimated greed and political interposition on the part of those whose job it is to disseminate justice. In a different context, Nicholas Watson argues that the line, "locke not þis chartre in þi coffre," points to the inclusiveness of "vernacular" spirituality. He argues more problematically, however, that it is antithetical to the actions of 1381: "The images of charter and coffer, both connected with the secular world of wealth, are used not to exclude all but the privileged from ownership – in the rebellion of 1381 it was this identification of the charter with privilege which led to systematic burning of charters – but to confer the status of freeman on all."[41] Granted, some rebels were bent on destroying

and extent of the power behind them: if only St. Peter had possessed God's plenitude of power he might have been able to will temporal dominion to the representatives of the established Church (19).

[40] See D. Vance Smith's discussion of charters and beginnings in *The Book of the Incipit*, 141–8. Smith argues that Mede's charter, when viewed in light of Lollard objections to indulgences, suggests a nostalgia for earlier documents, that a "prior ordinance" has a stronger claim to authority that a "recent depositing."

[41] Watson, "Conceptions of the Word: The Mother Tongue and the Incarnation of God," 109.

the middlemen of the judicial system and their written instruments, but the chroniclers were impressed more by the rebels' demands that ancient charters be liberated from monastic archives, or royal confirmations of privileges be issued from the long-obsolete Domesday Book, or that a new charter of manumission be issued by King Richard himself, than they were by acts of destruction. Indeed, even when the Abbot of St. Alban's offered the rebels a new charter of privileges they continued to agitate for King Offa's eighth-century "original."[42]

The rebels claimed that these liberated documents would reveal the truth about their privileges, and in doing so, restore a commonwealth in which service was owed directly to the king, and in which the king was the sole and unmediated dispenser of justice.[43] What the marginal note ("lettres of fraternite") from the "Charter of Heaven" manuscript suggests, then, is that the rebels' nostalgia for authentic royal documents anticipates in many ways the Lollard "free" brotherhood founded by Christ's charter and opposed to ecclesiastical letters, which withhold spiritual and economic profit from the meritorious poor. This is not to imply that Lollard writers, by appropriating Christ's charter, were advocating revolt.[44] It is to say, rather, that the radical political implications of Christ's charter are brought into focus by Lollard adaptations and annotations; they are importantly not antithetical. When taken to its logical extreme, Christ's charter represents theories of textual authority and of political and spiritual organization that informed Lollard and rebel ideologies alike.

The capacity of a divine charter to convey radical politics in terms of ecclesiological ideals, to arbitrate between theories of clerical wealth and royal dominion, can be seen especially well in an early Wycliffite tract, "The Grete Sentence of Curs Expouned" (dated by Arnold to ca. 1383). This tract invokes Christ's charter to accuse the orthodox clergy of treason and to demonstrate royal sovereignty over the temporal possessions of the Church. We have already seen that Lollards condemned pardons and fraternal letters as "singular," selfish, or self-ruled acts. "The

---

[42] Walsingham, *Gesta abbatam monasterii Sancti Albans*, ed. Riley, 308, 317–22.

[43] See Hilton, *Bondmen Made Free*, 229.

[44] Medieval chroniclers easily lumped together "Lollards, traitors, and rebels," but modern scholars have discredited any collusion between Wyclif's early followers and the 1381 leaders. See, for example, Aston, "Lollardy and Sedition."

Grete Sentence" turns singularity into sedition by creating an analogy between Christ's charter (the gospels) and the king's charter (Magna Carta). It begins by arguing that worldly clerks, "bi fals prechynge... bi sikernesse of letteris of fraternyte and synguler preieris," teach all men to be "rebel aȝenis þe kyng and lordis" and to destroy the "pees of þe kyng and his rewme."[45] It then compares the king's charter to the gospels and contrasts both to the "singular" and unauthorized claims of canon law. According to the Magna Carta, the king donates temporal goods to the Church as alms, but some clerks deceive the king and malign his charter by styling themselves as sovereign lords. They are subsequently cursed every time the Magna Carta is publicly proclaimed: "alle þe þat falsen þe kyngis chartre and assented þerto ben cursed solempnely of God and man, puppliched foure tymes in þe ȝeer" (306). By analogy, they are even more cursed by "þe *chartre of alle kyngis, þat is holy writt*," in which God commands all priests to live "in honest poverte and forsake seculer lordischip... as crist and his apostlis diden" (306, emphasis mine). By impugning the Magna Carta, in other words, the clergy necessarily impugn Christ's charter as well; the two documents together attest to royal sovereignty, but also to the primacy and generosity of royal documents, as contrasted with the treasonous, newfangled, and self-interested texts of the institutional church. In light of the analogy drawn between Christ's charter and the king's charter, it is noteworthy that the *Charters of Christ* scribes often gave them titles that deliberately evoked the Magna Carta, such as *magna carta saluatoris* and *magna carta libertationis et remissionis*.[46]

LANGLAND AS CENSOR?

So far I have been concerned to show the place of documentary rhetoric within vernacular literatures of piety, and particularly the ways that heterodox authors re-contextualize Christ's charter in order to refute orthodox notions of textual authority and spiritual community. In a moment we will discover the logic of the *Long Charter* revisions with

---

[45] Arnold, ed., *Select English Works*, 298 (hereafter cited in the main text by page number).

[46] In Middle English texts "Magna Carta" or "gret chartre" nearly always refers to the baronial document, usually in contradistinction to the Charter of the Forest (*Middle English Dictionary*, s. v. "chartre").

which this chapter began. First, however, I would like to suggest that those revisions very much resemble some of the changes that took place between the B-text and C-text of *Piers Plowman*. Early Protestant reformers, instrumental in rescuing *Piers Plowman* from literary oblivion, made much of what they took to be its proto-protestant sympathies. Modern scholars of Lollardy have also remarked upon the numerous correspondences between Lollard concerns and their expression in *Piers Plowman*, and they have put forward plenty of literary and codicological evidence to suggest that Lollards owned and read Langland's poem.[47] Of course Langland himself, writing the B-text in the late 1370s, could not have foreseen the impact of Wycliffism and the tremendous reaction that it triggered. As David Lawton has so influentially commented, Langland did not have Lollard sympathies; "the Lollards had Langlandian sympathies."[48] By the time Langland was writing the C-text, however, Wycliffite ideas were clearly gaining currency, and the revisions to documentary references in C give us some insight into the ways that Langland functioned as both internal and external censor of his own work.

In the case of Christ's charter, Langland anticipates the Lollard opposition between indulgences and an original divine pardon, an opposition that effectively undermines the authority of ecclesiastical letters. If his version of this opposition is functionally ambiguous, it nevertheless makes connections that, in a slightly later period, would be considered heretical and seditious. We have already seen in chapter 3 that Truth's Pardon, like other fictive charters, evokes but deliberately exceeds contemporary indulgences, both in the sense that it represents the absolute pardon of the Atonement, and in the sense that it reveals the indulgence to be an incomplete descriptor of divine legislation. The Pardon offers *venia*, the pardon for original sin, and a concomitant system of works by which one may attain heaven, but it only conditionally promises *indulgentia*, the final pardon and the eschatological separation of the *boni* and *mali*. In this way, Langland makes the very indeterminacy of a divine document central to the Pardon episode. After Piers tears the

---

[47] For correspondences between Lollardy and *Piers Plowman*, see Gradon, "Langland and the Ideology of Dissent"; von Nolken, "*Piers Plowman*, the Wycliffites, and *Pierce the Plowman's Creed*"; Scase, *Piers Plowman and the New Anticlericalism*, 120–60; and Bowers, "*Piers Plowman* and the Police."

[48] Lawton, "Lollardy and the *Piers Plowman* Tradition," 793.

Pardon at the end of B. 7, the dreamer ruminates on Piers's response and concludes that it shows the insufficiency of papal and ecclesiastical pardons to guarantee salvation. Nor can other spiritual works, such as prayers and masses for the dead, ever measure up to the kind of Dowel described by the Pardon:

> Al þis makeþ me on metels to þynke,
> And how þe preest preued no pardon to dowel
> And demed þat dowel Indulgences passe[þ],
> Biennals and triennals and Bisshopes lettres.
> Dowel at þe day of dome is digneliche vnderfongen;
> [He] passeþ al þe pardon of Seint Petres cherche. (7. 173–8)

Will then nervously retracts his bold criticism, conceding that the pope has the power to pardon temporal penance ("And so I leue leelly, lor[d] forb[e]de ellis" [182]), but he takes it up once more at the end of the passus ("A pokeful of pardon þere, ne prouincial lettres,/Thei3 [þow] be founde in þe fraternite [among] þe foure ordres/And haue Indulgences doublefold, but dowel [þee] helpe/I sette youre patentes and youre pardon at one pies hele" [197–200]). Although the dreamer's indignant tone sounds authorial, his criticism of pardons is not especially dependable. Truth's Pardon is meant to shake the sinner out of sloth with the uncompromising severity of the Creed, but Will narrowly misreads it as a satire of ignorant preachers, indulgences, and other practices often grouped together in Lollard polemic. Whereas Piers immediately accepts the responsibility to do well as enjoined by the Pardon ("of preieres and of penaunce my plou3 shal ben herafter" [124]), the priest's misrecognition helping Piers to redefine the relationship between pardon and contract, Will foists blame on those ecclesiastical establishments whose spiritual works fail to measure up to the efficacy of Dowel. Yet despite Will's unreliability, his "strong reading" of Truth's Pardon is nonetheless powerful and resounds throughout the poem. Notably, too, his contrast between indulgences and Dowel, and his implicit association of Truth's Pardon with the Ten Commandments a few lines later ("Forþi I rede yow renkes þat riche ben on erþe... Be [þow] neuer þe bolder to breke þe x hestes," etc. [187, 189]), are reiterated, if much more explicitly, in the passage from the *Lay Folks' Catechism* discussed above ("And also sekyr as god ys god. 3if þou kepe wel þese comaundementis þou schalt haue þe blysse of heuyn in body and sowle with-owten ende. þow þou haue neuer bulle of pardoun. ne letter of fraternite. Ne Chauntre aftyr þy deþ").[49] Like Will, too, another early Lollard writer contrasts indulgences with the Creed, objecting that the former distracts people from the latter and thus from heaven: "Also þese indulgencis maken men for to bileve not to þeir crede... Ffor God gyves none indulgencis from everlastyng peyne, no but til hym þat fynaly endis in charite" (Arnold, 459–60). Langland did little to minimize this contrast in C, possibly because Will's retraction was itself sufficient apology, or because the elimination of the tearing of the Pardon in C was enough to defuse the contentiousness of the scene.

Although Langland didn't revise this passage in any meaningful way, he was clearly aware of the difficulties of using the image of a divine document in the first place. He does make serious changes to B. 13 and 14, in which Hawkyn, Will's alter ego, questions the efficacy of indulgences and is never directly contradicted. Hawkyn belittles the pope's "gift" as "a pardon wiþ a peis of leed and two polles amyddes" (13. 246), referring to the pope's leaden seal or bull which was stamped with the heads of Saints Peter and Paul. Hawkyn's strategy here is to undermine indulgences by reducing them to their material components, the same strategy that Lollard writers would use in anti-pardon polemic. Hawkyn further quips that if the pope really had curative powers he would rid society of plague sores ("bocches"):

> Hadde ich a clerc þat couþe write I wolde caste hym a bille
> That he sente me vnder his seel a salue for þe pestilence,
> And þat his blessynge and hise bulles bocches myȝte destruye.
>
> (247–9)

If anything, Hawkyn's criticism of indulgences here is more powerful than Will's. His has the added punch of stereotypically lay and anti-literate disobedience (where it means to be comic it is also seditious), whereas Will's criticism is intellectually conflicted and subordinated to an academic discussion of the authority of dream-visions. Like Will, however, Hawkyn's spiritual bankruptcy seriously undermines his criticism of indulgences. Hawkyn is particularly susceptible to the sin of

---

[49] Simmons and Nolloth, ed., *Lay Folks' Catechism*, 57, ll. 882–7.

pride, revealed most tellingly in his refusal to submit to the correction of the church. Will observes him to be "singuler," an "ordre by hymselue/Religion saunȝ rule [and] resonable obedience" (13. 284–5), a charge of which Will himself is also accused. Like Will, too, Hawkyn is quick to blame church authorities for the problems of his society instead of examining his own conscience. Natural disasters are often linked to sin in *Piers Plowman*; Reason proves in his sermon, for example, that "þise pestilences were for pure synne,/And þe Southwestrene wynd on Saterday at euen/Was pertliche for pride and for no point ellis" (5. 13–15). Hawkyn's suggestion that the pope use pardons to combat the plague further attests to his prideful disobedience as well as to his sullen literalness; he refuses either to assume responsibility for his own sins or to acknowledge that the healing of the world depends not just on the pope's "pot with the salue," but on the reformation of the individual soul. To a certain extent, Hawkyn, by criticizing papal pardons, only reveals his chronic disobedience and should by no means be trusted.

Just as Will does in the Pardon episode, Hawkyn briefly and unconvincingly retracts his criticism of papal pardons, acknowledging that the pope cannot heal Christian society until the people reform (13. 256–60). Yet, just like Will's subversive musings, Hawkyn's vicious denunciation of pardons lingers on in B, checked by nothing except his own half-hearted retraction. Moreover, when Patience urges Hawkyn to confess and not despair, he draws on the image of Christ's original pardon manufactured on the cross, rather than drawing on the gifts of the institutional church, which Hawkyn has already rejected. This "acquitaunce," already discussed at length in chapters 3 and 4, protects all penitent sinners from the devil (the "pouke"), who would plead against them in the heavenly court: "A[c] if þe [pouke] wolde plede herayein, and punysshe vs in conscience,/[We] shoolde take þe Acquitaunce as quyk and to þe queed shewen it:/ *Pateat, &c: Per passionem Domini* (Let it be manifest, etc: Through the passion of the Lord)" (14. 189–90a). The poem generally supports institutional works, but in describing Christ's pardon as a freely and universally available document Patience underscores Hawkyn's criticism of pardons and ecclesiastical authority. Although Patience's sermon is devoted to the sacrament of penance and is generated by pastoral concerns, the image of Christ's Passion as the only necessary legal document might suggest to an errant reader a system of salvation and textual authority outside the purview of the institutional church. Like Truth's Pardon, Hawkyn's quittance seems deliberately to exceed indulgences; it invokes the notion of papal pardon but rephrases it in absolute and more secular terms, once again blurring the boundaries between heterodoxy and sedition. Like Truth's Pardon, moreover, this pardon may be acquired and displayed by any faithful and patient layman who needs to defend himself against the devil. But whereas the Pardon at least retains the trappings of ecclesiastical authority (in the A-text, for example, it is sent by the pope), this pardon is ambiguously produced by all those who strive to live according to the model of Christ, a harbinger of Lollardy's "trewe parfit men."

Langland clearly recognized the dangerous contrast that could be made between Christ's pardon and the pope's pardon and made the necessary revisions in the C-text. He made Hawkyn's (now called *Activa Vita*) speech less acerbic by omitting his insult to papal pardons and by transforming his insolence into a more willing (if still qualified) statement of obedience:

> Y fynde payn for þe po[p]e, and pre[y]en hym ych wolde
> That pestilenc[e] to pees and parfyt loue turn[e].
> For founde y þat his blessynge and his bulle myhte [destruye],
> Lette this luythere eir and leche þe sike –
> ....
> And þenne wolde y be bysy and buxum to helpe
> Vch a kyne creature þat on crist leueth. (C. 15. 216–19, 222–3)[50]

If the failure of papal bulls still resonates in C, it is nonetheless significant here that Hawkyn asks the pope not to cure the plague but to convert it into peace and perfect love – a safely spiritual redefinition of natural disasters and papal authority.

In the same spirit, Langland omits the entire description of Christ's quittance drawn up on the cross and reduces it to a one-line description of an ambiguous charter made jointly by Holy Church and charity: "And holy churche and charite herof a chartre made..." (C. 16.35).

---

[50] Text in *'Piers Plowman': The C-Version*, ed. Russell and Kane (hereafter cited in the main text by line number).

By replacing Christ's quittance with Holy Church's charter, Langland redefines the saving document as a gift from the institutional church, one alliteratively tied to Holy Church and charity, as if inseparable from the institutions that produced it. Whereas in the B-text Christ's quittance is presented as the ultimate remedy against the devil and comfort to the conscience, here it is reduced to one line, very awkwardly attached to the lines around it, and subordinated to a larger discussion about the three stages of penance. Langland has also replaced the impassioned lines about Christ comforting "alle maner peple" which precede Hawkyn's pardon in the B-text with a pedantic explanation of penance as the source of Dowel for both the ignorant and the learned: "Thise thre [stages of penance] withoute doute tholieth alle pouerte/And lereth lewed and lered, hey and lowe to knowe/Ho doth wel or bet or beste aboue alle" (C. 16. 32–4). If Hawkyn in the B version doubts that the pope's pardon "my3te lechen a man" (B. 13.253), in this passage penance, not Christ's pardon, becomes the soul's remedy at the day of judgment: "And bote these thre þat y spak of at domesday vs defende…" (C. 16.36).

All these revisions, then, make more explicit statements about the role of the church and the sacraments in salvation, and they do so by sacrificing the personal and unmediated comfort of Christ's Passion. Russell and Kane attribute the rewriting of B. 14.164–98 (including Hawkyn's quittance) to corruption in the reviser's B copy.[51] Be that as it may, one consequence of this rewriting is to reassert ecclesiastical authority by shifting the terms of documentary culture. In the oft-cited opinion of E. T. Donaldson, the C-reviser's "art" is characterized by "the desire to rid the poem of elements that might be misconstrued by the ignorant or give offense to the learned."[52] As a result, perfectly coherent if institutionally challenging passages are frequently replaced with blunter statements of orthodox doctrine. Significantly, Christ's charter is one of these passages that required revision precisely because it could be – and indeed was – read as a heterodox image. Perhaps by the 1380s, when the C-text was likely produced, Christ's charter had already begun to be co-opted for Lollard polemic.

---

[51] Russell and Kane, *Piers Plowman*, 73.
[52] Donaldson, *'Piers Plowman': The C-Text and Its Poet*, 163.

RECLAIMING THE CHARTER OF CHRIST

The Lollard appropriations of Christ's charter and Langland's changes in the C-text place us in a better position to understand the peculiar revisions of the *Long Charter*. Together, they clarify the issues at stake in the idea of a divine charter, and, consequently, they help to explain why the revisions might have had the dual effect of censoring the poem to meet orthodox requirements and defending it from outside, heterodox "censorship." To my knowledge, only one Lollard manuscript, Rawlinson C. 751, the manuscript containing the sermon for Quinquagesima Sunday, actually contains a version of the *Long Charter* (A), along with a collection of Lollard sermons and an interpolated "Charter of Heaven." Few fifteenth-century writers, however, could have been ignorant of some form of Christ's charter, and, as we have just seen, Lollard polemicists freely adapted it to fit their own ideological agendas. The *Long Charter* was revised in two stages, the first revision (B) surviving in nine manuscripts, the earliest of which was copied around 1400 in Harvard W. K. Richardson 22; and the second revision (C) uniquely surviving in BL Royal 17. C. xvii, a manuscript probably compiled by a parish priest before 1425, to judge from the other items. Both revisers attempted to prevent possible misreadings of the poem by showing that the terms of Christ's charter cannot be grasped or even approached without clerical mediation, nor can they be met without fulfilling the sacraments of the church. Certainly, not all the revisions of the *Long Charter* should be attributed solely to an anti-Lollard agenda. The C-reviser, for example, who added over three hundred lines to the B-text, seems to have wanted to make the poem more didactic and less meditative, and many of the additions merely flesh out the gospel narrative, which is presented schematically in the original. On the whole, though, most of the revisions to the *Long Charter* – the fictive narrator, rambling digressions on orthodox doctrine, and attempts to re-historicize Christ's charter – seem tailored to discourage the kinds of readings found in the Lollard sermons discussed above.[53]

[53] The difficulties of dating vernacular Wycliffite texts make it impossible to establish a direct causal relationship between these heterodox appropriations of Christ's charter and the *Long Charter* revisions that reassert its orthodoxy. I am suggesting that the *Long Charter* revisers were responding to this kind of interpretation, if not to my particular examples.

The implicit challenge of Lollardy was the reorganization of a spiritual community around an original text to the exclusion of other texts, and the devaluation of other practices and mediators.[54] Lollard appropriations of Christ's charter thematize this vexed question of textual authority by usurping the language of mainstream piety and documentary culture. The fifteenth-century revisers of the *Long Charter*, like their Lollard counterparts, recognized how Christ's charter figured in the making of textual community into spiritual community, and they reshaped the poem accordingly. Most significantly, both the B and C-revisers inserted a new narrator and commentator, a peevish and bossy preacher whose voice frames the poem and frequently interrupts to comment on the narrative. This clerical persona is inconsistent and by no means suggests that the poem was reworked simply for oral delivery, as we might suspect. Rather, the overall effect of the fictive preacher is to control access to Christ's voice and charter; neither reader nor listener can receive Christ's voice without taking into account the preacher's distinctive interjections. At the beginning of this chapter, we saw that the speaker of the first four lines of B and C warns his readers not to stray to that "other scole." This admonitory voice goes on to present Christ as if he were the poem's guest speaker: "Now ye shal here anon-righte,/your sauyour speke to yow as-tyte/wordes of a chartour þat he hath wroght," and, a few lines later, "Now y wil begynne to rede þeron;/ his pes he yeue [peace he give] vs euery-chon!" (B. 13–15, 23–4). Likewise the C-text narrator soberly introduces his text, "Now sal ȝe here with-outyn delyte/ȝoure sawyour [savior] spek to ȝou als-tyte [just so]" (C.13–14). In the original poem, Christ is the only speaker, but as the revised versions progress, it becomes increasingly difficult to distinguish between Christ's voice and that of the fictive preacher. By intervening in this way, the fictive preacher immediately re-establishes the clergy as scriptural interpreters and spiritual policemen, and by doing so he diminishes the agency of Christ's document by reading it aloud and subjecting it to commentary. Or, to put it another way, the fictive preacher effectively assumes the power to effect the linguistic performance of the divine charter, replacing

[54] Lollards did have spiritual leaders who disseminated information aurally to a group that valued lay literacy but probably remained at least ocularly illiterate. For more information about Lollard literacy, see Hudson, "Laicus Litteratus"; and Aston, "Lollards and Literacy," in *Lollards and Reformers*.

Christ not only as the primary speaker but also as the dispenser and enactor of spiritual legislation.

The revisers further reshaped the textual community of the *Long Charter* by turning Christ's universal charter into a private conversation between Christ and preacher. Whereas in the A-text Christ explains the significance of the Last Supper directly to the reader – "And þis I made for Monkynde,/Mi loue-dedes to haue in mynde: *Hoc facite in meam commemoracionem*" (Do this in memory of me) (A. 61–2) – in the B-text Christ addresses the narrator as a sermon-writer would a practicing preacher: "Here wol y foure wordes *yow* teche/and to þe peple loke *ye* hem preche: *Hoc facite in meam commemoracionem*/that *they* heue hem euer in mynde" (B. 111–13, emphases mine). Just as the preacher replaces Christ as primary speaker, so he replaces the reader as Christ's primary interlocutor. As such, he transforms the audience from active participants into passive receivers of doctrine. The fictive preacher acknowledges that textual dissemination is in some sense beyond his control; the poem might be perused silently or communicated aurally by any reader. "Wo-so wil ouer-rede this boke and with gostly eyen ther-on loke," (B. 1–2) he begins, and a few lines later adds, "who this boke can vnderstonde,/teche it forth thurgh al the londe" (B. 17–18). At the same time, he repeatedly insists upon his role as preacher expounding a text to an audience which must be exhorted, cajoled, and quieted. "Herken now to my word hende!" exclaims the narrator several times, as if addressing a noisy, bustling crowd (B. 92, C. 130). The C-reviser goes to greater lengths to portray his audience as an unruly mob. In every B-text manuscript the fictive preacher blesses his imaginary audience with the conventional phrase, "his pes he yeue vs euery-chon!" (B. 24–5). By contrast, the C-text narrator demands silence: "Ald youre pese now euer-ilkon!" (C. 29–30). Thus, if aural reading forges communal bonds between speaker and audience, as Joyce Coleman has argued about Chaucer, the revised *Long Charter* drastically reconfigures these bonds.[55] Rather than binding Christ and "alle folk," or Christ and the reader-at-large, Christ's charter has become the text that binds preacher and congregation.

---

[55] Coleman, *Public Reading and the Reading Public*, 108.

Interestingly enough, the *Long Charter* A-text is the only example of a supernatural charter in which Christ appeals directly to the individual reader without an authoritative intermediary. There is, in fact, a conspicuous absence in the original *Long Charter* of the kinds of mediating voices – narrative, clerical, allegorical – that usually accompany fictive documents. In Deguileville's *Pèlerinage de la vie humaine* and its English adaptations, Charity reads aloud Christ's last will and testament to a parliament of pilgrims, and in the sequel, the *Pèlerinage de l'âme*, Mercy delivers Christ's charter of pardon to the Archangel Michael and his heavenly court. Likewise, in the Faustian *Miracle de Théophile* literature, Théophile signals humility and obedience by surrendering his devil's charter to the bishop, who assumes the responsibility of reading and interpreting it to the entire community. If, in these examples, reading a charter aloud could be interpreted as charitable or instructive – it relays important information to people who are not able or have not had the chance to read the document – in the context of the *Long Charter*, reading aloud could also be seen as a safety measure in the guise of pastoral beneficence. It ensures that the power of textual transmission, interpretation, and implementation remains with an authorized, usually clerical, intermediary.

Notably, the original version of the *Long Charter* is the only example of a fictive document that lacks an intermediary of some sort, and in other examples of fictive documents the intermediary – the bearer or reader of the document – is there primarily to preside over the dissemination and interpretation of the document. For example, in a scene from the *Pilgrimage of the Lyfe of the Manhode*, the scene between Reason and the churl already discussed in chapter 1, the documentary *perlector* serves not just to convey authority but also to overcome resistance to it, a resistance conceived specifically as lay. In the English prose version, Grace Dieu sends Dame Reason with a divine commission to Rude Understanding, a character probably based on Dangier in the *Roman de la rose* and perhaps a model for Langland's Hawkyn as well. This churlish highwayman has tried to obstruct the narrator's pilgrimage because he presumes that the pilgrim has broken the king's (Christ's) law by carrying a stick and satchel. Reason's commission orders him to desist from his behavior or else appear in court.[56] Reason takes her commission out of a box and proffers it to Rude Understanding, who disparages the letter and tells her to read it aloud if she wishes: " 'I am non clerk, ne I can nothing in þi leves; rede hem as þou wolt, for wite wel I preyse hem litel' " (2822–4).[57] Reason then calls upon the lettered pilgrim to read the commission aloud, so that Rude Understanding will be forced to acknowledge her authority: " 'Come forth clerk,' quod she to me: 'vndoo þese letteres out of plyt, rede hem bifore þis bachelere þat weeneth he be a lord. Whan he heereth hem red, if God wole he shal answere me' " (2828–31). In this passage, two representatives of the clergy – Reason who, though female, is some sort of royal official, and the pilgrim who, like Deguileville, is a monk – together enforce Reason's authority by reading her commission aloud. These acts illustrate the power of documentary performance to eliminate lay dissent, and the pilgrim, as a clerk, is invited to participate in that power (or, allegorically speaking, he is invited to subdue his inward churl through grace). Documentary performance is thus shown to be not only helpful but also politically and morally necessary. Interestingly, in the second recension of *Pilgimage of the Life of Man* translated by Lydgate, Reason reads her commission herself and does not involve the pilgrim who, in this version, is a layman. In Lydgate's version, too, Rude Understanding is immediately subdued by Reason's reading: "And she yt radde wyth good wylle:/The cherl was coy & stood ful stylle . . . And off desput to gruchche sore,/Whan she hath maad, ope &cler,/Al theffect off hyr power."[58] Although the *Long Charter* preacher does not anticipate resistance in quite the same way as Deguileville, he fulfills some of the same functions as Reason and the pilgrim. He insists on painting his audience as an uneducated and unruly crowd and, by doing so, shows how important the *perlector* is to implementing the law properly, to subdue skeptics, or to prevent misreadings.

Langland, perhaps following Deguileville, also assigns an official intermediary to every one of his documents: Christ's charter of pardon is successively disseminated by the priest, Moses, and Peace. Yet in all

---

[56] *The Pilgrimage of the Lyfe of the Manhode*, vol. 1, ed. Henry, 67, ll. 2272–3 (hereafter cited in the main text by line number).

[57] Lydgate's translation of the second recension of the *Pelerinage de la vie humaine* reads: "I koude neuere yet clergye/And yiff thy power shal be wyst/Red yt thy sylff, yiff that the lyst" (*Pilgrimage of the Life of Man*, ed. Furnivall, 287, ll. 10464–6).

[58] Lydgate, *Pilgrimage of the Life of Man*, ed. Furnivall, 287, ll. 10468–9, 10474–6.

three episodes, this mediating presence is unraveled by competing readers and detractors, and overshadowed by the document itself. In the
episode of Truth's Pardon, the priest reads the Pardon aloud to an assembled company, but he and Piers quarrel over the meaning of the
Pardon's two lines as well as the right to interpret Scripture. Their bit-
ter confrontation leaves Will ambivalent about the proper meaning of
the Pardon, and he is forced subsequently to draw his own problematic
conclusions. Similarly, in the episode of Moses's maundement, Moses
offers Will a patent with all the markings of an official document and
Abraham attests to its truthfulness, but Will remains skeptical that the
patent really contains the "lordes lawes." Mediation breaks down a third
time in *Piers Plowman* when Lady Peace reads Love's patent aloud to
her sisters. Although Peace has, in fact, read and interpreted her patent
correctly, Rightwisnesse immediately challenges her authority: "What,
ravestow...or þow art riʒt dronke!" (B. 18.187). To be sure, in each
of these episodes, dissension drives the narrative forward, forcing the
reader and Will to seek out new perspectives and to progress spiritually.[59]
Nor is skepticism necessarily contagious; Langland's reader, cued in to
familiar themes and characters, may be a few steps ahead of Will, just
as Deguileville's reader is miles ahead of Rude Understanding. Yet, by
allowing these intermediaries to be challenged, Langland anticipates the
questions that surely preoccupied the *Long Charter* revisers: who may
legitimately be an official *perlector* and when may that role be contested? How may the public proclamation of legal documents be rightly
compared to the performance of the spiritual law, and does that proclamation necessarily oppose secular to spiritual authority, and clerical to
lay reading practices?

By creating this fictive preacher, moreover, the revisers of the *Long
Charter* brought the poem in line with some of the concerns expressed
by the Oxford debates on bible translation that took place during the
first decade of the fifteenth century, the same period in which the *Long
Charter* B-reviser probably set to work. As Watson has so influentially
argued, vernacular English literature before 1350 enjoyed the "relatively
uncomplicated position...of being able to express a concrete relationship between a defined author and a defined audience." After 1350,

---

[59] On this point, see Middleton, "Narration and the Invention of Experience: Episodic
Form in *Piers Plowman*," 100.

however, vernacular authors were increasingly aware of "presenting an ever wider array of theological concerns to an ever larger and less clearly defined group of readers."[60] Although English writers had been translating parts of the Bible into vernacular literature for centuries (from apocryphal narratives to contemplative treatises), the nebulous and variable character of vernacular reception was thrown into relief by the Wycliffite Bible and by the corresponding backlash of the orthodox clergy. Those opposing translation in the Oxford debate fully recognized the interpretative dislocations of translation and deemed it to be spiritually and politically destabilizing. It could, argued one opponent, enable any fool or woman to usurp the role of preacher and lead himself and his followers to heretical or seditious conclusions.[61] Another debater, William Butler, recommended that the laity gain biblical knowledge through hearing rather than reading, the former being less dangerous since it involves the testimony of preachers who function as "living holy books."[62]

During the half century in which the *Long Charter* was composed, disseminated, and revised, scriptural translation changed dramatically from being a pastoral imperative to a site of major ideological conflict. Conversely, the legal document was becoming linguistically and socially accessible, an accessibility that was bitterly contested in the 1381 revolt, but which spread inexorably in the Englishing and expansion of the royal bureaucracy, the wider circulation of documentary culture (especially in wills), and the literary appropriation of documentary forms. To be sure, documentary Latin preserved its monumentality and conventionality beyond the Middle Ages, but it also became subject to discursive and linguistic experimentation and could be re-contextualized to serve a variety of literary and ideological agendas. The fact that scripture could be depicted as a vernacular charter publicly proclaimed and openly displayed on the cross entailed a heady juxtaposition of two official discourses. The analogy between charter and scripture still worked, in other words, but it had come to represent an increasingly problematic relationship between official texts and their readers which Lollard readers were eager to exploit. In the *Charters of Christ* literature, moreover, Christ's charter represents spiritual agency as well as textual authority

---

[60] Watson, "Censorship and Cultural Change," 838.
[61] Ibid., 843.   [62] Ibid., 842.

(it depicts Christ as both the authenticating agent and written contract of salvation); in short, it represents the effective performance of the Word that Lollards refused to limit to the institutional priesthood.[63] The fictive preacher of the *Long Charter* thus served not only as a means of reasserting clerical authority, but also as the vessel through which Christ's charter might be both legitimately transmitted and ritually performed.

To return briefly to some of the other *Long Charter* revisions, it should be added that just as the fictive preacher can be understood as a legitimate way of transmitting official texts, whether legal or scriptural, so he can also be understood as a means of marking the text as orthodox: his very presence discourages heterodox readers. The revisers further mark the *Long Charter* as an orthodox text by making it overtly polemical. For example, the metaphor of Christ's charter-body is implicitly eucharistic, but the revisers dwell upon transubstantiation at every conceivable opportunity, as if anticipating a Lollard reader. The A-text records that Christ made a supper for friends and fed them with "holi word [his] flesch and blode" so that humankind might remember his "loue-dedes" (A. 57ff). The B-reviser takes this opportunity to remind readers that this story refers to the Eucharist ("thes wordes twocheth þe sacrament/that men receueth, verrament") and offers his readers a catchy mnemonic on transubstantiation: "it semeth many, & is but one;/it semeth bred, & it is none;/it is quyk, & semeth ded:/ it is my body in fourme of bred" (B. 117–20). The C-reviser omits the Last Supper passage altogether, embarking instead on a tedious speech about the dangers of believing that the Host is not Christ's body (C. 135–66). First Christ (or the preacher-narrator) hastily explains that he is discussing this subject in English only to reinforce the faith of the laity ("þis wordys are þus to vnderfong/to lewed men in ynglys tong" [133–4]); he then warns his readers that transubstantiation is the best lesson one can learn, and the best defense against the devil:

> It es þe best leson þat þou may lere
> þi gostly enmy aw [always]to fere;
> for þe grettest temptacyon,
> wyt þis þou may lay all don.
> Af [have]it in mynde stedfastly,
> And þou sall af [shall have]þi purpos, trewly. (C. 159–64)

[63] See Hudson, *Premature Reformation*, 324–7.

This move illustrates the C-reviser's general method of seizing upon opportunities for didacticism and directing them toward Lollard-sensitive issues. Such excessive commentary also has the effect of creating a structurally orthodox text. Where the sparer *Long Charter* A-text threatens to take biblical (and legal) quotations dangerously out of context, the revised versions encase Christ's charter in more traditional biblical narratives and buffer it with expositions on the sacraments. A similarly proactive revision occurs in the metaphor of the indenture discussed several times above. The A-text compares the Eucharist to an indentured copy of Christ's crucified charter-body, a duplicate copy of the same substance. The B-reviser considered this indenture metaphor to be a sufficient explanation of transubstantiation and saw fit only to add the warning that "who-so-euer be-leveth ther-on,/endeles payn shal he fynde non" (B. 357–8). This clever indenture metaphor proved too abstruse, however, for the C-reviser, who apparently judged it safer to compare the Eucharist to the original charter than to an indentured copy. An indentured copy, after all, might undermine the sacramental nature of the Eucharist or suggest that there are multiple available copies. Christ says that he will leave the sealed charter in the priest's hands: "þis charter þus celyd [sealed] leve I wyll þe,/ware-by þu sall ay sekyr [secure] be: /My precyus body, of þe preste hande" (C. 557–9), and he insists that his body is the sacrament performed simultaneously by different priests at different altars: "My precyus body es þe sacrament, /þat [at] many a autyre verament/þe prestes sakyre [consecrate]at þer messe" (C. 561–3).

Finally, if the original *Long Charter* seemed to promise unmediated access to divine revelation, as suggested above, this problem was further exacerbated by its peculiar transhistoricity. As suggested above, the appeal of Christ's charter stemmed, in part, from its fiction of authorial presence – it purports to be perpetually issued by Christ at an originary moment on the cross. This fiction appealed to Lollard fundamentalist historicism – it illustrated the "contrast between the modern corrupt church and the apostolic church"[64] – and convinced some more "mainstream" readers that Christ's charter was a talisman imbued with divine presence (both approaches eliminating the need for human

---

[64] Leff, *Heresy in the Later Middle Ages*, vol. 2, 526.

intermediaries or textual glosses). Correspondingly, the *Long Charter* revisers, and particularly the C-reviser, attempted to mediate the effects of the charter by restoring temporal and textual boundaries. The A and B-texts, for example, make no distinction between Christ as narrator and Christ as charter, moving seamlessly through literary, liturgical, and documentary modes. Beginning with Christ's first-person narration ("To shewen on alle my loue-dede,/Miself I wole þis chartre rede" [A. 91–2]), the poem swiftly moves to his scriptural lament from the cross ("*O [v]os omnes qui transitis per viam attendite & vidite, etc.* / Ye Men þat gon bi þis weye,/A-bydeþ a luytel [little], I ow preye,/And redeþ alle on þis parchemyn,/Yif eny serwe beo lyk to myn" [A. 93–6]); and, finally, to the alternating first-third person voice of his charter ("*Sciant presentes et futuri,*/Wite ye þat are and schal be-tyde,/þat Jhesu crist wiþ blodi side…Made a sesyng whon I was born…" [A. 98–105]). As a result, Christ's charter-voice seems to be perpetually present, forever regenerating itself and its terms to new readers and listeners; indeed, it is the documentary transportation of the sacred past that makes the charter at once foundational and accessible. In the C-text, however, the narrator interrupts at this pivotal place to explain that Christ issued his charter at a historical moment on the cross, not to the present readers and listeners: "Goddis son of heuen, þe sothe to say,/þis wordy[s] spake on gode fryday,/pyned on þe mounte of calwery,/to þe pepull þat passyd hym by" (C. 253–6). The charter, in other words, is not a timeless communiqué from Christ to a modern-day audience. It merely reports Christ's speech on the cross to a past "pepull" – it is a fiction of historical beginning – and consequently must be glossed by the ordained clergy as represented by the preacher-narrator. The audience should not think to draw directly upon an original document, however open and immediate it may claim to be, because both its text and authorizing body have been consigned to a sacred past.

Whereas his opponents in the Oxford Bible debate disparaged the laity as an unruly and unpredictable mob, one debater named Richard Ullerston praised them as the "people of God to whom Christ preached in the mother tongue and who both need and are fit to receive God's law translated into that tongue."[65] For Ullerston, then, the vernacular

---

[65] Watson, "Censorship and Cultural Change," 846.

forged a revelatory link between Christ's historical audience and the present lay audience. And, as mentioned above, it was exactly this nostalgic link between past and present audiences that was advertised by the conventional salutations of Latin charters and their fictive English counterparts. Ullerston's position may seem socially progressive, but by the early fifteenth century it was untenable and politically naïve. Both he and the *Charters of Christ* belonged to an earlier period in which legal documents could be drafted incontestably into the service of vernacular piety. But starting in the 1380s or 1390s, Lollard writers began to appropriate documentary culture for their own ends: to devalue the "new" documents of the institutional church and to fashion an "open" spiritual community based on scriptural authority and vernacular translation. The original *Long Charter* was thus doubly implicated: first, by its inherent claims to immediacy and authenticity; and second, by Lollard appropriations of orthodox imagery for heterodox polemic.

In conclusion, the revisers of the *Long Charter* were not concerned simply to delete or conceal heterodox positions but also to insulate the poem from misreadings and appropriations. For them, censorship was not simply the influence of legislation or social mores on literary production, but rather a creative impulse, and a competition for language and symbols at a time when the written vernacular was at once expanding and newly circumscribed. The charter, which embodied all the expectations and fears of vernacular literary production, became such a symbol.

6

Lollard rhetoric and the written record:
Margery Baxter and William Thorpe

I argued in the last chapter that medieval writers produced an alternative version of documentary culture that enabled them to articulate controversial ideas about private religions, indulgences, scriptural authority, and royal sovereignty. More surprisingly, perhaps, Lollards' appropriations of fictive documents were paralleled by similar strategies in their encounters with episcopal officers. Like other contemporary polemicists, self-identified Lollards on trial positioned themselves against documentary culture to contest orthodox ideas of textual authority. But just as their contemporaries borrowed the image of Christ's charter to discredit indulgences and formulate heterodox notions of political and spiritual community, so Margery Baxter and William Thorpe used documents to rescue Lollard rhetoric from the evidentiary language of written record and to rehabilitate a distinctly Lollard hermeneutic. For Baxter and Thorpe, just as for the Lollard sermon-writers, documentary culture set the terms for which a debate on textual authority could take place. Fifteenth-century sermons and trial records show that medieval documentary culture served as an easy target for criticism of bureaucratic corruption and institutional oppression. It also provided its critics, however, with rhetorical alternatives with which that criticism might be effectively deployed.

Between 1428 and 1431 a notary named John Excestr copied the records of the Norwich heresy trials into a court-book or personal *dictamen*.[1] His book suggests that the majority of the trials most likely consisted of a routine exchange of documents. The presiding bishop probably presented the defendant with a Latin deposition (perhaps read aloud in English)

---

[1] Justice, "Inquisition, Speech and Writing: A Case from Late Medieval Norwich."

listing the defendant's heretical beliefs or practices. Witnesses would be called in, if necessary, to corroborate or expand on the document. The defendant would admit to statements as charged, formally retract them, and state his or her intention to submit to the correction of the Church under pain of burning. An official abjuration would subsequently be drawn up in duplicate and sealed by the confessed heretic, who swore to keep his or her copy forever ("That other partie indented Y receyve undir the seel of office... to abide with me unto my lyves ende").[2] Nearly all of the abjurations were written in English ("in ydiomate Anglicano concepto") as well as Latin, and in the first person so that the defendant understood what he or she was retracting and might take legal responsibility for it.[3] Both the Latin certifications and English abjurations are fairly standardized – the English idiom here is neither creative nor unruly – and generally efface idiosyncratic comments that may have cropped up during the trial. Most of the defendants could read neither English nor Latin and were consequently assigned proxies who read their abjurations aloud for them.[4]

The deposition of the Lollard hostess and household preacher Margery Baxter differs from the others in its idiomatic English expressions of Lollard doctrine, some of them appearing to have seeped unintentionally into the Latin record. Baxter's friend Joan reported her to have said, for example, that when relics are worshipped Lucifer enjoys on earth the honor that he lost after his fall, "*in adoracione* of stokkes and stones and ded mennes bones" (42). This phrase "stokkes and stones"

---

[2] Tanner, ed., *Heresy Trials in the Diocese of Norwich*, 187 (hereafter cited in the main text by page number).

[3] Other Latin documents refer to the accused in the third person. The only exception to this rule is the case of the chaplain Robert Cavell whose Latin abjuration is addressed in the first person, presumably because as a cleric he understood the Latin of his abjuration and was thus able to take legal responsibility for it: "Cuius scripti indentati unam partem idem Robertus Cavell in manibus suis tenens coram dicto patre legit publice" (Tanner, ed., *Heresy Trials in the Diocese of Norwich*, 94).

[4] The following formula is typical: "Quem tenorem per magistrum Johannem Wylly, notarium publicum, tunc Ibidem presentem, publice perlectum idem Willelmus asseruit se de verbo ad verbum totaliter audivisse et plenarie intellexisse. Et quia idem Willelmus Bate asseruit se fore laicum, ipsam abiuracionem legere nescientem propria in persona, ipse constituit prefatum magistrum Johannem Wylly organum vocis sue" (Tanner, ed., *Heresy Trials in the Diocese of Norwich*, 159).

recalls typical Lollard iconoclasm: one early Lollard writer exclaims in disgust, "What almes is it to peynte gayly dede stones and roun stokkis wiþ such almes þat is pore mennus good and lyfelode?", and mocks those pilgrims who "cleuen sadly strokande and kyssand þese olde stones and stokkis."[5] It is not clear why Excestr recorded these statements; it may be that the idiom testified to the speakers' heterodoxy or was too exciting to render into Latin, or, as Steven Justice has argued, the notary was merely bored.[6] Whatever his reasons, these statements certainly disrupt the written record while at the same time making visible its purpose: to convert Lollard idiom into conventional – and punishable – English formulas.

This rhetorical challenge to documentary culture illuminates a more deliberate challenge that John Excestr did not see fit to relay in English. Baxter was reported to have said that even if she was convicted of heresy, she should not be burnt because she has had and still has ("habuit et habet") a charter of salvation in her womb ("unam cartam salvacionis in utero suo" [49]). If Baxter really made this strange pronouncement (and in a certain sense, of course, it matters only that it was reported to have been said), it can be interpreted in a number of different ways. Most obviously, Baxter intended to disparage the inquisitors' documentary authority by claiming to possess a superior charter, one that effectively nullified or superseded the one that she was being coerced into producing against herself. The bishop's document may be narrowly incriminating (it might send her to the stake), but hers is more largely redemptive: it will save her not only from temporal fire but also from the devil and eternal punishment. And where his is punitive, hers is continually generative. As one reader has proposed, Baxter may have been posing

---

[5] "Images and Pilgrimages," Hudson, ed., *Selections from English Wycliffite Writings*, 85, ll. 72–4; 87, ll. 159–60.

[6] Justice argues in "Inquisition, Speech and Writing" that the trials had become so routine that Excestr was momentarily roused by "outcroppings of idiosyncrasy" (305). He dismisses a few important considerations, however: first, that these stray expressions only appear in *reported* speech, either attributed by the defendant to other people or by a witness to a defendant; and second, that English could be an evidentiary language. Any defendant who could not understand Latin had his abjuration recorded in English so that he could swear to its contents. Clearly, in this instance, an English document was as binding and enforceable as a Latin one.

as a Marian figure harboring the Word in her womb like a charm, thus inuring herself to physical violence.[7]

Baxter's statement further shows that she is drawing from the textual materials of royal and ecclesiastical bureaucracies, but she is using them to produce an alternate document. She does this, notably, by borrowing the rhetoric of Christ's charter, a rhetoric that gestures to hermeneutic exclusivity at the same time that it invites all passersby to participate directly in a redemptive contract. Her charter of salvation, like Mary's womb, advertises the impenetrability as well as the sanctity of her bodily enclosure; Baxter uses it to posit a closed rather than an open spiritual community, one tantalizingly unavailable to the orthodox clergy.[8] The idea of a divine charter openly inscribed upon, but also mystically contained within a sacred body, can also be seen in the passage from the "The Charter of Heaven" which warns that Christ's charter is too precious to be locked in a chest: "þis scripture is oure lord Ihesu crist: chartre & bulle of oure eritage of heuene! Locke not þis chartre in þi coffre: but sette it eiþir write it in þin herte," but yet, at the same time, Christ is the very "cofre in whom is closid & loken: al þe tresoure of witte & wisdom of god."[9] Christ as the redemptive Word should be available to all, but as the sublime container of that Word he is in some way his own mediator, precious and secretive. We might say, then, that by advertising her own charter of salvation, Baxter is in some sense imitating Christ himself as the original preacher and material text of the contract of the Redemption, and she is doing so in such a way as to counter the trial documents of the institutional Church.

Like the polemical sermons discussed in the last chapter, Baxter's claim also criticizes both the authority and reading practices of the orthodox clergy. It suggests, for example, that textual authority – and particularly the authority to preach – is located not in the documents of the

---

[7] For Baxter as a Marian figure, see Copeland, "Why Women Can't Read: Medieval Hermeneutics, Statuary Law, and the Lollard Heresy Trials." For more information on women Lollards, see Cross, "'Great Reasoners in Scripture': the Activities of Women Lollards, 1380–1530."

[8] I am grateful to Bruce Holsinger for helping me to see this point.

[9] Spalding, ed., *Middle English Charters*, 101. Baxter clearly had a flair for lay *imitatio christi*. According to her witnesses, she once spread her arms out in imitation of the crucifixion and declared that this was the image of the crucifix that should be worshipped (Tanner, ed., *Heresy Trials in the Diocese of Norwich*, 44).

institutional church but in the body of the laity on the one hand (whether individual or corporate), and in the gospels (Christ's charter) on the other.[10] Not only does this suggestion evoke specifically Lollard notions of authority, but it also refers to local practices in which the demand for written texts and secrecy necessitated household-oriented textual communities which depended, in part, on Lollard women's aural transmission of scripture. As Ralph Hanna III writes about the Lollard women from Norwich, "They embodied texts and transported them in their corporeal persons, gave to them a life beyond mere vellum and thus attained a flexibility... of writing that their coreligionists might not have achieved."[11] Baxter's claim suggests even more significantly, however, that the scriptures of the orthodox clergy *are* the literal documents of the law, evidentiary records that must be metaphorically "glossed" by the faithful in order to be transformed into a charter of salvation, a legitimizing and doctrinally significant text. And it is this ironic critique of orthodox hermeneutics that really enabled Baxter to elude her trial, to go beyond what otherwise appears to be mere posturing and threats. Whatever its consequences, her citation of Christ's charter shows how trial documents might be subjected to and might generate infinite glosses. It implies, that is, that the ecclesiastical record does not authoritatively designate subjects – it is not a fundamental text – but rather its supposed subjects continually supply corrective glosses by physically embodying the text of scripture: Christ's original charter.

Baxter's deposition demonstrates how Lollard rhetoric might disrupt the conventions of the written record by invoking an alternate documentary culture, and how in doing so it might complicate or distort relationships between rhetoric, genre, and authority. William Thorpe's 1407 *Testimony* constitutes a more comprehensive example of how an unorthodox preacher might manipulate documentary rhetoric to critique and elude his trial. According to Thorpe, his *Testimony* is an accurate transcript of a trial that took place in the palace of Archbishop Arundel, the ostensible grounds for which was Thorpe's unauthorized preaching of heretical doctrine in Shrewsbury. If the trial really took place, it could certainly never have done so in the form reported by Thorpe (Arundel

[10] Hanna, "The Case of the Lollards and the Difficulty of Ricardian Prose Translation," 336.
[11] Hanna, "Some Norfolk Women and Their Books," 292.

plays an unlikely straw man to Thorpe's erudite martyr), and whether it was conducted in Latin or English – the text survives in both languages – is impossible to determine decisively.[12] The question of historical authenticity aside, Thorpe's *Testimony* is remarkable for the way that it interrogates the language of trial documents, such as those found in the Norwich court-book. In doing so, it simultaneously excavates a specifically Lollard rhetoric and proclaims the superiority of Lollard exegesis. In this respect, the *Testimony* is strikingly sympathetic to Dominick LaCapra's assertion that "the one thing a trial must repress is the way style…may be a politically subversive or contestatory force."[13] Indeed Thorpe, as will become clear, recovers the political and spiritual potency of Lollard "style" by inverting and subverting the written records of the institutional Church.

From the very beginning, Thorpe presents his *Testimony* as an alternative document: a self-made testament to his life and beliefs, but also a public sermon instructing present and future audiences. In his prologue he offers a traditional apology for revealing the sins of others, explaining that the book is intended to instill virtue in his readers and to comfort those in bad circumstances. He begins his account of his interrogation, moreover, with another conventional literary strategy:

> Knowen be it to alle men þat reden or heeren þis writinge byneþforþ þat, on þe Sondai next aftir þe faste Petir þat we clepen Lammasse, in þe ʒeer of oure lord a þousand foure hundred and seuene, I, William of Thorpe… was brouʒt bifore Tomas of Arundel, Archebischop of Cauntirbirie and chaunceler þanne of Yngland.[14]

This salutation suggests that Thorpe's self-writing has the status of a public proclamation worthy of trust and remembrance; it is, importantly, the document about his trial, in contradistinction to those documents produced by or occasioning the trial. It is, from that perspective, a legacy rather than an account of the self. Rita Copeland provocatively asks how

---

[12] Anne Hudson tentatively makes an argument for English based upon Thorpe's exhortation to his intended audience in the prologue. See also her comments on the historicity of the text (which she defends) in the introduction to her edition, *Two Wycliffite Texts: The Sermon of William Taylor 1406 and the Testimony of William Thorpe 1407*, xlii–liii. On Thorpe's use of the conventions of standard academic debate, see Fiona Somerset, *Clerical Discourse and Lay Audience in Late Medieval England*, 179–215.

[13] LaCapra, *Rethinking Intellectual History: Texts, Contexts, Language*, 47.

[14] Hudson, ed., *Two Wycliffite Texts*, ll. 6–71 (hereafter cited in the main text by line number).

Thorpe, as an academic and clerical insider, can offer a true model of dissent: how can he represent his own life and still speak on behalf of other Lollards?[15] She goes on to argue that he fashions a dissenting self through intellectual labor, that is, through the violence of his interrogation. It should be added, however, that this salutation offers a more conventional way of representing and reaching out to a larger audience, and of converting insider into oppositional politics. At first glance the salutation may seem to perpetuate an orthodox (and in the context of the trials, oppressive) model for public writing, but it actually works to rewrite the heresy documents found in a standard trial. As we saw earlier, first-person English documents were used only for abjurations, and thus the defendant spoke only through an incriminating and coerced confession. By contrast, Thorpe's first-person salutation is close to standard for a patent (i.e., "Sachez ke nus volons et otrions," or in Latin, "omnibus hanc cartam visuris vel auditoris"), not an abjuration, confession, or petition, and thus it effectively reinscribes the dissenting subject into an assertive public document.[16]

Thorpe further invokes and contests documentary culture by forcing Arundel to lay out several trial documents which Thorpe systematically undermines. He seems, in fact, to have deliberately provoked each step of the proceedings in order to contest the preaching authority of the institutional Church and to expound on the basic tenets of Lollardy. For example, Arundel begins the interrogation by asking Thorpe to renounce his beliefs in exchange for clemency ("wiþouten ony feynynge knele doun and leie þin hond vpon a book and kisse it, bihoting feithfulli … þat þou wolt submytte þee to my correccioun and stonde to myn ordinance" [190–3]). Thorpe uses this opportunity to deliver a suspect version of the Creed, at the end of which he asks if he may lay his hands on the Book. "Of course," says the archbishop, and Thorpe immediately protests that the book is a created thing and therefore cannot be sworn by. He then disingenuously asks Arundel to tell him the procedure by which he must submit (345–8). The archbishop promptly

---

[15] See Copeland, "William Thorpe and His Lollard Community: Intellectual Labor and the Representation of Dissent."

[16] Compare Thorpe's salutation, for example, with the first few lines of Jack Upland's "petition": "To veri god & to alle trewe in Crist, I Iacke Vplond make my moone, þat Anticrist and hise disciplis bi coloure of holynes wasten & disceiuen Cristis chirche bi many fals signes" (*Jack Upland, Six Ecclesiastical Satires,* ed. Dean, 54, ll. 1–3).

recites a list of formulas, repeating the exact order and language of the Norwich abjurations: Thorpe is to disavow his heretical beliefs, cease from holding them either privately or openly ("priuyli" or "appertli"), stop consorting with or aiding heretics ("neither þou schalt fauoure man ne woman ... þat holdiþ ony of þese forseide opynynouns"), and deliver the names of heretics to episcopal officers ("þou shalt putten [them] vp, pupblischinge her names, and make hem knowen to þe bishop of þe diocise þat þese ben inne, eiþer to þe bishopis mynystris" [357–60]). Similarly at Norwich, the defendants were first to lay their hands on the Gospels ("Y abjure and forswere, and swere be these holy Gospels be me bodely touched"), abjure their heretical beliefs, and promise to hold those beliefs neither "opinly ne prively," nor give help or favor to those who do so (in Latin, "auxilium vel favore publice vel occulte") (87). A typical Norwich abjuror likewise ends his retraction by promising that he will turn over any other Lollards to the authorities: "Yf Y knowe ony heretik or of heresie ony man or woman suspect ... Y shal late you, worshipfull fadir, or your vicar generall in your absens or the diocesans of suche men have soone and redy knowyng" (87).[17] What is remarkable in Thorpe's account is not so much his familiarity with these formulas but the way that he deliberately glosses them to extricate himself rhetorically and ideologically from the proceedings. He explains that if he were to swear to what Arundel has set forth, he would undermine the faith of true Christian men, condemn innocent people to their deaths, and damn himself to hell. Thus the abjuration that formed the basis for the heresy trials becomes in Thorpe's *Testimony* a virtual outline for Lollard doctrine.

When Thorpe again refuses to submit, Arundel becomes angry and orders his clerk to take out a certificate sent by the bailiff of Shrewsbury, which has been stored in a cupboard with "dyuerse rollis and other writingis" (621–3). This "litil rolle," as Thorpe calls it, reports the heretical statements preached by Thorpe in Saint Chad's church and is meant to be an intimidating and irrefutable record. Thorpe, however, has goaded the archbishop into taking it out of the cupboard in the first place, and indeed this certificate turns out to be another text from

---

[17] Thorpe's version of the abjuration differs only slightly from the Norwich, perhaps because he was loosely translating from or remembering a Latin version; the content of both is remarkably the same.

which to launch the Lollard counter-offensive. Arundel reads it aloud, ticking off five stereotypical Lollard positions on the Eucharist, images, pilgrimages, tithes, and swearing, and using the formulas that would become standard in the Norwich trials. Thorpe immediately denies having preached these statements "priuyli ne apeertly" (638), not in order to protest his innocence but to elaborate on the statements. An improbable dialogue follows in which Arundel puts each of the five statements to Thorpe and allows him five times to rephrase each statement in a more learned and nuanced fashion, in effect turning them into mini-sermons. Concerning the third statement on pilgrimage, for example, Arundel asks him, " 'What seist þou now to the þridde poynt þat is certified aȝens þee, preaching at Schrouesbirie opinli þat pilgrimage is vnleeful?' " and Thorpe responds,

> "Sere, bi þis certificatioun I am acused to ȝou þat I schulde teche þat no pilgrimage is leeful. But, ser, I seide neuere þus ... And þerfore, ser, howeuere myn enemyes haue certified to ȝou of me, I toolde at Schrouesbirie of two manere of pilgrimagis, seiinge þat þer ben trewe pilgrimes and fals pilgrimes." (1221–4)

Tales of martyrdom are often, of course, about frustrating the legal system, about turning official procedure into a forum for narrative and debate. But by interrogating documentary culture – both the abjuration that Arundel wants him to sign and the certification against him – Thorpe restores doctrinal complexity to Lollard beliefs and proves the irreducibility of Lollard rhetoric. In this way, he inverts the process of the heresy records; rather than letting his sermon be converted into documentary formulas, he converts the language of legal record into a vernacular sermon on Lollard beliefs – a written transcript, that is, of the sermon for which he was arrested!

Thorpe's strategy also reveals a more general concern of his *Testimony* – and, indeed, its ostensible reason for being – that authority can be supported, not by the prescription of prelates, but rather by the truth of scripture and the witnessing of true Christian men. Unlike Margery Kempe, who seems to have spent days on end collecting official letters of credence and safe-conduct, Thorpe wants to prove that his arrest for preaching without a license is doctrinally illegitimate. When Arundel warns that Thorpe had no right to preach because neither he nor any other prelate "'wol admitte or graunte þee for to preche bi witnesse of her lettris'" (745–6), Thorpe predictably responds that Lollard preachers, unlike friars, do not want to be bound by the terms of "'ȝoure lettre neiþer lettris of oþir bishopis writun wiþ enke vpon parchemyne,'" the authority of which is not supported in the gospels (759–62). Furthermore, the evidence of their right to preach consists of the people to whom they preach rather than official letters: "'ȝhe, þe peple to who we prechen, be þei feiþful either vnfeiþful, schulen be oure lettris that is oure witnesse-berer'" (774–5). Peculiarly, Thorpe's objection to ecclesiastical letters does not extend to secular letters as well. Later, in a debate about images, Arundel argues in favor of religious images on the grounds that they signify the authority of those whom they represent. Hoping to ensnare Thorpe in a critique of secular authority, he offers an analogy from aristocratic practice: lords customarily seal their letters with their coats of arms so that their subjects recognize their authority and obey the letters ("'in worschip of her lordis þei don of her cappis or her hoodis to her lettris'" [1090–1]). Thorpe refuses to rise to the bait, replying tersely that the representative authority of secular letters does not apply to religious practices: "'þis worldli vsage of temperal lordis . . . is no symylitude to worschipe ymagis maad bi mannes hond'" (1096–8).

Arguably Thorpe is doing much more in his *Testimony*, however, than refuting the authority of ecclesiastical letters and locating authority in the gospels. We have seen that by interrogating legal documents, Thorpe, like Margery Baxter, emancipates himself rhetorically, and consequently sets an example for other convicted Lollards. He further puts the ecclesiastical bureaucracy on trial by opposing a Lollard hermeneutics to what might be called the evidentiary hermeneutics of the archbishop and his clerks. Like Margery Baxter, he attacks the fundamentalism of episcopal officers and, by doing so, ironically turns legal documents into Arundel's *scriptura sola*. If Lollards were accused of interpreting the Bible literally to their own advantage, in the *Testimony*, Arundel's major proof-texts become the abjuration and certification to which he adheres literally, and which Thorpe must "gloss" in order to excavate their true sense. In a typical moment in the trial, the archbishop's clerks prompt him to stick to the certification when Thorpe's explication of Holy Church leaves him speechless:

"Ser, he seide riȝt now þat þis certificacioun þat cam to ȝou from Schrouesbirie is vntruli forgid aȝens him. þerfore, ser, appose ȝe him now here in alle the poyntis which ben certified aȝens him" ... "And þe Archebischop took þanne þe certificacion in his hond and he lokide þerevpon a while, and so þanne he seide to me ...". (924–9)

Arundel's problem, in other words, is that he and his clerks refuse to distinguish between the literal accusations listed on the certification and Thorpe's subtle exegesis of those accusations. Nor can they reconcile the two truths that Thorpe so plainly exploits: the evidentiary truth of the certification (whether or not Thorpe illicitly preached heretical doctrine at Shrewsbury) and the truth of the statements themselves. In the *Testimony*, Arundel reminds Thorpe that he represents the two spheres of the English "clergie" or "written church": he is *both* archbishop and chancellor, the arbiter of religious doctrine but also the purveyor of legal documents, the means by which doctrinal opinions may be formalized, legitimized, or punished.[18] By performing Lollard exegesis on ecclesiastical documents, Thorpe crucially divides the two spheres of "clergie," the scriptural and the documentary, which Arundel and the heresy trials threatened to conflate.

Like the *Charters of Christ* discussed in chapter 5, the testimonies of William Thorpe and Margery Baxter show that in late medieval England documentary culture always constituted the matter from which even an anti-establishment agenda could proceed. As in Baxter's deposition, official letters remain in the *Testimony* the dominant points of reference both for naming an oppositional voice and for contesting orthodox ideas of textual authority. Indeed, the literature of this period suggests more broadly that legal culture was subject to a larger cultural appropriation in which its official instruments were converted to serve vernacular piety, whether the practice of that piety or its criticism. Late medieval documentary culture provided a language with which to discuss the rhetorical, evidentiary, and foundational claims of official texts, a language that in certain hands might be used to rewrite documentary culture itself.

---

[18] See Justice's illuminating comments on Langland, Ball, and the "written church" in *Writing and Rebellion*, 116–18.

Epilogue

"My lordys lettyr & the seel of Cawntyrbery"

The Book of Margery Kempe (probably written in the 1430s) is a work written to authorize an exceptional life. It narrates the life of a laywoman from her own perspective, a life dedicated to communing with Christ and confronting those around her. It is a work that ultimately aspires to be a saint's life – it argues for the exemplary – and it is concerned with the condition of medieval society only insofar as that society attests to the identity of Margery Kempe herself. We saw that the poetry in the *Piers Plowman* tradition deliberately subordinates the historical identity of the subject to the textual modes of public writing – material legal documents. By contrast, *The Book of Margery Kempe* relentlessly pursues the identity of its subject, whose shocking costume and outrageous "roaring" provoked both criticism and praise. Consequently, much recent scholarship on Margery Kempe has considered either her historical self-presentation or the rhetorical devices by which she confects herself within her narrative.

One of the most dramatic aspects of Kempe's identity, however, is the one least remarked upon: her collection of legal documents. During the period before she retired to her hometown of Bishop's Lynn, she successfully obtained letters of safe-conduct and credence from the bishops of Leicester and Lincoln, an archbishop of York, and two archbishops of Canterbury. In fact, a sizable section of her *Book* (chapters 49–55), the account of her travels around England, is almost entirely devoted to stories about collecting official documents; by the end of her life she must have amassed a sizable personal archive. In her account of her travels to Germany, Jerusalem, Venice, and Rome, she doesn't mention a single document. In England, however, it is clear that documents gave her the license to travel freely, as well as protection against those who questioned her orthodoxy or chastity.

Interestingly, the very documents that locate Kempe's identity within the confines of ecclesiastical authority, which confirm her identity by classifying the unclassifiable, are the same ones that give textual expression to an exemplary life. Practically speaking, of course, without a letter to guarantee her person, she would have been imprisoned or molested by local townspeople and officials. After all, she was a woman loudly professing the divine word, not only outside her own parish but also in two different dioceses; and she had to win the confidence of ecclesiastical overlords in order to avoid martyrdom or social death. She is convincingly distraught, for example, when the Archbishop of York's servant, who accompanies her out of the diocese, returns to York with her safe-conduct, leaving her stranded: "And so sche passyd forth wyth a man of the Erchebischop, beryng the lettyr whech the Erchebishop had grawntyd hir for a recorde, and he browt hir to the Watyr of Humbyr, and ther he toke hys leve of hir, returnyng to hys lord and beryng the sayd lettyr wyth hym ayen, so was sche left a-lone wythowtyn knowl-ache of the pepyl."[1] Her need for written protection and identification is especially acute in her hometown of Bishop's Lynn, where documents not only shield her from accusations of heresy or prostitution, but they also give her the right to participate in ordinary rituals from which she would otherwise be firmly excluded. Once she has the Archbishop of Canterbury's letter in hand, for example, local clerics have no choice but to let her hear mass and sermons, even though her "gift of tears" annoys other congregants. The prior of Saint Margaret's in Bishop's Lynn tries to prevent her from taking communion in the chapel after he learns that a new brother refuses to enter the chapel with her present. The parish priest reminds the prior, however, that Kempe possesses "my Lordys lettyr of Cawntyrbery and hys seel" and is therefore entitled to every pastoral service (4681–2).

Significantly, however, Kempe ascribes enormous importance to these documents, without the least concern that they might cast doubt on her divine election. We assume that an exemplary life guarantees itself

---

[1] *The Book of Margery Kempe*, ed. Windeatt, ll. 4530–5. (hereafter cited in the text by line numbers).

without catering to institutional recognition. But Kempe gloats in her mastery of ecclesiastical bureaucracy, not simply because she has won the approval of those in power and put minor officials in their place, but also because she believes that an exceptional life may be textually constituted through the acquisition of legal instruments. When the exasperated archbishop of York throws his hands in the air and asks her (rhetorically) what he should do with her ("I wite not what I schal don wyth the!"), she promptly replies, "My Lord, I pray yow late me have yowr lettyr and yowr seyl into recorde that I have excusyd me ageyn myn enmys and nothyng is attyd ageyns me, neithyr herrowr ne heresy that may ben prevyd upon me" (1409–13). Likewise she refuses to come home to Bishop's Lynn without a letter from the Archbishop of Canterbury; as she triumphantly declares, the Archbishop of York, in her own diocese, would not ȝeue credence to [her] wordys" without "my Lordys lettyr and seel of Cawntyrbery" and has made her promise not to return home "tyl I had my lordys lettyr and the seel of Cawntyrbery" (4581–5).

Certainly, one way of explaining her penchant for legal instruments would be to point out that she is often strategically conflicted: she will gesture to an approved category (e.g., marriage, illiteracy, transubstantiation) while at the same time subverting that category (e.g., chastity, bible-thumping, swearing). By doing so, she avoids punishment but also articulates a subjectivity by challenging contemporary institutions.[2] But additionally, for Kempe, legal documents seem to have struck the right balance between official approbation and personal magnetism without which a saint's life cannot properly come into being. The virtue of the saint depends upon both the willingness of the biographer to make a case for canonization (usually after the death of the saint) and the personal magnetism of the saint, which inspires the biographer to write in the first place. In traditional hagiography this balance is tacitly expressed through the conventions of genre: the disinterested third-person narrator, the distancing of the hagiographic subject, and the conformation of the saint's life to the *miracula* of romance. As others have noted, *The Book*

---

[2] See Ruth Shklar [Nissé]'s excellent article, "Cobham's Daughter: *The Book of Margery Kempe* and the Power of Heterodox Thinking." Nissé argues that Margery uses Lollard rhetoric to critique institutional models of defining and interrogating heresy, while at the same time defending her orthodoxy. See also Staley's thoughtful discussion of Kempe's screening strategies in *Margery Kempe's Dissenting Fictions*, 1–38.

of Margery Kempe approximates but finally confounds its own generic conventions, most notably by telling the story from the perspective of the still active and therefore barely credible female saint. Yet in many ways Kempe's documents work to restore the identity fashioned through traditional hagiography. For Kempe, her ability to secure documents is evidence at once of official written approbation and of divine favor or personal magnetism; consequently they become in her narrative both institutional tokens and charismatic artifacts. In one episode, for example, the mayor of the town of Leicester refuses to release her without a letter from the bishop of Lincoln excusing her release. After a number of interrogations, she is able to procure from the abbot of Leicester "a lettyr...to my Lord of Lyncolne, into record [in] what conversacyon sche had ben the tyme that sche was in Leicetyr." The dean of Leicester is equally happy to "recordyn and witnessyn wyth hir" in her solicitation of the bishop "for he had gret confidens that owre Lord lovyd hir" (3892–6). Her efforts to corroborate election and bureaucracy finally pay off when the bishop of Leicester hands her a letter admonishing the mayor of Leicester that "he schulde not vexyn hir ne lettyn hir to gon & comyn whan she wolde" (3946–7). She is finally delivered from Leicester, however, by a combination of factors: unusually bad weather, the superstitions of the townspeople, and the bishop's letter.

> Than ther fellyn gret thunderys and levenys and many reynes, that the pepil demyd it was for veniawns of the sayd creatur, gretly desyryng that she had ben owt of that cuntre. And sche wolde in no wise gon thens tyl that sche had hir scryppe ageyn. Whan the seyde meyr receyved the forseyd lettyr, he sent hir hir skryppe and leet hir gon in safte wher sche wolde. (3948–53)

In this wonderfully packed passage the bishop's letter is notably on par with more experiential forms of evidence: climate, public opinion, and divine retribution. In a similar episode, after Kempe has obtained an especially coveted letter from the Archbishop of Canterbury in London, a lone man on horseback accosts her and her husband outside of Ely, menaces them, and threatens to drag them off to prison. She begs her husband to show the man "my Lordys lettyr of Cawtirbery" (4596–7), at which point the assailant suddenly, almost miraculously, backs off: "Whan the man had redde the lettyr, than he spak fayr and goodly unto hem, seying: 'Why schewyd me not yowr lettyr beforn?'" (4597–9). Kempe tells this story like an exemplum in a sermon, the letter taking the place of the crucifix, Host, or other holy image that might convert doubters or detractors. She clearly considered these ecclesiastical letters to be an integral part of her confessional autobiography and as quasi-sacred objects to be exhibited in the larger trial staged by her *Book*. They are, we might say, textual incarnations of her worldly charisma: the man's credulity has as much to do with Kempe's "shewing" of her letter as it does with the routine functioning of ecclesiastical bureaucracy.

By arguing that Kempe's documents restore the balance between official approbation and personal magnetism, I am further proposing that they represent in textual form the generic aspirations of the *Book*, the text that is at once officially composed and charismatically inspired. In the process, these documents model ideal modes of reading and writing. It is as if the way that Kempe wants her book to be received has become a collection of textual objects confidently paraded within the *Book* itself. It is not so much that the *Book* extends the ecclesiastical authority that Kempe so persistently seeks out; it is rather that it places inside the text what traditional hagiography places outside. I am not saying that Kempe's documents exist merely for authorial reflection; on the contrary, they are the most straightforward representations of medieval practice that the *Book* has to offer. I am saying, rather, that to collect documents is to guarantee one's physical safety or license a behavior, but it is also to figure one's religious identity through generic means otherwise unavailable. The drive to collect documents is the same drive to narrow the limits of hagiography into material texts presentable in one's own life and on one's own person. It is telling, in this respect, that Kempe is accused not only of being a Lollard, but of distributing messages for the notorious Lollard Sir John Oldcastle: "than cam tho too men whech had arestyd hir, seyng wyth the frer that sche was Combomis [Cobham's] dowtyr and was sent to beryn lettrys abowtyn the cuntre" (4419–21). Clearly, this accusation reflects many things about Kempe and her book: her strategy of self-interrogation, her fascination with slander, and the difficulties of being a woman at large in late medieval England. But it also suggests that she imagined herself as someone who deals in documents and who keeps them quite literally on her peripatetic person. It would seem that the Lollard letters are the obverse of Kempe's safe-conducts – whereas the non-conformist usurps textual authority, the conformist cheerfully seeks it out – but in fact they add up to much the same thing: they show that the textual forces that shape religious identity emerge both in the way a person's story is told and as the material texts that that person collects within the story of his or her own life.

This last example also shows why it is significant that Kempe collects documents only on her English pilgrimage. That she does so, of course, has something to do with the fact that she was from England and could appeal to the jurisdiction of English ecclesiastics, who, during the course of Kempe's lifetime, wielded ever more control over vagrants, heretics, and itinerant preachers. But more importantly, by locating documents in England in the particular way it does, the *Book of Margery Kempe* attests to the intersection of documentary culture and literary practice which is the subject of this book. I chose to end this book with the *Book of Margery Kempe*, not because it exemplifies a documentary poetics, but because it doesn't. By documentary poetics I mean the mutual shaping of literary texts and documentary culture, and specifically the ways that writers use documentary practices to think through problems of textual production. It is this awareness, that documents exemplify what it means to write a text in late medieval England, that makes documentary poetics largely a literary concern, whether that concern is intricately formal, such as the relation of narration to performance within the lyric (chapter 2), or more broadly theoretical, such as the question of how the document may represent competing definitions of textual community (chapter 5). By documentary poetics I also mean the tendency of English authors to borrow from and contribute selectively to documentary culture, in order to express ideas about textuality relevant to vernacular literature in late medieval England.

Margery Kempe never claims to carry a charter of Christ in her womb, nor does she use documents explicitly to call attention to her own literary project. She pursues her own identity textually, but not imaginatively, through the acquisition and possession of legal documents. Yet her *Book* brackets and extends the curious intersection between literature and documents by accounting for narratives of everyday life. It shows in a broad way how the amassing of documents, the collection and display of legal instruments, characterizes literary practice in fourteenth and early fifteenth-century England, not through analogy but through reciprocity. It is precisely the reciprocity between documentary culture and literary culture that allowed late medieval English authors to visualize new relationships between form and practice, identity and community, and text and self.

Bibliography

PRIMARY SOURCES

MANUSCRIPTS

CAMBRIDGE

Cambridge University Library MS Ff. 6.34, "Charter of Heaven"
Cambridge University Library MS Additional 6686, *Short Charter*
St. John's College MS B.15, *Short Charter*
St. John's College MS D.8, *Carta libera*
St. John's College MS E. 224, *Carta libera*

LONDON

British Library MS Additional 21253, *Carta Domini nostri Iesu Christ*
British Library MS Additional 37049, *Short Charter*
British Library MS Additional Charter 5960, *Short Charter*
British Library MS Cotton Caligula A, II, *Long Charter*
British Library MS Harley 2322, "Charter of Heaven"
British Library MS Harley 2382, *Long Charter*
British Library MS Harley 6848 Ar. 36, *Short Charter*
British Library MS Rawlinson poet. 175, *Long Charter*
British Library MS Sloane 3292, *Short Charter*
British Library MS Stowe 620, *Short Charter*
Lambeth Palace Library MS 408, *Lay Folks' Catechism* (interpolated)

NEW YORK

The Pierpont Morgan Library MS M.772, *Le pèlerinage de la vie humaine*

OXFORD

Bodleian Library MS Additional C. 280, *Long Charter*
Bodleian Library MS Douce 13, "Charter of Heaven"
Bodleian Library MS Douce 104, *Piers Plowman*

Bibliography

Bodleian Library MS Douce 274, *Lay Folks' Catechism* (interpolated)
Bodleian Library MS Douce 300, Guillaume de Deguileville, *Le pèlerinage de la vie humaine*
Bodleian Library MS Kent Charter 233, *Carta Dei*
Bodleian Library MS Rawlinson C. 209, "Charter of Heaven"
Bodleian Library MS Rawlinson C. 751, "Charter of Heaven", *Long Charter*
Bodley MS 89, *Long Charter*

PRINTED TEXTS

Augustine of Canterbury. *Opera Omnia*, vol. 1. Ed. Francis Schmitt. Stuttgart: Frommann-Holzboog, 1984.

Augustine of Hippo. *Enarrationes in Psalmos*. Ed. Eligius Dekkers and John Fraipont. CCSL, vols. 38–40. Turnhout: Typographi Brepols, 1956.

An Alphabet of Tales: An English Fifteenth-Century Translation of the Alphabetum Narrationum of Etienne de Besançon. Ed. Mary Macleod Banks. EETS OS 126–27. London: K. Paul, Trench, Trübner & Co., 1904.

Ancrene Wisse: Parts Six and Seven. Ed. Geoffrey Shepherd. London: T. Nelson and Sons Ltd., 1959.

Arnold, Thomas (ed.). *Select English Works of John Wyclif*. 3 vols. Oxford: Clarendon, 1869–71.

The Anonimalle Chronicle, 1333–1381. Ed. V. H. Galbraith. New York: Barnes and Noble, 1970.

Barr, Helen (ed.). *The 'Piers Plowman' Tradition: A Critical Edition of 'Pierce the Ploughman's Crede,' 'Richard the Redeless,' 'Mum and the Sothsegger,' and 'The Crowned King.'* London: J. M. Dent, 1993.

Biblia Latina cum Glossa ordinaria: Facsimile Reprint of Editio Princeps Adolf Rusch of Strassburg [1480–81]. 4 vols. Intro. Karl Froehlich and Margaret T. Gibson. Turnhout: Typographi Brepols, 1992.

Biblia Sacra vulgatae editiones. Paris: Lefevre Bibliopolam, 1843.

The Book of Vices and Virtues. Ed. W. Nelson Francis. EETS OS 217. London: Oxford University Press, 1942.

Bozon, Nicole. *Les contes moralises*. Ed. Lucy Toulmin Smith and Paul Meyer. Paris: Firmon Didot, 1889.

Bracton, Henry de. *De legibus et consuetudinibus Angliae*. Trans. Samuel E. Thorne. Cambridge: Belknap Press of Harvard University Press, in association with The Selden Society, 1968.

Camargo, Martin (ed.). *Medieval Rhetorics of Prose Composition: Five Medieval 'Artes Dictandi' and Their Tradition*. Binghamton: Medieval and Renaissance Texts and Studies, 1995.

Charles D'Orléans. *Fortunes Stabilnes: Charles of Orleans's English Book of Love, A Critical Edition*. Ed. Mary-Jo Arn. Binghamton: Medieval and Renaissance Texts and Studies, 1994.

Chaucer, Geoffrey. *The Riverside Chaucer*. Gen. ed. Larry D. Benson. 3rd edn. Boston: Houghton Mifflin, 1987.

Bibliography

Cigman, Gloria (ed.). *Lollard Sermons*. EETS OS 294. Oxford: Oxford University Press, 1989.

Crow, Martin M., and Clair C. Olson (eds.). *Chaucer Life-Records*. Oxford: Clarendon, 1966.

Davies, R. T. (ed.). *Middle English Lyrics: A Critical Anthology*. Chicago: Northwestern University Press, 1968.

Dean, James (ed.). *Six Ecclesiastical Satires*. Kalamazoo: Medieval Institute Publications, 1991.

Denholm-Young, Noel. *The Liber epistolaris of Richard de Bury*. Oxford: Roxburghe Club, 1950.

Durandus, Guillelmus. *Rationale divinorum officiorum*. Ed. A. Davril and T. M. Thibodeau. CCSL, vol. 140. Turnhout: Typographi Brepols, 1995.

Earliest English Wills. Ed. F. J. Furnivall. EETS OS 78. London: Trübner and Co., 1882.

The Early English Versions of the Gesta Romanorum. Ed. Sidney J. H. Herrtage, EETS ES 33. London: Oxford University Press, 1879.

Fasciculi zizaniorum magistri Johannis Wyclif cum Tritico. Ed. W. W. Shirley. Rolls Series vol. 5. Her Majesty's Stationary Office, 1858.

Fasciculus morum: A Fourteenth-Century Preacher's Handbook. Ed. and trans. Siegfried Wenzel. University Park: Pennsylvania State University Press, 1989.

The French Text of the 'Ancrene Riwle'. Ed. J. A. Herbert. EETS OS 240. London: Oxford University Press, 1944.

Gower, John. *The Complete Works of John Gower*, Ed. G. C. Macaulay. 4 vols. Oxford: Clarendon, 1899–1902.

Gower, John. *The Major Latin Works of John Gower*. Trans. Eric Stockton. Seattle: University of Washington Press, 1962.

Guillaume de Deguileville. *Le pèlerinage de la vie humaine*. Ed. J. J. Stürzinger. London: Printed for the Roxburghe Club by Nichols & Sons, 1893.

Guillaume de Deguileville. *The Pilgrimage of the Life of Man, Englisht by John Lydgate, A.D. 1426, from the French of Guillaume de Deguileville*. Ed. Frederick J. Furnivall and K. B. Locock. EETS ES 77, 83, 92. London: Trench, Trübner, 1899–1904.

Guillaume de Deguileville. *Pilgrimage of the Life of the Manhode*. Ed. Avril Henry. 2 vols. EETS OS 288. London: Oxford University Press, 1985.

Guillaume de Deguileville. *Pilgrimage of the Soul, A Critical Edition of the Middle English Dream Vision*. Ed. Rosemarie Potz McGerr. New York: Garland Pub, 1990.

Hoccleve, Thomas. *Hoccleve's Work*. Ed. Frederick J. Furnivall and I. Gollancz. Rev. edn. Jerome Mitchell and A. I. Doyle. EETS ES 61, 73. London: Kegan Paul, 1892. Rev. repr. Millwood, NY: Kraus Reprint, 1987.

Hoccleve, Thomas. *Regement of Princes*. Ed. Charles Blyth. Kalamazoo: Medieval Institute Publications, 1999.

Horstmann, Carl (ed.). *Yorkshire Writers: Richard Rolle of Hampole and His Followers*. 2 vols. London: Swann Sonnenschein & Co., 1895–6.

Horstmann, Carl, and Frederick J. Furnivall (eds.). *The Minor Poems of the Vernon Manuscript*. 2 vols. EETS OS 98, 117. London: Oxford University Press, 1892, 1901.

Hudson, Anne (ed.). *Selections from English Wycliffite Writings*. Cambridge: Cambridge University Press, 1978.

Hudson, Anne (ed). *Two Wycliffite Texts: The Sermon of William Taylor 1406 and the Testimony of William Thorpe 1407*. EETS OS 301. Oxford: Oxford University Press, 1993.

Hudson, Anne, and Pamela Gradon (eds.). *English Wycliffite Sermons*. Oxford: Clarendon, 1983.

Hugh of St. Cher. *Postilla super Psalterium*. Nurenberg: Anton Koberger, 1498.

Jacobus de Voragine. *The Golden Legend: Readings on the Saints*. Trans. William G. Ryan. 2 vols. Princeton: Princeton University Press, 1993, 1995.

Jeffrey, David, and Brian J. Levy (eds. and trans.). *The Anglo-Norman Lyric: An Anthology*. Toronto: Pontifical Institute of Mediaeval Studies, 1990.

John of Garland. *Parisiana Poetria of John of Garland*. Ed. and trans. Traugott Lawler. New Haven: Yale University Press, 1974.

Jones, Michael and Simon Walker (eds.). "Private Indentures for Life Service in Peace and War, 1278–1476." *Camden Miscellany* 32, 5th series. London: Royal Historical Society, 1994, 1–190.

Kempe, Margery. *The Book of Margery Kempe*. Ed. Barry Windeatt. New York: Longman, 2000.

Knighton, Henry. *Knighton's Chronicle 1337–1396*. Ed. and trans. G. H. Martin. Oxford: Clarendon, 1995.

Langland, William. *'Piers Plowman': The B Version*. Ed. George Kane and E. Talbot Donaldson. London: Athlone Press, 1975.

Langland, William. *'Piers Plowman': An Edition of the C-Text*. Ed. Derek Pearsall. Berkeley: University of California Press, 1978.

Langland, William. *'Piers Plowman': The A Version*. Ed. George Kane. London: Athlone Press, 1960. Rev. edn. 1988.

Langland, William. *'Piers Plowman': The C Version*. Ed. Geoffrey Russell and George Kane. London: Athlone Press, 1997.

Latham, R. E. *Revised Medieval Latin Word-List from British and Irish Sources*. London: Oxford University Press, 1965.

The Latin Text of Ancrene Riwle. Ed. Charlotte D'Evelyn. EETS OS 216. London: Oxford University Press, 1944.

The Lay Folks' Catechism. Ed. Thomas F. Simmons and Henry E. Nolloth. EETS OS 118. London: K. Paul, Trench, Trübner, 1901.

Legenda aurea. Ed. Giovanni Paolo Maggioni. Tavarnuzze: SISMEL – Edizioni del Galluzzo, 1998.

Lincoln Wills, vol. 1, *1271–1526*. Ed. and trans. C. W. Foster. Lincoln: J. W. Ruddock & Sons for the Lincoln Record Society, 1914.

Matthew, F. D. (ed.). *The English Works of John Wyclif Hitherto Unprinted*. London: Oxford University Press, 1880.

Bibliography

Mirk, John. *Festial*. Ed. Theodor Erbe. EETS ES 96. London: Oxford University Press, 1905.

Paschasius Radbertus. *Expositio in Matheo Libri XII*. Ed. Bede Paul. CCSL, vol. 56. Turnhout: Typographi Brepols, 1984.

Raymo, Robert R. (ed.). "A Middle English Version of the *Epistola Luciferi ad Clericos*." In Derek Pearsall and R. A. Waldron (eds.). *Medieval Literature and Civilization, Studies in Memory of G. N. Garmonsway*. London: The Athlone Press, 1969, 233–48.

Richard of Bury. *Richard D'Aungerville of Bury, Fragments of His Register and Other Documents*. Ed. Dean of Durham. London: Andrews & Co. for the Surtees Society, 1910.

Richard of Bury. *Philobiblon*. Ed. and trans. E. C. Thomas, rev. edn. by M. Maclagan. Oxford: Oxford University Press, 1960.

Rutebeuf. *Le miracle de Théophile*. Ed. Jean Dufournet. Paris: Flammarian, 1987.

Skeat, W. W. (ed.). *The Complete Works of Geoffrey Chaucer*. 5 vols. Oxford: Clarendon, 1897.

The South English Legendary. Ed. Charlotte D'Evelyn and Anna J. Miller. EETS OS 235, 236, 244. London: Oxford University Press, 1956–9.

Speculum Christiani: A Middle English Religious Treaty of the Fourteenth Century. Ed. Gustaf, Homstedt. EETS OS 182. London: Oxford University Press, 1933.

The Story off Theofle. Ed. Eugen Kolbing in "Die jungere engliche fassung der Theophilussage," *Englishe Studien* (1876): 30–57.

Tanner, Norman (ed.). *Heresy Trials in the Diocese of Norwich, 1428–31*, Camden Fourth Series, vol. 20. London: Royal Historical Society, 1977.

Walker, Greg (ed.). *Medieval Drama: An Anthology*. Oxford: Blackwell, 2000.

Walsingham, Thomas. *Gesta abbatum monasterii Sancti Albans*. Ed. H. T. Riley. Rolls Series 24.4., vol. 3. London: Longman, Green, 1869.

The Westminster Chronicle, 1381–94. Ed. and trans. L. C. Hector and Barbara F. Harvey. New York: Oxford University Press, 1982.

SECONDARY SOURCES

Adams, Robert. "Langland's Theology." In John Alford (ed.). *A Companion to 'Piers Plowman,'* pp. 87–114.

Adorno, Theodor W. *Notes to Literature*. 2 vols. Ed. Rolf Tiedemann, trans. Shierry Weber Nicholsen. New York: Columbia University Press, 1991–2.

Aers, David. "Christ's Humanity and *Piers Plowman*." *Yearbook of Langland Studies* 8 (1994): 107–25.

Aers, David. "*Vox populi* and the Literature of 1381." In David Wallace (ed.). *The Cambridge History of Middle English Literature*, pp. 432–53.

Alford, John. "Literature and Law in Medieval England." *Publications of the Modern Language Association* 92 (1977): 941–51.

Alford, John. *'Piers Plowman': A Glossary of Legal Diction*. Cambridge: D. S. Brewer, 1988.

Bibliography

Alford, John. (ed.). *A Companion to 'Piers Plowman.'* Berkeley: University of California Press, 1988.

Alford, John. *'Piers Plowman': A Guide to the Quotations*. Binghamton: State University of New York Press, 1992.

Alford, John. "The Scriptural Self." In Bernard S. Levy (ed.). *The Bible in the Middle Ages: Its Influence on Literature and Art*. Binghamton: Medieval and Renaissance Texts and Studies, 1992, pp. 1–21.

Alford, John. "Langland's Learning." *Yearbook of Langland Studies* 9 (1995): 1–17.

Alford, John. "Langland's Exegetical Drama: The Sources of the Banquet Scene in *Piers Plowman*." In John Alford and Richard Newhauser (eds.). *Literature and Religion in the Later Middle Ages: Philological Studies in Honor of Siegfried Wenzel*. Binghamton: Medieval and Renaissance Texts and Studies, 1995, pp. 97–117.

Allen, Judson Boyce. "Langland's Reading and Writing: Detractor and the Pardon Passus." *Speculum* 59 (1984): 342–62.

Allen, Judson Boyce. "Grammar, Poetic Form, and the Lyric Ego: A Medieval *A Priori*." In Lois Ebin (ed.). *Vernacular Poetics in the Middle Ages*, pp. 199–226.

Ames, Ruth. "The Pardon Impugned by the Priest." In Bernard Levy and Paul Szarmach (eds.). *The Alliterative Tradition in the Fourteenth Century*. Kent, OH: Kent State University Press, 1981, pp. 47–67.

Aston, Margaret. "Lollardy and Sedition, 1381–1431." *Past and Present* (1960): 1–39.

Aston, Margaret. *Lollards and Reformers: Images and Literacy in England*. London: Hambledon Press, 1984.

Baker, Denise. "The Pardons of *Piers Plowman*." *Neuphilologische Mitteilungen* 85 (1984): 462–72.

Baldwin, Anna. "The Debt Narrative in *Piers Plowman*." In Robert R. Edwards (ed.). *Art and Context*, pp. 37–50.

Barr, Helen. *Signes and Sothe: Language in the 'Piers Plowman' Tradition*. Cambridge: D. S. Brewer, 1994.

Barton, J. L. "The Mystery of Bracton." *Journal of Legal History* 14 (1993): 1–142.

Baswell, Christopher. "*Latinitas*." In David Wallace (ed.). *The Cambridge History of Medieval English Literature*, pp. 122–51.

Baugh, Albert C. and Thomas Cable. *A History of the English Language*. 3rd edn. Englewood Cliffs, NJ: Prentice Hall, 1993.

Beckwith, Sarah. "Problems of Authority in Late Medieval English Mysticism: Language, Agency, and Authority in the *Book of Margery Kempe*." *Exemplaria* 4 (1992): 172–99.

Beckwith, Sarah. *Christ's Body: Identity, Culture, and Society in Late Medieval Writings*. New York: Routledge, 1993.

Bedos-Rezak, Brigitte. "Diplomatic Sources and Medieval Documentary Practices." In John Van Engen (ed.). *The Past and Future of Medieval Studies*. Notre Dame: University of Notre Dame Press, 1994, pp. 313–43.

Bennett, Michael J. "Careerism in Late Medieval England." In Joel Rosenthal and Colin Richmond (eds.). *People, Politics and Community in the Later Middle Ages*. New York: St. Martin's Press, 1987, pp. 19–39.

Bibliography

Blamires, Alcuin. "*Mum & the Sothsegger* and Langlandian Idiom." *Neuphilologische Mitteilungen* 76 (1975): 583–604.

Boffey, Julia. "Lydgate, Henryson, and the Literary Testament." *Modern Language Quarterly* 53 (1992): 41–56.

Boureau, Alain. "The Letter-Writing Norm, A Mediaeval Invention." In Roger Chartier, Alain Boureau, and Cecile Dauphin (eds.). Christopher Woodall (trans.). *Correspondence: Models of Letter-Writing from the Middle Ages to the Nineteenth Century.* Princeton: Princeton University Press, 1997, pp. 1–58.

Bowers, John M. *The Crisis of Will in 'Piers Plowman'.* Washington, DC: The Catholic University Press, 1986.

Bowers, John M. "*Piers Plowman* and the Police: Notes Towards a Wycliffite Langland." *Yearbook of Langland Studies* 6 (1992): 1–50.

Boyle, Leonard E. "Diplomatics." In J. M. Powell (ed.). *Medieval Studies: An Introduction.* Syracuse: Syracuse University Press, 1992, pp. 69–101.

Brady, M. Teresa. "Lollard Interpolation and Omissions in Manuscripts of the *Pore Caitif.*" In Michael Sargent (ed.). *De cella in seculum: Religious and Secular Life and Devotion in Late Medieval England: an Interdisciplinary Conference in Celebration of the Eighth Centenary of the Consecration of St. Hugh of Avalon, Bishop of Lincoln, 20–22 July, 1986.* Cambridge: D. S. Brewer, 1989, pp. 183–203.

Brand, Paul. "'The Age of Bracton.'" In John Hudson (ed.). *The History of English Law: Centenary Essays on "Pollock and Maitland."* Oxford: Oxford University Press for the British Academy, 1996, pp. 65–90.

Brand, Paul. *The Origins of the Legal Profession.* Oxford: Blackwell, 1992.

Brownlee, Kevin. "The Problem of Faux Semblant: Language, History, and Truth in the *Roman de la Rose.*" In Marina Brownlee, Kevin Brownlee, and Stephen Nichols (eds.). *The New Medievalism.* Baltimore: Johns Hopkins University Press, 1991, pp. 253–71.

Burgess, Clive. "Late Medieval Wills and Pious Convention: Testamentary Evidence Reconsidered." In M. A. Hicks (ed.). *Profit and the Professions in Later Medieval England.* Wolfeboro Falls: A. Sutton, 1990, pp. 14–33.

Burrow, J. A. "Autobiographical Poetry in the Middle Ages: The Case of Thomas Hoccleve." *Proceedings of the British Academy* 68 (1982): 389–412.

Burrow, J. A. *Langland's Fictions.* Oxford: Clarendon, 1993.

Burrow, J. A. *Thomas Hoccleve.* Aldershot: Variorum, 1994.

Burton, Dorothy Jean. "The Compact with the Devil in the Middle English Version of *Piers the Plowman,* B. II." *California Folklore Quarterly* 5 (1946): 179–84.

Camargo, Martin. *Ars dictaminis, Ars dictandi.* Turnhout: Brepols, 1991.

Camille, Michael. "The Illustrated Manuscripts of Guillaume de Deguileville's 'Pèlerinages', 1330–1426." Unpublished doctoral dissertation, University of Cambridge, 1985.

Camille, Michael. "The Language of Images in Medieval England, 1200–1400." In J. J. G. Alexander and Paul Binski (eds.). *Age of Chivalry: Art in Plantagenet England, 1200–1400.* London: Royal Academy of the Arts, 1987, pp. 33–40.

Camille, Michael. "The Devil's Writing: Diabolic Literacy in Medieval Art." In Irving Lavin (ed.). *World Art: Themes of Unity and Diversity.* University Park: Pennsylvania State University Press, 1989, pp. 355–60.

Camille, Michael. "The Book as Flesh and Fetish in Richard de Bury's *Philobiblon.*" In Dolores Warwick Frese and Katherine O'Brien O'Keeffe (eds.). *The Book and the Body.* Notre Dame: University of Notre Dame Press, 1997, pp. 34–77.

Carruthers, Mary. *The Search for St. Truth.* Evanston: Northwestern University Press, 1973.

Carruthers, Mary. *The Book of Memory: A Study of Memory in Medieval Culture.* Cambridge: Cambridge University Press, 1990.

Catto, J. I., and Ralph Evans (ed.). *A History of the University of Oxford, vol 2: Late Medieval Oxford.* Oxford: Clarendon, 1992.

Chaplais, Pierre. *English Royal Documents: King John–Henry VI, 1199–1461.* Oxford: Clarendon, 1971.

Chaplais, Pierre. *Essays in Medieval Diplomacy and Administration.* London: Hambledon Press, 1981.

Chaplais, Pierre. *English Medieval Diplomatic Practice, Part I: Documents and Interpretation.* London: Her Majesty's Stationary Office, 1982.

Clanchy, M. T. "Archives and Memory in the Middle Ages." *Archivaria* 11 (1981): 115–25.

Clanchy, M. T. "Literacy, Law and the Power of the State." In Jean-Claude Vigueur, C. Pietri, and Jean-Paul Genet (eds.). *Culture et Idéologie dans la Genèse de l'Etat Moderne.* Paris: Collection de l'Ecole Française de Rome, 1985, pp. 25–43.

Clanchy, M. T. *From Memory to Written Record: England 1066–1307.* 2nd edn. Cambridge: Blackwell, 1993.

Coleman, Janet. "The Science of Politics and Late Medieval Academic Debate." In Rita Copeland (ed.). *Criticism and Dissent,* pp. 181–214.

Coleman, Joyce. *Public Reading and the Reading Public in Late Medieval England and France.* Cambridge: Cambridge University Press, 1996.

Colish, Marcia. "*Psalterium Scholasticorum*: Peter Lombard and the Emergence of Scholastic Psalms Exegesis." *Speculum* 67 (1992): 531–48.

Copeland, Rita. "Why Women Can't Read: Medieval Hermeneutics, Statuary Law, and the Lollard Heresy Trials." In Susan Sage Heinzelman and Zipporah Batshaw Wiseman (eds.). *Representing Women: Law, Literature, and Feminism.* Durham: Duke University Press, 1994, pp. 253–86.

Copeland, Rita. "William Thorpe and His Lollard Community: Intellectual Labor and the Representation of Dissent." In Barbara A. Hanawalt and David Wallace (eds.). *Bodies and Disciplines: Intersections of Literature and History in Fifteenth-Century England,* Minneapolis: University of Minnesota Press, 1996, pp. 199–221.

Copeland, Rita. (ed.). *Criticism and Dissent in the Middle Ages.* Cambridge: Cambridge University Press, 1996.

Copeland, Rita. *Pedagogy, Intellectuals, and Dissent in the Later Middle Ages: Lollardy and Ideas of Learning.* Cambridge: Cambridge University Press, 2001.

Crane, Susan. "The Writing Lesson of 1381." In Barbara Hanawalt (ed.). *Chaucer's England,* pp. 201–21.

Bibliography

Crane, Susan. "Anglo-Norman Cultures in England, 1066–1460." In David Wallace (ed.). *The Cambridge History of Medieval English Literature*, pp. 35–60.

Cross, Claire. "'Great Reasoners in Scripture': The Activities of Women Lollards, 1380–1530." In Derek Baker (ed.). *Medieval Women*. Oxford: Basil Blackwell, 1978, pp. 359–80.

Curtius, Ernst Robert. *European Literature and the Latin Middle Ages*. Trans. Willard R. Trask. Princeton: Princeton University Press, 1973.

Denholm-Young, Noel. "Richard de Bury, 1287–1345." In *Collected Papers on Mediaeval Subjects*. Oxford: Basil Blackwell, 1946, pp. 135–68.

Derrida, Jacques. *Of Grammatology*. Trans. Gayatri Chakravorty Spivak. Baltimore: Johns Hopkins University Press, 1976.

Derrida, Jacques. *Archive Fever*. Trans. Eric Prenowitz. Chicago: University of Chicago Press, 1996.

Dinshaw, Carolyn. *Chaucer's Sexual Poetics*. Madison: University of Wisconsin Press, 1989.

Donaldson, E. T. *'Piers Plowman': The C-Text and its Poet*. New Haven: Yale University Press, 1949.

Du Cange, Charles Du Fresne (1610–88). *Glossarium mediae et infimae Latinitatis*. Graz, Austria: Akademische Druck – u. Verlagsanstalt, 1954.

Duffy, Eamon. *The Stripping of the Altars: Traditional Religion in England, 1400–1580*. New Haven: Yale University Press, 1992.

Duranti, Luciana. *Diplomatics: New Uses for an Old Science*. London: Society of American Archivists and Association of Canadian Archivists, in association with the Scarecrow Press, 1998.

Dyer, Christopher. "Social and Economic Background to the Rural Revolt of 1381." In Rodney H. Hilton and T. H. Aston (eds.). *The English Rising of 1381*. Cambridge: Cambridge University Press, 1984, pp. 9–42.

Ebin, Lois (ed.). *Vernacular Poetics in the Middle Ages*. Kalamazoo: Medieval Institute Publications, 1984.

Economou, George. "Self-Consciousness of Poetic Activity in Dante and Langland." In Lois Ebin (ed.). *Vernacular Poetics in the Middle Ages*, pp. 177–98.

Edwards, Robert R. (ed.). *Art and Context in Late Medieval English Narrative: Essays in Honor of Robert Worth Frank Jr*. Rochester, NY: D. S. Brewer, 1994.

Faith, Rosamund, "The 'Great Rumor' of 1377 and Peasant Ideology." In Rodney Hilton and T. H. Aston (eds.). *The English Rising of 1381*, pp. 43–73.

Ferster, Judith. *Fictions of Advice: The Literature and Politics of Counsel in Late Medieval England*. Philadelphia: University of Pennsylvania Press, 1996.

Fisher, John. *The Emergence of Standard English*. Lexington: The University Press of Kentucky, 1996.

Foucault, Michel. *The Archeology of Knowledge*. Trans. A. M. Sheridan Smith. New York: Pantheon Books, 1972.

Fowler, Elizabeth. "Civil Death and the Maiden: Agency and the Conditions of Contract in *Piers Plowman*." *Speculum* (1995): 760–92.

Frank, Robert Worth, Jr. *'Piers Plowman' and the Scheme of Salvation*. New Haven: Yale University Press, 1957.

Galbraith, V. H. *Domesday Book: Its Place in Administrative History*. Oxford: Clarendon, 1974.

Galloway, Andrew. "*Piers Plowman* and the Schools." *Yearbook of Langland Studies* 6 (1992): 89–107.

Galloway, Andrew. "Writing History in England." In David Wallace (ed.). *The Cambridge History of Medieval English Literature*, pp. 255–83.

Galloway, Andrew. "Making History Legal: *Piers Plowman* and the Rebels of Fourteenth-Century England." In Kathleen M. Hewett-Smith (ed.). *William Langland's 'Piers Plowman'*. New York: Routledge, 2001, pp. 7–39.

Gellrich, Jesse. *The Idea of the Book in the Middle Ages: Language Theory, Mythology and Fiction*. Ithaca: Cornell University Press, 1985.

Goldberg, Jonathan. *Writing Matter: From the Hands of the English Renaissance*. Stanford: Stanford University Press, 1990.

Gradon, Pamela. "Langland and the Ideology of Dissent." *Proceedings of the British Academy* 66 (1980): 179–205.

Gradon, Pamela. "*Trajanus Redivivus*: Another Look at Trajan in *Piers Plowman*." In Douglas Gray and E. G. Stanley (eds.). *Medieval Studies Presented to Norman Davis in Honor of his Seventieth Birthday*. Oxford: Clarendon, 1983, pp. 93–114.

Grady, Frank. "*Piers Plowman, St. Erkenwald*, and the Rule of Exceptional Salvation." *Yearbook of Langland Studies* 6 (1992): 61–88.

Grady, Frank. "The Generation of 1399." In Emily Steiner and Candace Barrington (eds.). *The Letter of the Law*, pp. 185–229.

Gransden, Antonia. *Historical Writing in England ca. 550–1307*. Ithaca: Cornell University Press, 1974.

Green, Richard Firth. "Lydgate and Deguileville Once More." *Notes and Queries*, n.s. 25, 233:2 (1978): 105–6.

Green, Richard Firth. *Poets and Princepleasers: Literature and the English Court in the Late Middle Ages*. Toronto: University of Toronto Press, 1980.

Green, Richard Firth. "John Ball's Letters: Literary History and Historical Literature." In Barbara Hanawalt (ed.). *Chaucer's England*, pp. 76–200.

Green, Richard Firth. *A Crisis of Truth: Literature and Law in Ricardian England*. Philadelphia: University of Pennsylvania Press, 1999.

Green, Richard Firth. "Medieval Literature and Law." In David Wallace (ed.). *The Cambridge History of Medieval English Literature*, pp. 407–31.

Griffiths, Jeremy, and Derek Pearsall (eds.). *Book Production and Publishing in Britain 1375–1475*. Cambridge University Press, 1989.

Griffiths, R. A. "Public and Private Bureaucracies in England and Wales in the Fifteenth Century." *Transactions of the Royal Historical Society*. 5th series. 30 (1980): 109–30.

Hagen, Susan. *Allegorical Remembrance: A Study of 'The Pilgrimage of the Life of Man' as a Medieval Treatise on Seeing and Remembering*. Athens: University of Georgia Press, 1990.

Hall, Hubert. *Select Formulas of English Historical Documents*. New York: Burt Franklin, 1969 [1908–9].

Hallam, Elizabeth. *Domesday Book Through Nine Centuries*. New York: Thames and Hudson, 1986.

Hanawalt, Barbara (ed.). *Chaucer's England: Literature in Historical Context*. Minneapolis: University of Minnesota Press, 1992.

Hanna, Ralph, III. "The Difficulty of Ricardian Prose Translation: The Case of the Lollards." *Modern Language Quarterly* 51 (1990): 319–40.

Hanna, Ralph, III. "Some Norfolk Women and Their Books." In June Hall McCash (ed.). *The Cultural Performance of Medieval Women*. Athens: University of Georgia Press, 1996, pp. 208–305.

Hanna, Ralph, III. "Will's Work." In Steven Justice and Kathryn Kerby-Fulton (eds.). *Written Work*, pp. 23–66.

Harding, Alan. *A Social History of English Law*. Baltimore: Penguin Books, 1966.

Harding, Alan. *England in the Thirteenth Century*. Cambridge: Cambridge University Press, 1993.

Harding, Alan. *Medieval Law and the Foundations of the State*. Oxford: Oxford University Press, 2002.

Hartung, Albert (gen. ed.). *A Manual of the Writings in Middle English*, vol. 23. New Haven: The Connecticut Academy of Arts and Sciences, 1986.

Harvey, Barbara. "Draft Letters Patent of Manumission and Pardon for the Men of Somerset in 1381." *English Historical Review* 80 (1965): 89–91.

Harvey, P. D. A., and Andrew McGuiness. *A Guide to British Medieval Seals*. Toronto: University of Toronto Press, 1996.

Henry, Avril. "The Illuminations in the Two Illustrated Middle English Manuscripts of the Prose *Pilgrimage of the Lyfe of the Manhode*." *Scriptorium* 37 (1983): 264–73.

Hiett, Alfred. "The Cartographic Imagination of Thomas Elmham." *Speculum* 75 (2000): 859–86.

Hilton, Rodney H. *Bondmen Made Free: Medieval Peasant Movements and the English Rising of 1381*. New York: Temple Smith, 1973.

Hilton, Rodney H., and T. H. Aston (eds.). *The English Rising of 1381*. Cambridge: Cambridge University Press, 1984.

Holsinger, Bruce. "Langland's Musical Reader: Liturgy, Law, and the Constraints of Performance." *Studies in the Age of Chaucer* 21 (1999): 99–141.

Holsinger, Bruce. "Vernacular Legality: The English Jurisdictions of *The Owl and the Nightingale*." In Emily Steiner and Candace Barrington (eds.). *The Letter of the Law*, pp. 154–84.

Hudson, Anne. "The Expurgation of a Lollard Sermon-Cycle." In Anne Hudson (ed.). *Lollards and Their Books*. London: Hambleton Press, 1985, pp. 201–16.

Hudson, Anne. "A New Look at *The Lay Folks' Catechism*." *Viator* 16 (1985): 241–58.

Hudson, Anne. *The Premature Reformation: Wycliffite Texts and Lollard History*. Oxford: Clarendon, 1988.

Hudson, Anne. "'*Laicus litteratus*': The Paradox of Lollardy." In Peter Biller and Anne Hudson (eds.). *Heresy and Literacy, 1000–1530.* Cambridge: Cambridge University Press, 1994, pp. 222–36.

Hughes, M. E. J. "'The Feffment that Fals Hath Ymaked': A Study of the Image of the Document in Some Literary Analogues." *Neuphilologische Mitteilungen* 93 (1992): 125–33.

Hussey, S. S. "Implication of Choice and Arrangement of Texts in Part 4." In Derek Pearsall (ed.). *Studies in the Vernon Manuscript.* Cambridge: D. S. Brewer, 1990, pp. 61–74.

Jager, Eric. "The Book of the Heart: Reading and Writing the Medieval Subject." *Speculum* 71 (1996): 1–26.

Jameson, Frederic. *The Political Unconscious.* Ithaca: Cornell University Press, 1981.

Jeffrey, David. *The Early English Lyric & Franciscan Spirituality.* Lincoln: University of Nebraska Press, 1975.

Jones, H. S. V. "Imaginatif in *Piers Plowman*." *Journal of English and Germanic Philology* 13 (1914): 583–8.

Justice, Steven. "The Genres of *Piers Plowman*." *Viator* 19 (1988): 291–306.

Justice, Steven. *Writing and Rebellion: England in 1381.* Berkeley: University of California Press, 1994.

Justice, Steven. "Inquisition, Speech and Writing: A Case from Late Medieval Norwich." In Rita Copeland (ed.). *Criticism and Dissent*, pp. 244–63.

Justice, Steven, and Kathryn Kerby-Fulton (eds.). *Written Work: Langland, Labor, Authorship.* Philadelphia: University of Pennsylvania Press, 1997.

Kaulbach, Ernest. *Imaginative Prophecy in the B-Text of Piers Plowman.* Cambridge: D. S. Brewer, 1993.

Keen, Jill Averil. "Documenting Salvation: Charters and Pardons in 'Thou Wommon Boute Vere,' the *Charters of Christ* and *Piers Plowman*." Unpublished doctoral dissertation, University of Minnesota, 1995.

Ker, N. R. *English Manuscripts in the Century after the Norman Conquest.* Oxford: Clarendon, 1960.

Kerby-Fulton, Kathryn, and Denise Dupres. *Iconography and the Professional Reader: The Politics of Book Production in the Douce 'Piers Plowman'.* Minneapolis: University of Minnesota Press, 1999.

Kerby-Fulton, Kathryn, and Steven Justice. "Langlandian Reading Circles and the Civil Service in London and Dublin, 1380–1427." *New Medieval Literatures* 1 (1997): 59–83.

Kibbee, Douglas A. *"For to Speke Frenche Trewely": The French Language in England, 1000–1600: Its Status, Description and Instruction.* Philadelphia: John Benjamins Publishing, 1991.

Kirk, Elizabeth. "Langland's Narrative Christology." In Robert R. Edwards (ed.). *Art and Context*, pp. 17–35.

Knapp, Ethan. "Bureaucratic Identity and the Construction of the Self in Hoccleve's *Formulary* and *La Male Regle*." *Speculum* 74 (1999): 357–76.

Kuczynski, Michael P. *Prophetic Song: The Psalms as Moral Discourse in Late Medieval Literature*. Philadelphia: University of Pennsylvania Press, 1995.

Kurath, Hans, and Sherman Kuhn (eds.). *Middle English Dictionary*. Ann Arbor: University of Minnesota Press, 1952 – present.

LaCapra, Dominick. *Rethinking Intellectual History: Texts, Contexts, Language*. Ithaca: Cornell University Press, 1983.

Lawler, Traugott. "The Pardon Formula in *Piers Plowman*: Its Ubiquity, Its Binary Shape; Its Silent Middle Term." *Yearbook of Langland Studies* 14 (2000): 117–52.

Lawton, David. "Lollardy and the *Piers Plowman* Tradition." *Modern Language Review* 76 (1981): 780–93.

Lawton, David. "*Piers Plowman*: On Tearing – or Not Tearing – the Pardon." *Philological Quarterly* 60 (1981): 414–22.

Leff, Gordon. *Heresy in the Later Middle Ages*. 2 vols. Manchester: Manchester University Press, 1967.

Lerer, Seth. *Literacy and Power in Anglo-Saxon England*. Lincoln: University of Nebraska Press, 1991.

Lewis, Flora. "Rewarding Devotion: Indulgences and the Promotion of Images." In Diana Wood (ed.). *The Church and the Arts*. Oxford: Blackwell, 1992, pp. 179–94.

Lindenbaum, Sheila. "London Texts and Literate Practice," In David Wallace (ed.). *The Cambridge History of Medieval English Literature*, pp. 284–309.

Lochrie, Karma. *Margery Kempe and Translations of the Flesh*. Philadelphia: University of Pennsylvania Press, 1991.

Marx, C. W. *The Devil's Rights and the Redemption in the Literature of Medieval England*. Cambridge: D. S. Brewer, 1995.

McNiven, Peter. *Heresy and Politics in the Reign of Henry IV: The Burning of John Badby*. Woodbridge, Suffolk; Wolfeboro, NH: Boydell, 1987.

Middleton, Anne. "The Idea of Public Poetry in the Reign of Richard II." *Speculum* 53 (1978): 94–114.

Middleton, Anne. "The Audience and Public of *Piers Plowman*." In David Lawton (ed.). *Middle English Alliterative Poetry*. Cambridge: D. S. Brewer, 1982, pp. 101–23.

Middleton, Anne. "Narration and the Invention of Experience: Episodic Form in *Piers Plowman*." In Larry D. Benson and Siegfried Wenzel (eds.). *The Wisdom of Poetry: Essays in Early English Literature in Honor of Morton Bloomfield*. Kalamazoo: Medieval Institute Publications, 1982, pp. 81–122.

Middleton, Anne. "Acts of Vagrancy: The C-Version 'Autobiography' (C. 5.1-108) and the Statute of 1388." In Steven Justice and Kathryn Kerby-Fulton (eds.). *Written Work*, pp. 208–317.

Minnis, Alistair. "Langland's Ymaginatif and Late-Medieval Theories of Imagination." *Comparative Criticism* 3 (1981): 71–103.

Minnis, Alistair. *Medieval Theories of Authorship: Scholastic Literary Attitudes in the Later Middle Ages*. 2nd edn. Philadelphia: University of Pennsylvania Press, 1988.

Shklar, Ruth [Nissé]. "Cobham's Daughter: *The Book of Margery Kempe* and the Power of Heterodox Thinking." *Modern Language Quarterly* 56.3 (1995): 277–304.

O'Keeffe, Katherine O'Brian. *Visible Song: Transitional Literacy in Old English Verse*. Cambridge: Cambridge University Press, 1990.

Orme, Nicholas. *English Schools in the Middle Ages*. London: Methuen and Co. Ltd., 1973.

Orme, Nicholas. "Indulgences in the Diocese of Exeter 1100–1536." *Transactions of the Devonshire Association for the Advancement of Science, Literature, and Art* 120 (1988): 15–32.

Palmer, Robert. *English Law in the Age of the Black Death, 1348–1381: A Transformation of Governance and Law*. Chapel Hill: The University of North Carolina Press, 1993.

Parkes, M. B. "The Literacy of the Laity." In D. Daiches and A. Thorlby (eds.). *The Medieval World*. London: Aldus Books, 1973, pp. 555–77.

Patterson, Lee. *Negotiating the Past: The Historical Understanding of Medieval Literature*. Madison: University of Wisconsin Press, 1987.

Pearsall, Derek. *The Life of Geoffrey Chaucer*. Oxford: Basil Blackwell, 1992.

Phillips, Helen. "Chaucer and Deguileville: The *ABC* in Context." *Medium Aevum* 62 (1993): 1–19.

Pollack, Frederick, and F. W. Maitland. *A History of English Law Before the Time of Edward I*, 2nd edn. London: Cambridge University Press, 1968.

Pollard, A. W., and G. R. Redgrave (eds.). *A Short-Title Catalogue of Books Printed in England, Scotland, and Ireland 1475–1640*. 2nd edn. rev. and enlarged by W. A. Jackson, F. S. Ferguson, and Katharine F. Pantzer. 3 vols. London: Bibliographical Society, 1976, 1986, and 1991.

Rice, Nicole, "Spiritual Ambition and the Translation of the Cloister: *The Abbey* and *Charter of the Holy Ghost*." *Viator* 33 (forthcoming, 2002).

Richardson, H. G. "Business Training in Medieval Oxford." *American Historical Review* 46 (1941): 259–78.

Richardson, Malcolm. "The Fading Influence of the Medieval *Ars Dictaminis* in England After 1400." *Rhetorica* 19 (2001): 225–47.

Rothwell, William. "Language and Government in Medieval England." *Zeitschrift Für Franzosische Sprache und Literatur* 93 (1983): 258–70.

Rothwell, William. "The Legacy of Anglo-French: *Faux Amis* in French and English." *Zeitschrift Für Romanische Philologie* 109 (1993): 16–46.

Rothwell, William. "The Trilingual England of Geoffrey Chaucer." *Studies in the Age of Chaucer* 16 (1994): 45–67.

Russell, J. Stephen. "Allegorical Monstrosity: the Case of Deguileville." *Allegorica* 5 (1980): 95–103.

Salter, Elizabeth. *'Piers Plowman': An Introduction*. Cambridge, MA: Harvard University Press, 1962.

Savage, Anne, and Nicholas Watson. *Anchoritic Spirituality: Ancrene Wisse and Associated Works*. New York: Paulist Press, 1991.

Sayers, Jane. "The Medieval Care and Custody of the Archbishop of Canterbury's Archives." In *Law and Records in Medieval England: Studies on the Medieval Papacy, Monasteries and Records*. London: Variorum Reprints, 1988, pp. 95–109.

Bibliography

Scase, Wendy. *Piers Plowman and the New Anticlericalism*. Cambridge: Cambridge University Press, 1989.

Scase, Wendy. "Writing and the Plowman: Langland and Literacy." *Yearbook of Langland Studies* 9 (1995): 121–39.

Scase, Wendy. "'Strange and Wonderful Bills': Bill-Casting and Political Discourse in Late Medieval England." *New Medieval Literatures* 2 (1998): 225–47.

Scattergood, John. *The Lost Tradition: Essays on Middle English Alliterative Poetry*. Dublin: Four Courts, 2000.

Simpson, James. *'Piers Plowman': An Introduction to the B-Text*. New York: Longman, 1990.

Simpson, James. "The Constraints of Satire in *Piers Plowman* and *Mum and the Sothsegger*." In Helen Phillips (ed.). *Langland, the Mystics, and the Medieval English Religious Tradition, Essays in Honour of S. S. Hussey*. Cambridge: D. S. Brewer, 1990, pp. 11–30.

Smith, D. Vance. *The Book of the Incipit: Beginnings in the Fourteenth Century*. Minneapolis: University of Minnesota Press, 2001.

Somerset, Fiona. *Clerical Discourse and Lay Audience in Late Medieval England*. Cambridge University Press, 1998.

Spalding, M. C. *The Middle English Charters of Christ*. Bryn Mawr: Bryn Mawr College, 1914.

Spearing, A. C. "Prison, Writing, Absence: Representing the Subject in the English Poems of Charles D'Orléans." *Modern Language Quarterly* 53 (1992): 83–99.

Spitzer, Leo. "A Note on the Poetic and Empirical 'I' in Medieval Authors." *Traditio* 4 (1946): 414–22.

Staley, Lynn. *Margery Kempe's Dissenting Fictions*. University Park: Pennsylvania State University Press, 1994.

Steiner, Emily, and Candace Barrington (eds.). *The Letter of the Law: Legal Practice and Literary Production in Medieval England*. Ithaca: Cornell University Press, 2002.

Stewart, Susan. *On Longing: Narratives of the Miniature, the Gigantic, the Souvenir, the Collection*. Durham, NC: Duke University Press, 1993.

Stock, Brian. *Listening for the Text: On the Uses of the Past*. Baltimore: Johns Hopkins University Press, 1990; rev. edn. Philadelphia: University of Pennsylvania Press, 1996.

Strohm, Paul. *Hochon's Arrow: The Social Imagination of Fourteenth-Century Texts*. Princeton: Princeton University Press, 1992.

Strohm, Paul. "Chaucer's Lollard Joke: History and the Textual Unconscious." *Studies in the Age of Chaucer* 17 (1995): 23–42.

Strohm, Paul. *Theory and the Premodern Text*. Minneapolis: University of Minnesota Press, 2000.

Tavormina, M. Teresa. *Kindly Similitude: Marriage and Family in 'Piers Plowman'*. Cambridge: D. S. Brewer, 1995.

Taylor, John. *English Historical Literature in the Fourteenth Century*. Oxford: Clarendon, 1987.

Bibliography

Tout, T. F. "Literature and Learning in the English Civil Service in the Fourteenth Century." *Speculum* 4 (1929): 365–89.

Tout, T. F. *Chapters in the Administrative History of Medieval England*, vol. 5. Manchester: Manchester University Press, 1920–33.

Turner, Victor. *The Anthropology of Performance*. New York: PAJ Publications, 1988.

Uhlman, Diana. "The Comfort of Voice, the Solace of Script: Orality and Literacy in *The Book of Margery Kempe*." *Studies in Philology* 91 (1994): 50–69.

von Nolken, Christina. "*Piers Plowman*, the Wycliffites, and *Pierce the Plowman's Creed*." *Yearbook of Langland Studies* 2 (1988): 71–102.

Waldron, R. A. "Langland's Originality: The Christ-Knight and the Harrowing of Hell." In Gregory Kratzmann and James Simpson (eds.). *Medieval English Religious and Ethical Literature: Essays in Honor of G. H. Russell*. Cambridge: D. S. Brewer, 1986, pp. 66–81.

Wallace, David. *Chaucerian Polity: Absolutist Lineages and Associational Forms in England and Italy*. Stanford: Stanford University Press, 1997.

Wallace, David. (ed.). *The Cambridge History of Medieval English Literature*. Cambridge: Cambridge University Press, 1999.

Walls, Kathryn. "Did Lydgate Translate the *Pèlerinage de la vie humaine?*" *Notes and Queries*, n.s. 24, 222:2 (1977): 103–5.

Watson, Nicholas. "Censorship and Cultural Change in Late Medieval England: Vernacular Theology, the Oxford Translation Debate, and Arundel's Constitutions of 1409." *Speculum* 70 (1995): 822–64.

Watson, Nicholas. "Conceptions of the Word: The Mother Tongue and the Incarnation of God." *New Medieval Literatures* 1 (1997): 85–124.

Watson, Nicholas. "Visions of Inclusion: Universal Salvation and Vernacular Theology in Pre-Reformation England." *Journal of Medieval and Early Modern Studies* 27 (1997): 145–87.

Wenzel, Siegfried. *Verses in Sermons: "Fasciculus morum" and its Middle English Poems*. Cambridge, MA: The Mediaeval Academy of America, 1978.

Wenzel, Siegfried. "Langland's Troianus." *Yearbook of Langland Studies* 10 (1996): 181–5.

Westrem, Scott. *The Hereford Map*. Turnhout: Brepols, 2001.

Woolf, Rosemary. "Tearing the Pardon." In S. S. Hussey (ed.). *"Piers Plowman": Critical Approaches*. London: Methuen, 1969, pp. 50–75.

Woolf, Rosemary. *Art and Doctrine: Essays on Medieval Literature*. Ed. Heather O'Donoghue. London: Hambledon Press, 1986.

Index

abjurations 230
Adorno, Theodor 61
Alford, John 11, 123
allegory of the book 18, 71 *see also* "material textuality"
Allen, Judson Boyce 67, 123
Ambrose, saint 104, 128
Ancrene Wisse 115–118
Anglo-Norman, and law French 54
Anselm of Canterbury, saint, *Cur Deus homo* 100–101
Archives
    collecting and storage 4, 32, 36–38, 73, 96, 174, 188–189, 209–210, 236, 240–242
    theories of 93–94, 120, 182
Ars dictaminis, and autobiography 58, 59–60; *dictamen* and trial records 229; as literary exercise 56–58
Arundel, Thomas, Archbishop of Canterbury 196, 233–239
Augustine of Hippo, saint, *Ennarrationes in Psalmos* 100, 121–139
    influence on medieval writers: *Fasciculus morum* 123; William Langland 121–139; John Lydgate 123; Francis Petrarch 123; Richard Rolle 123; Wycliffite Psalter 123

Baldwin, Anna 118
Baker, Denise 115
Barr, Helen 177, 179
Baxter, Margery 12, 230–233
Bedos-Rezak, Brigitte 13
Black Death 5
Boffey, Julia 59, 152
Book of Vice and Virtues 6
Boureau, Alain 66–67
Bozon, Nicholas 103
Bracton, Henry de 5, 21
    De legibus et consuitudinibus Angliae 10, 20, 21–28, 47, 65, 72, 122, 140
brevity 3–4

broadsides and bill-casting 184–185, 186
    see also "1381 Revolt"
Brownlee, Kevin 46
bureaucracy, English *see also* "documents"
    growth of 5, 53–57
    languages of 54–55, 193, 229–231
Burgess, Clive 153
Burrow, J. A. 59

Cade, John 184
Camargo, Martin 53, 55, 57, 58
Camille, Michael 18
Carruthers, Mary 137
censorship
    and fifteenth-century legislation 196, 228
    and the *Long Charter* 197–198, 218–228
    and revisions to *Piers Plowman* 211–217
certificates 236–237
chancery 3, 5, 21, 56
Charles d'Orleans, *Fortunes Stabilnes* 31, 60
charms *see* "talismans and charms"
Charter of the Abbey of the Holy Ghost 68, 97–99, 204
Charters of Christ 10–11, 50–53, 159–161
    illustrations of 75–90, 159–161, 199–200
    texts:
        Carta dei 52, 66, 71–72, 74, 90, 205
        Carta domini nostri Iesu Christ 51
        Carta libera 52, 87
        "Charter of Heaven" (*Pore Caitif*) 52, 70, 71, 162–163, 195, 199, 205, 206, 207–210
        Long Charter 50, 65, 69–70, 76–77, 84, 112, 113, 130, 142, 194–200, 207, 218–228
        Short Charter 52, 66, 74, 77, 80, 195, 199
charters of feoffment 50, 83, 97
charters of manumission 8, 24, 210
charters of pardon 7–8, 32–35, 83
"charter of salvation" (Margery Baxter's) 231–233

Chaucer, Geoffrey 20, 55
works:
"ABC" hymn 29, 48–49
Book of the Duchess 30
Pardoner's Prologue 164–165
Troilus and Criseide 60
chirographs 50, 102, 140–142, 198, 207, 226 *see also* "indentures of service and maintenance," "*chirographum decreti*" and "*chirographum dei*"
chirographum decreti 53, 100–105, 134–135
chirographum dei 104–105, 127–132, 134–135
historical writing, medieval 4, 94, 95–96
citationality 3–4
Clanchy, Michael 4, 22, 54, 172
Coleman, Joyce 13, 220
commissions 36–40, 114–115, 222
Confirmation of the Provisions of Oxford 54, 73
contract, breach of 5–6; and memory 69–70
Copeland, Rita 234–235
counsel 177–189
Crane, Susan 193
Creed, Apostles 235
Creed, Athanasian 111–114, 124, 126, 128, 131, 132, 139, 214
Curtius, Ernst 18

Deguileville, Guillaume de 10, 20, 29–46
illustrations of works 33, 36–38, 43, 79, 159–161
reception of works 29–31, 48–49
works:
Pèlerinage de la vie humaine: Reason's commission 35–46, 222; Charity's testament 49, 159, 221; Tribulation's commission 114–115
Pèlerinage de l'âme: Mercy's charter of pardon 32–35, 111, 112, 125, 221
Derrida, Jacques 120
devil's record 32–33, 100–103, 106, 183
Dinshaw, Carolyn 165
diplomacy 2
"documentary poetics" 10, 29, 47–48, 245
documents *see also* "legal formulas" and "bureaucracy, English"
definition of 3–4, 19–20
performance of 23, 26–28, 39–43, 68, 148–149, 157–158, 221–223
production of 19–20, 79, 133, 135, 147, 157–158, 229–233
proliferation of 4–5, 95, 193
Domesday Book 8–9, 210
dominion 21, 22, 28, 42–44
Donaldson, E. Talbot 217
Donation of Constantine 208, 209

Durandus of Mende 138
Dyer, Christopher 7

Epistola Luciferi 103
Epistola Sathanae ad clericos 103
Eucharist, sacrament of 207, 225; fracture of the host 50, 138, 198, 207, 226
Excestr, John 229–231

Faith, Rosamund 7, 172
Fasciculi zizanorum 203
Fasciculus morum 50–52, 62–64, 74, 105, 112, 132, 133–135, 159
Ferster, Judith 184
forgery 3, 6, 8, 48, 141
formularies 56–57, 58
Foucault, Michel 93–94
Fowler, Elizabeth 44
Franciscan spirituality 18, 50–52, 68
Frank, Robert Worth, Jr. 138
Friar Grimestone's Commonplace Book 61–62
Fulbert of Chartres 102

Galloway, Andrew 95
genre *see also* "romance," "satire" and "hagiography"
document as a "genre of social action" 173–177
and material textuality 19–20
relationship between charters and lyrics 75–90
Gesta Romanorum 102
Glossa ordinaria 101
Gower John, *Cronica tripertita* 6; *Vox clamantis* 175
Grady, Frank 184
Green, Richard Firth 5–6, 186–187, 193
"Grete Sentence of Curs Expouned" 210–211

Hagen, Susan 31
hagiography 242–244
Hanna, Ralph III 126, 233
Herebert, William 18
Hereford Mappamundi 1–3
Hoccleve, Thomas 55, 59, 196
works:
Pilgrimage of the Soul 30
Regement of Princes 190
Holsinger, Bruce 193

indentures of service and maintenance 6, 141
indulgences, papal or ecclesiastical 77–79, 110, 127, 132–133, 134, 155, 157–158, 164, 199–200, 202, 212–215
indulgentia vs. *venia* (conditional vs. absolute pardon) 125, 126–127, 212

Inns of Court 21
instrumentality 3–4

Jack Upland 196, 201
Jacobus de Voragine 101
Jager, Eric 18
Jameson, Fredric 90
John of Garland 56
Justice, Steven 7, 56, 170, 172–173, 176, 177, 193, 231

Keen, Jill Averil 115, 163
Kempe, Margery, *The Book of Margery Kempe* 13, 180, 240–246
Ker, Neil 123
Kerby-Fulton, Kathryn 56, 155, 157
"key text" 93–94, 109
Knighton, Henry 7, 8, 171

LaCapra, Dominick 234
Langland, William 56
   Piers Plowman 11–12, 20, 30, 93–142, 143–190, 222–223; illustrations of 155; revisions to 212–217
   A-text: 108, 150, 155
   B-text: Hawkyn's quittance 106–107, 110, 161, 214–217; Imaginatif 148–149, 167–168, 180–182; Lewte 165–167; Mede's marriage charter 107, 110, 154; Moses's maundement 115–120, 150–152, 161–163, 223; Peace's patent 115–120, 223; Piers's testament 151–153; Trajan 146–148; Truth's Pardon 95, 109–115, 125–127, 135–142, 154–155, 181, 205, 212–214, 223
   C-text: 181–182
Latinity
   and administration 54, 193, 230
   and authority 52, 224
   Latin tags 65–66, 107, 154
Lawton, David 137, 212
Lay Folks' Catechism 204–206, 207, 213
Le roman de la rose 30–31, 46, 221
legal agency 21, 25–26
legal fictions
   of absence 26–28, 34–35, 72, 122
   of person 34–46, 174–175
   of publicness or accessibility 157–163, 176, 204
legal formulas 23–26, 51, 52, 53, 68, 72–74, 87–90, 97, 107, 134, 154, 158, 171, 176, 204, 227, 229–231, 234–235, 237 *see also* "bureaucracy, English," "documents," "Latinity" and "literacy and illiteracy"
legal will 22–28, 65–66
letters and briefs 60–61, 244–245
letters close 115, 158
letters of fraternity 201–210

letters patent 33, 72–74, 115–118, 155, 158–163, 183, 235
Lewis, C. S. 31
Lindenbaum, Sheila 186–187
literacy and illiteracy 7–8, 39–43, 111, 145–153, 157, 171, 172, 187, 214
liturgy 62–67, 138, 148, 227
livery of seisin 4–5, 22, 47, 50, 83
Lollardy 12–13
   on the antiquity and authority of scripture 202–203, 208–209, 219, 232–233, 237–238
   iconoclasm and anti-materialism 199, 203, 231, 238
   against indulgences and letters of fraternity 201–210
   polemic and rhetoric 194–228, 229–239
   on predestination 202, 206, 210
   and schools 198
   and trials 229–239
Love, Nicholas 196
Lydgate, John, *Pilgrimage of the Life of Man* 30, 36–41, 45, 48–49, 222
lyric
   and address 61–90, 227
   and metaphor 70–75, 85–87

Magna Carta 54, 157, 203, 211
mainprises 117
material textuality
   and anti-materialism 203, 214
   and genre 18–20, 75–90
   and legal will 24
   and maps 2
   and personification allegory 33–35
   as public ("obtrusive") writing 153, 185–189
   as textual gloss 127, 162
Matheson, Lister 56
Merke, Thomas 56
Middleton, Anne 42, 98, 140, 144, 170, 177, 181
Mirk, John 105
Mum and the Sothsegger 9, 11–12, 177–189
   "bag of books" episode 182–189
   "safe-conduct" episode 179–182

Norwich heresy trials 229–233
Novatian 104

"obtrusive" vs. "intrusive" writing 11, 144, 145, 146, 152–153, 154–155, 169–170, 185–189
Oldcastle, Sir John 244–245
Oxford debate on bible translation 223–224, 227–228

Palmer, Robert 5
pardons *see* "indulgences"

parliament, languages of 54; parliamentary commons 178, 188
patents *see* "letters patent"
Pecham, John 103
personification allegory 31–46
Piers Plowman see "Langland, William"
"*Piers Plowman* Tradition" 177
Privy Seal 5, 55
psalms, commentaries 123, 128 *see also* "Augustine of Hippo, saint, *Ennarrationes in Psalmos*"
public writing 153, 185–189 *see also* " 'obtrusive' vs. 'intrusive' writing"

quittances 49, 106, 215–217

Rabanus Maurus 100
relics 4, 9, 73
Richard of Bury 58
    works:
    Philobiblon 18, 59–60
    Liber epistolaris 58
romance 2; and documentary practice 96–99, 115–120
Russell, J. Steven 31
Rutebeuf, *Le miracle de Théophile* 102–103, 107–109, 221

safe-conducts and letters of credence 2, 179–180, 181, 240, 243–244
Salter, Elizabeth 116
Sampson, Thomas 55, 57
    Modus dictandi 58

satire, documents as social satire 48, 103; as a moral quandary 165–170, 178–189
Scase, Wendy 145, 170, 184, 186–187
scriveners 55, 57
seals 1–2, 25, 34, 74–75, 77, 84–85, 87–90, 96, 110, 117–118, 134, 158, 159–163, 207, 238
Simpson, James 121, 163, 168, 178
Sixteen Points of Lollard Belief 201
Spearing, A. C. 60
Stock, Brian 13, 93, 194 (*see also* "key text" and "textual community")
Strohm, Paul 197

talismans and charms 74, 77, 85, 243–244
testaments 49, 151–153
"textual community" 194, 195, 204, 206, 210, 219, 232–233 *see also* "Lollardy, on the antiquity and authority of scripture"
1381 Revolt 7–8
    letters of John Ball 11–12, 171–177, 186, 193, 209
Thorpe, William, *Testimony* 12, 233–239
trial records 12–13, 229–239
Turner, Victor 173–177

Usk, Thomas, "Appeal" 95

Walsingham, Thomas 8, 96, 171
Watson, Nicholas 193, 209, 223–224
writs 27, 83
Wyclif, John *see* "Lollardy"

York Play of the Crucifixion 62

CAMBRIDGE STUDIES IN MEDIEVAL LITERATURE

1 Robin Kirkpatrick *Dante's Inferno: Difficulty and Dead Poetry*
2 Jeremy Tambling *Dante and Difference: Writing in the "Commedia"*
3 Simon Gaunt *Troubadours and Irony*
4 Wendy Scase *"Piers Plowman" and the New Anticlericalism*
5 Joseph Duggan *The "Cantar De Mio Cid": Poetic Creation in its Economic and Social Contexts*
6 Roderick Beaton *The Medieval Greek Romance*
7 Kathryn Kerby-Fulton *Reformist Apocalypticism and "Piers Plowman"*
8 Alison Morgan *Dante & the Medieval Other World*
9 Eckehard Simon (ed.) *The Theatre of Medieval Europe: New Research in Early Drama*
10 Mary Carruthers *The Book of Memory: a Study of Memory in Medieval Culture*
11 Rita Copeland *Rhetoric, Hermeneutics and Translation in the Middle Ages: Academic Traditions and Vernacular Texts*
12 Donald Maddox *The Arthurian Romances of Chrétien de Troyes: Once and Future Fictions*
13 Nicholas Watson *Richard Rolle and the Invention of Authority*
14 Steven F. Kruger *Dreaming in the Middle Ages*
15 Barbara Nolan *Chaucer and the Tradition of the "Roman Antique"*
16 Sylvia Huot *The "Romance of the Rose" and its Medieval Readers: Interpretations, Reception, Manuscript Transmission*
17 Carol M. Meale (ed.) *Women and Literature in Britain, 1150–1500*
18 Henry Ansgar Kelly *Ideas and Forms of Tragedy from Aristotle to the Middle Ages*
19 Martin Irvine *The Making of Textual Culture: Grammatica and Literary Theory, 350–1100*
20 Larry Scanlon *Narrative, Authority and Power: the Medieval Exemplum and the Chaucerian Tradition*
21 Erik Kooper *Medieval Dutch Literature in its European Context*
22 Steven Botterill *Dante and the Mystical Tradition: Bernard of Clairvaux in the "Commedia"*
23 Peter Biller and Anne Hudson (eds.) *Heresy and Literacy, 1000–1530*
24 Christopher Baswell *Virgil in Medieval England: Figuring the "Aeneid" from the Twelfth Century to Chaucer*
25 James Simpson *Sciences and Self in Medieval Poetry: Alan of Lille's "Anticlaudianus" and John Gower's "Confessio Amantis"*
26 Joyce Coleman *Public Reading and the Reading Public in Late Medieval England and France*
27 Suzanne Reynolds *Medieval Reading: Grammar, Rhetoric and the Classical Text*
28 Charlotte Brewer *Editing "Piers Plowman": the Evolution of the Text*

29 Walter Haug *Vernacular Literary Theory in the Middle Ages: The German Tradition in its European Context*

30 Sarah Spence *Texts and the Self in the Twelfth Century*

31 Edwin Craun *Lies, Slander and Obscenity in Medieval English Literature: Pastoral Rhetoric and the Deviant Speaker*

32 Patricia E. Grieve *"Floire and Blancheflor" and the European Romance*

33 Huw Pryce (ed.) *Literacy in Medieval Celtic Societies*

34 Mary Carruthers *The Craft of Thought: Meditation, Rhetoric, and the Making of Images, 400–1200*

35 Beate Schmolke-Hasselman *The Evolution of Arthurian Romance: The Verse Tradition from Chrétien to Froissart*

36 Siân Echard *Arthurian Narrative in the Latin Tradition*

37 Fiona Somerset *Clerical Discourse and Lay Audience in Late Medieval England*

38 Florence Percival *Chaucer's Legendary Good Women*

39 Christopher Cannon *The Making of Chaucer's English: a Study of Words*

40 Rosalind Brown-Grant *Christine de Pizan and the Moral Defence of Women: Reading Beyond Gender*

41 Richard Newhauser *The Early History of Greed: the Sin of Avarice in Early Medieval Thought and Literature*

42 Margaret Clunies Ross *Old Icelandic Literature and Society*

43 Donald Maddox *Fictions of Identity in Medieval France*

44 Rita Copeland *Pedagogy, Intellectuals, and Dissent in the Later Middle Ages: Lollardy and Ideas of Learning*

45 Kantik Ghosh *The Wycliffite Heresy: Authority and the Interpretation of Texts*

46 Mary C. Erler *Women, Reading, and Piety in Late Medieval England*

47 D. H. Green *The Beginnings of Medieval Romance: Fact and Fiction 1150–1220*

48 J. A. Burrow *Gestures and Looks in Medieval Narrative*

49 Ardis Butterfield *Poetry and Music in Medieval France: From Jean Renart to Guillaume de Machaut*

9 780521 110532